p.6 - GDPS - all do "sirens"
have also.

The Triumph of Emptiness

The Triumph of Emptiness

Consumption, Higher Education, and Work Organization

Mats Alvesson

OXFORD
UNIVERSITY PRESS

OXFORD
UNIVERSITY PRESS

Great Clarendon Street, Oxford, OX2 6DP,
United Kingdom

Oxford University Press is a department of the University of Oxford.
It furthers the University's objective of excellence in research, scholarship,
and education by publishing worldwide. Oxford is a registered trade mark of
Oxford University Press in the UK and in certain other countries

First Edition published in 2013
Impression: 1

British Library Cataloguing in Publication Data

Data available

ISBN 978–0–19–966094–0

Printed in Great Britain by
CPI Group (UK), Croydon, CR0 4yy

Contents

List of Abbreviations

CSR	corporate social responsibility
DN	*Dagens Nyheter*
HRM	human resources management
MBA	Master of Business Administration
PBO	post-bureaucratic organization
SDS	*Sydsvenska Dagbladet Snällposten*
TFL	transformational leadership

List of Figures

Preface

In today's society, a strong emphasis on 'it must look good', and preferably even shine, is vital for the success of individuals, occupational groups, and organizations. Considerable time is devoted to the right visual approach, the right jargon, and the right mass-media focus, while less attention is paid to considerations about substance, practical viability, and quality. The brand is often more crucial than the actual product, and the CV is more important than expertise and ability. The focus is on the surface. The ambition is to put a gilt edge on life by applying attractive indicators that often have no or little substance. I refer to this as grandiosity. A world in which certification and branding are increasingly emphasized and dominate over more substantive issues gives rise to uncertainty and scepticism and even outright cynicism. This is what I characterize as the triumph of emptiness. This is certainly not a completely new phenomenon, but it has been accelerating in terms of intensity and scope, and now appears to be a key characteristic of 'advanced' society.

In this book, I take a broad approach to certain contemporary phenomena. I highlight how consumption is becoming an increasingly crucial and widespread factor, without achieving greater consumer satisfaction, how the knowledge ideal and qualifications for higher education are becoming undermined, and how people in organizations and working life concentrate on developing and copying dubious recipes and impressive representations to ensure that everything looks good.

Some of my criticisms are hardly new, but my thesis is in direct contradiction to the main track in management and sociological research where knowledge society, professionalism, leadership, entrepreneurship, strategic human resource management, and other impressive framings are popular. Alternative, down-to-earth representations (post-affluent society, occupations, supervision, small businesses, and personnel administration) are less so.

This book is a contribution to academic research, but it is also an expression of a critical concern for society as a whole. I am more interested in contributing to a critical understanding than in indicating some specific solutions. Critical insight is often the major result of social science and this is normally

[handwritten margin notes: "Cop out of live better" / "analysis of action?"]

preferable to a blueprint for change, in particular when problems are deeply embedded in culture and there are no easy policy or technical fixes. As with all critical research, the purpose is not to offer maximum empirical accuracy in description so much as a framework for challenging and rethinking dominant lines of understanding. My goal is productive provocation. I am less interested in details and nuances than conveying a strong message about our existence, whether as institutions or individuals, in contemporary, affluent societies. I have tried to tame the inclination of the contemporary academic to be specialized, cautious, and not say 'too much'. My personal attitudes are relatively clearly marked in this book, although it is largely based on research—by both myself and others. I have personally been engaged in organization, management, and working life research for twenty-five years, and a fair proportion of the conclusions reached by my research groups, and myself, are cited in this book, together with the results of other research, of course. I have, however, tried to avoid overburdening the manuscript with too many references.

I should mention that part of this work is inspired by observations in Sweden, although I have considerable international experience and affiliations with universities in the UK and Australia. Sweden is fairly egalitarian and less overtly commercial than many other capitalist countries. That grandiosity is so visible also in Sweden gives credibility to my thesis and I don't think that frequent use of observations from Swedish contexts diminishes the book's general relevance—on the contrary, I think they underscore it. The book is mainly restricted to covering affluent societies—e.g., most of Europe, North America, Australia, as well as other countries—or groups and institutions within countries. The exact relevance of a theory or a framework is partly for the reader to assess. All theories and concepts work sometimes, and sometimes they don't. The value is in challenging established assumptions and offering new ways of seeing, which sensitize us as to how to approach and act in the world.

I have benefited from the efforts of a number of colleagues from the United States, UK, New Zealand, Austria, and Sweden, who have read and commented on this manuscript. There are too many to mention here, but I am particularly grateful to Christian Berggren, Jon Bertilsson, Yvonne Due Billing, Carys Egan-Wyer, Yiannis Gabriel, Allanah Johnson, Bernadette Loacker, Wolfgang Meyrhofer, Helen Nicholson, Sonia Ospina, André Spicer, Kate Sullivan, and Sofia Ulver-Sneistrup for reading the whole or parts of the draft to this book.

I am grateful to the Swedish Council for Working Life and Social Science and Handelsbankens Research Foundations for support for various research projects and to David Canter and Joan Fälldin for translation and language editing.

Mats Alvesson
Lund, August 2012

1

Introduction

Zero-sum games, grandiosity, and illusion tricks

[handwritten margin note: Status claim in zero sum in each dimension.]

Modern society is characterized by grandiose self-personifications and claims on a large scale. There is a strong desire to be labelled in the most attractive and pretentious terms. This applies to individuals, occupations, organizations, and political elites. One problem is that the struggle for the most coveted sugar plums—high professional status, conspicuous consumption, 'world-class education', 'excellence', and so on—involves a zero-sum contest. This means that a benefit for one specific individual or group is gained at the expense of another. Not everybody can be excellent or afford high-status goods or get a degree from a high-status university. Grandiose projects occupy an ever-increasing proportion of the time, commitments, and resources of various elite groups, such as politicians, media people, corporate executives, union leaders, and other representatives of organizations and professional groups. But also the lives of common people increasingly circle around grandiosity. There is a strong emphasis on illusion tricks to back this up: CV improvement, title and grade inflation, organizations exhibiting impressive window-dressing through policy formulation and executive development programmes, and occupations re-launched as professions. This book focuses on the hollowness of such grandiosity and illusory projects, and emphasizes the zero-sum games involved, and also the destructive social and psychological consequences of such phenomena.

Based on these concepts, I will develop a framework for understanding the contemporary age and its institutions. I will examine critically some predominant ideas about management, organizational structure, working life, consumption, and education, which are often taken for granted:

[handwritten margin note: a grandiose undertaking indeed!]

- Economic growth and higher consumption are key sources of increased satisfaction.
- Education is something positive that leads to higher qualifications, and is needed to a greater and greater extent by both individuals and society.
- Current and future working life is permeated by views of a knowledge economy and a knowledge-intensive society, a greater degree of professionalization, and an emphasis on leadership in the creation of effective organizations.

I will show that many conditions and developments in these three areas, which may appear to be positive and socially functional, can be better understood in terms of grandiosity, illusion tricks, and zero-sum games.

My personal viewpoint is rather sceptical, perhaps on the verge of cynicism. My interest lies more in puncturing myths than in the dissemination of optimism or a social engineering philosophy. Like Habermas (1972), I see the raison d'être for social science as critically examining dominant institutions and broadly shared assumptions in order to point out how they constrain our ability and willingness to think through social issues and personal choices in order to arrive at conclusions grounded in reflective reasoning and sensitive ethical considerations. This often means struggling, not only with what appears to be repressive and bad, but also with what seems attractive and good.

Let me start by recounting an episode that will throw light on some of the aspects this book tackles.

> I am on my way to a major conference on knowledge society and education. Being familiar with the conference's location, I decide to take an overnight train and a sleeping berth. After a night of relatively undisturbed sleep, I dress, brush my teeth quickly, and step down from the train whilst nodding to the guard—who is probably called a senior conductor these days, or maybe even a Train Master. At the Central Station in Stockholm, I push my way through the swarming crowds of commuters and make my way to the café in the main hall that serves porridge for breakfast. I wait for the young man who clears the tables to make a space for me. After a rapid breakfast, it is time to move on. Outside the station, I pass a long line of taxis waiting for customers. I cross the street and glance in a few shop windows. I see vans and other vehicles passing by, and a few street workers in the distance— some of them are emptying waste-paper baskets. My bus arrives and I get on it. We pass a number of shops. Employees are busy preparing the day's sales work. I get off the bus close to the hotel where I am heading. Once inside the hotel, I ask the receptionist how to find the conference hall. Outside the conference hall, waiters are preparing for the coffee break. I enter the hall. Now it is time for the 'knowledge society'.

In the course of the early morning, I have observed a mass of people at work. But soon I will be faced with another kind of work: conferencing on a knowledge society. Here they will be talking eagerly about 'competence', the importance of higher education and innovation, and suggesting that we can only cope with international competition if we have access to knowledge and quality. IT, high tech, and pharmaceuticals industries are heavily stressed. This knowledge-intensive society is far more acutely present in the conference room than in the working life that I observed in the street outside, which is notably absent in the context of the conference. And the converse also applies: all these transport, service, and retail employees can probably perform their tasks without worrying too much about all this talk about a knowledge society. Or maybe they can't? I will come back to this question.

Sources of inspiration

I am inspired, in particular, by Fred Hirsch, the economist, *Social Limits to Growth* (1976) and by Daniel Boorstin, the historian, *The Image* (1961). These works were published some years ago, but they appear to be even more relevant today. Further, somewhat more general inspiration comes from the Frankfurt school's critical theories—well known for attacking ideologies and 'truths' that lock people into taken-for-granted assumptions and societal forms misleadingly seen as given, rational, and superior. The key names are Horkheimer, Adorno, Marcuse, Fromm, and Habermas. I have also drawn upon Lasch (1979), *The Culture of Narcissism*; Klein (2000), *No Logo*; Sennett (2006), *The Culture of New Capitalism*; and, to some extent, Foley (2010), *The Age of Absurdity*. There are frequent references to the field of 'Critical Management Studies' (CMS), although I make clearer use of the term 'new institutional theory' (John Meyer and colleagues; see, for example, Meyer and Rowan, 1977), which stresses that organizations develop structures to ensure that things look good so that others will think so too. This tradition is interpreted from a critical angle, however. The ideas expressed in Bourdieu (1984) about an economy with a social differentiation have also had an impact on this book. There are, of course, many others to refer to and draw upon, but I do not want to burden the text with too many references.

All the authors and theories that I have mentioned are in the business of unmasking myths, i.e., investigating dangerous 'truths'. This is the business in which I also consider myself. I am aware that my own truth may not be innocent either and hope that the book is very clear on this point. My aim is to offer a framework and concepts that may be useful, rather than to establish strong truth claims.

Zero-sum games

The first manifestation of the three contemporary conditions and developments I emphasize in this book is that, in an affluent society underpinned by economic growth, the satisfaction provided by consumption has increasingly strong social or relative characteristics. By this, I mean that personal utility/satisfaction is closely interwoven with that of others in the form of open or lightly disguised competition.

In this case, increased satisfaction results primarily from the way the individual ranks in relation to others. Almost all consumption involves both a personal and a social aspect. However, people often think of consumption mainly, or even solely, in individual terms—the preferences and wishes of individuals are satisfied via consumption. This is a 'private' matter, not directly related to the standing of others. If you are starving and receive food, the value and satisfaction involved is primarily individual, and is not related to hunger in the rest of society. The value of shelter as protection against the wind or cold is largely independent of your neighbour's situation—your own exposure to cold is not affected by whether your neighbour is freezing to a greater or lesser extent. Fundamental needs are of this nature, and they involve an 'independent', or absolute, degree of satisfaction. Economists refer to these as 'non-positional goods' (Hirsch, 1976).

However, consumption with strong or relative social orientation is different. Here we talk about positional goods, referring to 'those things whose value depends strongly on how they compare with things owned by others' (Frank, 1985: 101). Crucial here is not what you have and do, per se, but what you have and do in relation to others. Such consumption is part of a salient social context, and the satisfaction/utility depends on your position in relation to others' preferences and behaviour. Consumption involves a significant degree of demonstration to others and/or awareness of others' levels of consumption. The social aspect indicates that utility does not represent some absolute, independent value and independent satisfaction but is, instead, dependent on other people's consumption (or other living conditions). This includes, for example, road congestion—traffic queues depend on other people's actions. Status objects such as branded clothing are another example. Their value is largely a question of their ability to allow you to distinguish yourself from others—and overshadow them. Fashion provides a similar example. Clothes that you once regarded as beautiful and of high quality, and which you actually like, can soon lose their value if everyone else switches to a new style. And if you are the only one in the village with a bicycle, and the other villagers have to walk, you are probably very happy. But if most of the people in your surroundings have big new cars, while you are driving around in an old small one, you may well feel rather dissatisfied. (That is to say, if you don't belong to the tiny minority that enjoys marking its deviation from normal status patterns. This usually calls for some like-minded people to support you, as when one belongs to a counter-cultural group. Sometimes this means a specific form of 'anti-mainstream' consumption, including paying a lot for 'retro' things, but there are also people who are simply quite uninterested in spending much time or money on consumption.)

In *The Social Limits to Growth* (1976), Hirsch proposes that an ever-increasing proportion of growth in wealthy societies is devoted to goods and services with a strong positional aspect. Status, social differentiation, and conspicuous consumption have been part of most societies since the beginning of civilization. However, there have been drastic changes since the industrial revolution, and particularly since WWII, as a large majority of the population have experienced increases in material living standards. Positionality is no longer an issue for a small elite, nor is it a marginal phenomenon for the majority of people. It is a key element of social life for a significant part of all people today in North America, Europe, and many other countries. The satisfaction following from economic growth depends on how you relate to others in terms of buying power and consumption. It is hardly a question of some general improvement in well-being. We must invest more, for example, in education, if we are not to slip back in the job queue, and must pay more for an attractive house location if we don't want to be forced to live in some peripheral suburb with long commuter journeys. Consumption is, as much else, increasingly becoming a zero-sum game. There is considerable support for the thesis 'that relative standing is far more important than the absolute level of consumption in determining individual well-being' (Frank, 1985: 106). What many people regard as desirable becomes, virtually by definition, reserved for the few. Only a limited number can be educated in prestigious institutions, get the most attractive jobs, or have access to a lakefront house, and the number of inner-city apartments with a view is also limited. The price of such education, lakefront plots, or apartments is forced upwards in line with, or more than, the average increase in salaries. The attractiveness of and competition for positional goods increase with economic growth.

One alternative is to increase the supply, but this leads to a decline in value. With more apartments in the city centre, high-rise developments and congestion reduce the satisfaction of such locations. If many people purchase high-status branded products their 'value-creation' capabilities (to use modern business jargon) are reduced.

This line of argument may be illustrated in Figure 1.

A problem is that the limited impact of growth on increased satisfaction is not clear for the individual, and what appears to be rational if everyone applies their personal rationality becomes the converse at the aggregate level. People purchase the most sophisticated status gadgets, complete a protracted educa-

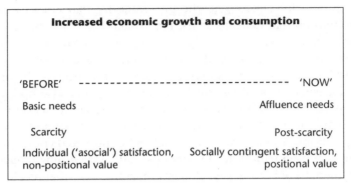

Figure 1. A simple overview of a trend from the centrality of non-positional goods in pre-affluent to positional goods in post-affluent society.

tion career, or drive their cars from the suburbs to the city centre to save time, only to discover too late that other people have also bought the same gadget, that there are hundreds of other job applicants with the same education, and that the traffic jams are interminable. Our individual and political thinking is rooted in an old economy composed primarily of private (non-positional) goods that are not affected by consumption by other individuals.

> The bedrock is valuation by individuals of goods and opportunities in the situation in which they find themselves. At any moment of time and for any person, standing on tiptoe gives a better view, or at least prevents a worse one. Equally, getting ahead of the crowd is an effective and feasible means of improving one's welfare, a means available to any one individual. It yields a benefit, in this sense, and the measure of the benefit from the isolated action is clear-cut. The sum of benefits of all actions taken together is nonetheless zero. (Hirsch, 1976: 7)

Improvements in the ability to consume are, per se, less relevant than a relative increase. According to this logic, it is better to receive a personal pay rise of 4 per cent if the average figure is 2 per cent than a pay increase of 6 per cent if everyone else is getting the same. This applies to an economy in which basic needs are already provided for and the focus is instead on the consumption of positional objects, and in which possessions and habitual actions have repercussions on benefits for the individual. This situation has applied for some time to the majority of the population in modern Western societies. (It should be clear that most of the points made in this book mainly refer to wealthy societies and wealthy groups across the globe.)

This reasoning explains the paradox that, notwithstanding increased productivity and economic growth, many people feel a strong need for more consumption. According to Hirsch, meeting these demands by means of higher growth is no solution. This is no better than urging people in a crowd to stand on their toes to get a better view. As we shall see in Chapter 2, a higher material standard of living in affluent societies has not resulted in greater satisfaction. When I refer to zero-sum games in this book, I am referring primarily to the sense that greater benefits for a specific individual mean a reduction in someone else's benefits. Sometimes this involves a clear zero-sum game in which one person's advantage corresponds directly to another person's loss. This certainly is the case in the sports world, but also in the ranking of universities and schools where success is only achieved at another's expense. This is normally, however, a question of tendencies towards a zero-sum game rather than an absolute phenomenon. Perhaps one might refer to the fact that one person's greater advantage involves an under-mining/weakening of another person's situation. In this case, the pluses and minuses involved are not necessarily equivalent. One might, in principle, imagine a considerable plus for someone at a somewhat lesser expense for someone else, for example, when money is redistributed from the rich to the poor. This can also involve a small plus for some people, but a larger minus for others as, for example, when many individuals acquire a car in a historic city centre. But, for the most part, it is difficult to quantify the advantages and the disadvantages. For those mathematically minded, preferring a strict—rather than my intended metaphorical—view of zero-sum games, one can talk about 'small net-sum' games instead, where the positive advantage of an outcome is met by a similar, larger or smaller, disadvantage. The key point is that a plus for someone is at the direct or indirect expense of someone else, and not whether the equation yields exactly zero.

One variation on this theme is 'mimetic rivalry'. This concept was coined by René Girard (Asplund, 1989) and is based on the idea that people demand what others desire. The other people concerned are not necessarily the entire population, but may consist of a group with which an individual identifies, for example, a class, a profession, or a neighbourhood. In other words, an individual is more likely to be influenced and motivated by the aims of such a group than by his or her own independent preferences. Since we identify and compete with others, they become simultaneously our models and rivals. Girard describes this:

> The subject desires the object because the rival desires it. Through desiring one or another object the rival presents it as desirable for the subject. The rival is the subject's model, but not only on the superficial level of behaviour or attitudes, but also on the more crucial level of desire. (quoted in van Reis, 1988: 64)

A simple example is an auction in which you may be only mildly attracted by an object until you notice that others are interested, and then your own interest increases. Travel destinations, objects with a desirable trademark, employers and jobs, and everything that has a fashion aspect involve a considerable degree of mimetic rivalry. But many things are durable and change slowly. Universities that have acquired elite status tend to hang onto it, and this also applies to many manufacturers of high-quality/high-status physical products. Our desires and perceived satisfactions depend on the corresponding desires and satisfactions of other people; what we want and we perceive outcomes of efforts to meet desire are very much group-related. While Hirsch emphasizes the centrality of the positional aspects, particularly with regard to economic growth and the affluent society, Girard sees mimetic rivalry as a more general human phenomenon. This does not prevent such aspects from becoming more significant in an epoch when the basic needs of the great majority of a society can be met with a fraction of the resources available. In such a situation, desires, motives, and energy are highly focused on aspects dependent on how personal achievement/consumption relates to that of other people. Mimetic rivalry reinforces the nature of existence as a zero-sum game, and societal development reinforces such mimetic rivalry.[1]

Grandiosity

The second manifestation of contemporary developments concerns living in a society where what I denote as 'grandiosity' is triumphing. This is perhaps the most important theme of this book. By grandiosity, I mean attempts to give yourself, your occupational group/organization, or even the society in which you live, a positive—if somewhat superficial—well-polished and status-enhancing image.

As much as possible is targeted and becomes symbolically upgraded and made remarkable and impressive, adding to status and self-esteem. Issues of substance (practices or tangible results) are marginalized. Grandiosity involves representing or loading phenomena such that they appear as attractive as possible within a framework of what seems to be reasonable.

In other words, grandiosity does not necessarily mean delusions of grandeur or something that is obviously mad. My interest does not lie in the obsession of dictators or other national leaders in the construction of monuments to commemorate themselves, or in the recognition of the value of major achievements, such as the Nobel Prize or Olympic championships. Contemporary grandiosity—at least in open, relatively equality-oriented (often high taxation)

---

[1] A possible counterargument is that the spreading Euro-crisis, and the increasing inequalities, may mean that it is once again becoming more difficult to satisfy the basic needs for sections of the population in many countries. But this would not undermine the relevance of the theme discussed. For the major part of the population in countries with a GNP significantly above world average, the positional goods and zero-sum games are significant part of consumption.

societies—is socially controlled, semi-realistic, and confined to loading an increasing number of phenomena with strongly positive, exaggerated meaning that generate attractiveness, success, and distance from the paltriness and mediocrity of everyday life. Grandiosity is being democratized. Everybody wants it and feels entitled to it. It is typically camouflaged and represented as a favourable, but not obviously misleading, representation of a phenomenon. Grandiosity gilds the lily by lending a golden haze to various phenomena. Since this involves considerable doctoring of a world that is not always beautiful, it also involves the application of smoke screens. Grandiosity is linked with an increasingly widespread 'narcissism' and a desire to enhance self-esteem. We want to be in the public eye, confirmed, associated with something prestigious, and to distance ourselves from what is trivial. The desire to be fascinating is not just an individual phenomenon, but also very much a collective one. It applies to various institutions and groups that acquire labels to boost themselves in terms of meaning, sophistication, and status. Let me give some examples of this phenomenon.

Our society has rapidly moved from being seen as industry- and service-oriented to one of information (during the 1970s) and, in the absence of more rapid upgrading, has wound up being identified as a 'knowledge' society. A similar, perhaps even more grandiose idea is the one of the rise and domination of 'the creative class' and 'the creative economy' (Florida, 2001). All this sounds great and is very popular to communicate. Thompson et al. (2000: 122) write: 'Policy-makers and academics alike . . . endlessly repeat the mantra that knowledge work offers a rationale for the development of capital in the workplace, a blueprint for the creation of "world class" firms, and a way of preventing advanced economies restructuring away their sunset industries from becoming peripheral low-wage, low skill national economies.' This new economy, which was so popular a few years ago, may be expected to make a new appearance, maybe equally triumphant and captivating as its impact in the late 1990s. In this dynamic knowledge society, it is essential to keep up with things. In the education world, the number of higher degrees has grown almost explosively.

Many societies are becoming academic on a broad front, with new additions such as gastronomy, fashion science, and competence science. Restaurant, hotel, and tourism studies are being turned into academic disciplines, with special programmes offered at university level.

In working life, bureaucracy and mass production have had to make way for so-called knowledge-intensive companies, dynamic networks, and flexible, customer-steered operations. And people are employed for 'value creation processes' rather than for the production of goods and services. Small businesses are now run by 'entrepreneurs', at least according to researchers and policy-makers. Maybe one or two bicycle repairers or hairdressers have failed to keep up with the times and still regard themselves as small business owners? Managers and supervisors are increasingly labelled as 'leaders'. Strategic visions and empowerment have pushed aside organizational management of a more conventional, more boring, nature. In the universities, a sluggish collegial spirit has been supplanted by academic leadership.

New occupations have emerged—executive coaches provide sparring partners for leaders (formerly called managers). There is considerable inflation of job titles: more and more people have become 'managers' and 'executives', and it is not particularly exclusive to have 'vice president' on your business card these days.

And this is not exclusive to individual titles. Groups have become teams; and when senior managers meet, they become 'executive teams'. Rationalization is now termed 'business process engineering'. Plans have become 'strategies'. Management training now takes the form of 'executive development programmes'. Giving advice is referred to as 'coaching', which has become a booming industry, supposedly helping a world increasingly in need of expert advice. Expressions like 'world class' and 'excellence' are used more and more frequently, often without much backup in terms of demonstrated qualities or accomplishments.

We also have had an upgrading of education programmes, job titles, and representations of activities that, while giving a better impression, does not actually involve any real improvement. This illustrates the workings of grandiosity.

There are similar trends in the consumer area, where the focus is on youth, beauty, physical fitness, and success. Fashion and brand names have a great impact, and products are associated with identity and are given a strong loading for expressing, or even creating, buyer personalities. Individuality is promoted as a question of adopting a particular consumption pattern, and travel increasingly involves trips to exotic, faraway places. Basic needs have become less important, while a higher proportion of consumption has narcissistic overtones. Goods and services have become levers for improving self-esteem and status. According to marketing and other lifestyle experts, products express your identity and enable you to realize yourself to the full.

These are all trends that involve enhanced status and self-esteem, improving the image of individuals, groups, organizations, and activities. These trends often mean a combination of something deviating from, and superior to, others. But such efforts have become increasingly desperate, as the space for and competition over grandiosity have become tight. Most efforts have failed or have been only partly successful. As I will elaborate, grandiosity is increasingly haunted by its own emptiness—the lack of concrete content can strike back. People will experience disappointment and frustration.

My thesis is that our era is becoming permeated by such grandiosity—and emptiness—although this is not to say that other ages and societies did not also exhibit similar traits. Grandiosity, of course, is hardly a new phenomenon. At the individual level, the tendency to heighten personal self-esteem by self-glorification may well be an intrinsic feature of human existence. This is what psychoanalysts call narcissism, quite a normal condition, although in extreme cases it sometimes takes pathological forms. Psychoanalysts refer to 'the grandiose self', which is characterized by fantasies of omnipotence, exhibitionism, and ambition. The grandiose self is very prominent in early childhood, when the individual experiences separation from the parents and compensates for the feeling of being little, marginalized, and dependent (Kohut, 1971, 1977). Successful development involves integration of these grandiose fantasies into a more positive, stable, and realistic self-image. In some cases, though, the development process goes awry and results in 'narcissistic personality disturbances'. In most cases, there is a vulnerability to frustration, involving swings between reasonable perceptions and expressions of grandiosity—omnipotence, perfection, and success—and the opposite, a sense of emptiness, meaninglessness, and failure. Such narcissistic problems appear to have increased in recent decades, however (Twenge and Foster, 2010), where immature, grandiose, idealizing fantasies, and an unstable self-image have become an increasing feature of 'problem-loaded normal psychology'. Psychologists claim that pathological narcissism is a prime candidate for late-capitalism's archetypal emotional disturbance (Kovel, 1981: 104) and that we live in a 'narcissistic culture' (Lasch, 1978), where people spend time building up a positive self-image—usually only with limited success—with the help of relationships, status symbols, consumption, identification with and admiration of idols, fantasies, and so on. One aspect of this is giving oneself and one's surroundings a grandiose overtone, where there is a strong dependence on a reflective and supportive environment, although this is often hidden and denied.

> Narcissism represents the psychological dimension of this dependence. Notwithstanding his occasional illusions of omnipotence, the narcissist depends on others to validate his self-esteem. He cannot live without an admiring audience. His apparent freedom from family ties and institutional constraints does not free him to stand alone or to glory in his individuality. On the contrary, it contributes to his insecurity, which he can overcome only by seeing his 'grandiose self' reflected in the attentions of others, or by attaching himself to those who radiate celebrity, power, and charisma. For the narcissist, the world is a mirror. (Lasch, 1978: 10)

Celebrity cultures and Facebook addictionados, etc. both reflect and reinforce such orientations. Uncertainties and doubts about one's own abilities—shortage of good feedback and reaffirmation such as reliable educational systems and cultural traditions offering stable reference points—also lead to a shaky sense of self and an exaggerated need for confirmation.

The grandiosity theme is not entirely new, even for the general public. Historical studies show that even in times of acute poverty, relatively poor people were prepared to devote some of their limited resources to luxury and status objects. There was no great change in the material standard of living between the sixteenth and nineteenth centuries, but nonetheless there was a marked increase in the consumption of 'luxury' goods. Söderberg (2002) refers to the increased importance of 'the narrow gilt edge'. Although the interest in gilding one's life is not a new phenomenon, economic growth and the ability of mass-media institutions to stimulate fantasies, ambitions, desires, and attractive ideals have made this a central life-concern for many people. Elite groups have faced competition from a wider circle in the luxury consumption area. The dynamism of the economy is increasing as the former try to maintain their advantage and the latter approach the former in terms of fashionable luxury consumption and high-status goods (Simmel, 1904). Conspicuous consumption has become more than an elite phenomenon, partly because the desire to become 'elite-like' is spreading.

Throughout history, collective phenomena have also been affected by grandiose ideas, and certain types of grandiosity were probably more marked in other eras. Pyramids, palaces, big statues of leaders, and other impressive monuments are largely a thing of the past and, to some extent, our own age is more modest when it comes to grandiose public excesses; there are exceptions, of course, such as the spectacular buildings in Dubai. Exaggerated status symbols in the form of 'monumental grandiosity' are considered slightly ridiculous in many countries, at least when associated with specific personas. But, of course, grandiose self-images also continue to flourish in the context of nationalism, colonialism, racism, and sexism. As grandiosity is everywhere, it would be presumptuous of me to deny such pretensions on my own part. Perhaps this book is also permeated by grandiose ambitions—if not in terms of glorification fantasies, then maybe in terms of grand claims to 'reveal everything'. So beware, dear reader!

Although grandiosity, as an individual and collective orientation, may go back to the Stone Age, this does not imply that it is a constant factor in human and social life. With increasing wealth, positional goods become more central than non-positional goods, and the former lead to a strong preoccupation with keeping up with, or being ahead of, the Joneses. Our time is characterized by a powerful accumulation of institutions and mechanisms that encourage grandiosity. They are perhaps less ostentatious than in the past—since formerly they were often associated with royalty, the nobility, or unabashed nationalism—but they nonetheless permeate our entire culture, sometimes in less obvious ways. In contrast with the 'monumental grandiosity' of another age, we note the distributed and, partially camouflaged, grandiosity of our own era. We can refer to the decentralization and cultural deep penetration of grandiosity, as well as its democratization—grandiose projects are no longer the preserve of an elite, but are now accessible to everyone, to some extent. Time, information, and money allow more groups to move from a focus on survival and comfort to grandiosity. And many occupational groups, organizational leaders, and individuals take this opportunity. The popularity of reality shows on TV suggests a widespread interest in ambitions and fantasies of winding up in the spotlight. The idea here is that anyone can acquire idol status—without the advantages of birth, talent, or actual achievement.

At the same time, these individual attempts to weld together an identity are often tied up with collective aspirations to upgrade projects undertaken by organizations and occupational groups. In this instance, there may be an emphasis on the feeling of belonging to a special species, since members of the group belong to a select category whose foremost qualities rub off on the individual concerned.

We can also refer to a strange mixture of fantasy and cravings as a unique feature of our age. The promoters of this process include politicians, the mass media, schools, universities and education institutions, marketers, therapists, and other experts on 'human improvement', and they are all selling a potentially better life—if you simply buy their products or utilize their services. The numbers and effects of various institutions creating and reinforcing fantasies and desires about creating and maintaining a happier and more impressive life are growing. The scope for increasing numbers of people to devote considerable time, energy, and resources to projects with grandiose implications is probably greater than ever before. Education, human improvement (development), travel, clothes, housing, and various gadgets offer ever-growing options. Telephony is a good example. A decade or so ago, it was mainly a question of having access to a telephone, and the opportunity to use it. Today, a mobile phone is a complex of opportunities to convince yourself and others about your degree of sophistication, technical know-how, economic resources, etc., involved in intensive competition for position and progress in terms of status and social differentiation. Thus, the mobile phone turns communication—and its associated sub-functions—into a strongly symbolic phenomenon in which opportunities for self-glorification and the admiring glances of others are an important factor. On the other hand, of course, I would not want to deny the practical advantages of mobile telephony. Probably seldom is it only a matter of showing off. More often, it is likely to constitute a complicated mix of motives and meanings where interest and practical advantage are difficult to sort out from the desire to keep up with, or preferably be ahead of, and admired by, others. Grandiosity seldom appears in a pure, naked form.

It is often claimed that modern society is populated, at least among the younger generation, by individualists who are different from previous generations (Cartwright and Holmes, 2006). It is doubtful whether there is much substance in this, but at any rate, it expresses a strong belief in an independent ability to form oneself and one's life. Narcissism encompasses denial of the attributes of a mass society and an exaggerated belief in people's ability to create themselves. Problems and attempted solutions are individualized, but the underlying attributes are collective and 'recipes' for solutions comply with social standards.

Standardization tendencies and conformism are certainly powerful in a mass communication society such as ours. One classic example is the McDonaldization of society, which suggests the direct opposite of individualism in the traditional sense (Ritzer, 2004). Some time ago, Riesman (1950) and Fromm (1955) identified a cultural shift from people who were controlled from within, permeated by internalized ideals and with relatively stable values that provided a clear sense of direction, to people who were externally controlled or market-oriented, sensitive to signals from their surroundings, and willing to comply with the expectations of others. This trend appears to be continuing. Riesman summarizes his account by saying that 100 years ago the individual functioned like a gyro-compass—internalized values set the direction—while radar man began to predominate from mid-twentieth century—with highly sensitive registration and adaptation to the norms and reactions to his surroundings. Team members and brand worshippers provide good examples of this. Perhaps external control is not the direct opposite of individuality but, to the extent that our age is characterized by individualism, it is largely a socially sensitive and adaptable kind of individualism. There are templates for individualism, contingent upon class, gender, ethnicity, age, etc. The scope for individual characteristics is limited in an organization and consumption-oriented society. But nonetheless, grandiose fantasies about being a unique individual are rather common.

Grandiosity is often at odds with the average, the trivial. It is an active force in the struggle against the privileges of others and the banality of life. Education, working life, and consumption as well as many other parts of society and life are, whenever possible, charged with this grandiosity. This is my main thesis, but it becomes particularly relevant when related to the zero-sum-game quality of the grandiose aspirations of various individuals and groups and linked to its companion piece—the illusion tricks.

Illusion tricks

A third key manifestation of contemporary development is a declining interest in 'substance' and a greater interest in conveying images and ideas that give the impression of something positive: progress, politically correct values, general rationality, and adaptive ability. It is important to do something that gives a good overall impression. Such images are independent of, or loosely linked to, what is actually happening at a more substantial level. Pseudo-events, pseudo-actions, and pseudo-structures are all example of illusion tricks. These concepts allude to the way in which activities and developed structures focus less on a substantial practice or quality (behaviour, results) than on signalling what is positive, impressive, and fascinating—or is at least legitimate and anticipated. There is a strong demonstration element, which claims to indicate substance or quality but which is weak or non-existent and is hence misleading, at least in part. This representation is out on a limb—it is a signifier without actually signifying much. Ethical principles, gender equality plans, and many 'quality assurance' initiatives and corporate social responsibility policies are good examples. In an 'audit society' it is important to exhibit the correct indicators to be ticked off when mass media or authorities pay a visit (Power, 2003). In working life and organizations, professionalization projects, leadership talk, and reorganizations are typically in accordance with the latest fashion. (This will be discussed at greater length in Chapters 6–9.)

Boorstin (1961) noted, more than fifty years ago, that our expectations of new developments clearly exceed the potential candidates for such achievements. Major natural disasters, war, drastic political reforms, and revolutionary scientific breakthroughs that attract the attention of more than a narrow group of specialists are relatively rare. They barely suffice to provide the media with enough 'news', i.e., easily interest-triggering, sellable items. According to Boorstin, the solution for a shortage of interesting news items was the pseudo-event. Pseudo-events are synthetic news items launched by the media or other actors—various elite groups—with the intent of arousing interest and providing an object for mass-media reporting. Public opinion polls are, for example, often produced or financed by media that want to have something to write about. A pseudo-event has the following characteristics:

- Non-spontaneous, but arranged because someone has planned, placed, or initiated it.
- Primarily (but not necessarily exclusively) planned to match an immediate mass-media reporting requirement; its news value is the decisive aspect.
- Only loosely linked with the underlying reality that it is supposed to reflect. A press conference may mention intentions, plans, or

opinions about something that has taken place, or perhaps may take place.

- Tendencies to promulgate self-fulfilling prophecies; the pseudo-event becomes part of reality and, as a result, has consequences.

Over the course of time, pseudo-events have tended to overshadow 'real' or spontaneous events. Since they are staged for the mass media and public consumption, they are easy to handle and report.

> Pseudo-events from their very nature tend to be more interesting and more attractive than spontaneous events. Therefore in American public life today pseudo-events tend to drive all other kinds of events out of our consciousness, or at least to overshadow them. Earnest, well-informed citizens seldom notice that their experience of spontaneous events is buried by pseudo-events. Yet nowadays, the more industriously they work at 'informing' themselves the more this tends to be true. (Boorstin, 1961: 37)

Pseudo-events are easy to grasp from the consumer viewpoint, but consumers fail to appreciate the pseudo aspect and accept them as genuinely important phenomena. And they can also be recycled in a new opinion poll that provides opportunities for reporting differences from the previous sounding. Pseudo-events are planned to be easy to understand—it is almost impossible for outsiders to grasp how suitable candidates for political posts really are, but we can readily form an opinion of their ability to make a good impression on TV. As Boorstin (1961) points out, having the ability to say something convincing in 30 seconds is hardly a good indicator of one's insights into complex questions or one's ability to make a complicated organizational structure function satisfactorily. Some consumers of mass media might, upon reflection, realize this, but this realization does not necessarily lead to a drop in the consumption of superficial TV programmes or news articles in favour of more serious knowledge seeking, i.e., the reading of serious journalistic articles or books on a subject matter.

An example of a pseudo-event was a press conference in Stockholm about HIV/AIDS, with Sharon Stone, a famous American actress, and four of Sweden's leading researchers in this area. All the questions were directed at Sharon Stone. A news agency interviewed a local celebrity in the audience who explained how important it was for famous personalities to be ambassadors in such fields as the general public accepts what they say in a different way. The problem is that pseudo-events are competing with other, more important events and information. Maybe some mass-media organs would be attracted by a press conference, even if there was no movie star, and then perhaps the focus would be on the HIV/AIDS issue. In the ensuing newspaper article, Sharon Stone got six lines (about friends having died from AIDS, etc.), the researchers got three, and the local celebrity in the audience got nine (SDS, 27 May 2005). This clearly indicates the importance of celebrities in this kind of context and, more broadly, how pseudo-issues easily attract more interest than 'substance'. The use of the celebrity to draw attention to HIV/AIDS transformed into the HIV/AIDS issue becomes a motive for paying attention to the movie star and celebrities more generally.

A more serious aspect is, perhaps, that aid organizations sometimes give more priority to their visibility than to encouraging support for those in need. In connection with the tsunami disaster that primarily affected Indonesia, Sri Lanka, and Thailand in 2005/6, it may be noted that the various voluntary 'organizations' efforts to achieve rapid results and promote themselves sometimes led to unsuccessful aid since there were obstacles to effective coordination. They were quickly building houses that could be photographed, inaugurated and handed over to grateful families, but when the rain comes they were often flooded' (DN Debate, 18 January 2006).[2] Similar observations were made in connection with the earthquake disaster on Haiti in 2010.

Most mass-media output involves speculations, rumours, denials, comments, political initiatives for media purposes, commercial events, news about celebrities, and so on. Maybe we should condemn the media, but we should probably also condemn—or deprecate—a population that has come increasingly to expect that the world should deliver interesting news at frequent intervals. One might also think that sensible people might be content with news once a week or so, with a greater emphasis on 'real' events. We have created a world of pseudo-events in order to avoid obviating 'spontaneous' news items, and this fits better into the news-reporting machinery. In Europe, we sometimes know more about the families of American presidential candidates than ethnic genocide and hunger disasters in Africa.

Not only mass media but also locally staged events often have a pseudo-nature. In an organizational context, we can refer to pseudo-structures as involving visible, formal structures, or tangible patterns of behaviour that lay claim to, and are often regarded as having an impact on results and behaviour. Yet they still operate primarily at the symbolic or ceremonial level. Such symbolism, which is intended to display something substantive, is different from 'pure' or clearly symbolic phenomena such as commemorative speeches, guards of honour, and awards. In such cases, it is explicit that such ceremonies are symbolic and no one expects any tangible results or

---

[2] Acronyms like DN and SDS followed by a date refer throughout this book to articles from Swedish newspapers. As most readers will not benefit from more detailed references, I only mention them with minimum information.

consequences. In this book, I am *not* addressing 'pure' forms of symbolism, easily recognized as entirely ceremonial.

Examples of pseudo-structures might be many quality-assurance projects, committees, leadership programmes, many political 'reforms', organizational changes, and so on. There are examples of a wide spectrum of quality-assurance activities in higher education. Programme evaluations and mandatory courses in pedagogy, or PhD supervision—sometimes strongly disliked by most people forced to participate but heralded as proof of quality and commitment to teaching by university management—are two examples that look good, although in many cases, such activities can be irrelevant or even counter-productive, other than performing a legitimizing function.

It may be difficult to identify pseudo-structures and distinguish them from structures that have a genuine impact on 'substantial' operations (i.e., the production that takes place as compared with purely symbolic activities). The litmus test of a pseudo-structure is that it is regarded as real and significant by some half-informed—but naïve—individuals, but that closer, critical examination reveals the structure to be primarily concerned with the symbolic and ceremonial. Like pseudo-events, pseudo-structures may be regarded as illusion tricks, normally with some degree of self-deception.

Grandiosity and illusion tricks are both in the field of presenting the world in a positive light, but there are differences. While grandiosity points to general attempts to redefine meanings, by giving something a gild-edged shimmer, illusion tricks involve specific events, arrangements, and texts. Illusion tricks are produced to signal something definite, but are in a dubious or misleading relationship with something 'substantive' (practices, behaviours, competence beyond impression management skills, tangible results). Illusion tricks do not necessarily have to give a particularly strong impression of attractiveness or success. They may just as well signal that the individual and others are 'following along' to avoid feeling shame for having failed to comply with the norm. An illusion trick involves small changes in the substantial content, while repackaging an object and presenting it in a more elegant form. A re-organization or a change of a title, which has limited effect on activities that go on more or less as before, could be an example. A change of the gender composition of the board of directors to display improved gender balance/equal opportunity, where the new female members do not represent anything qualitatively different or do not have much to say, is another illustration. Illusion tricks are particularly successful when the people concerned are not particularly well informed and, at least in some quarters, the intentions may be good. They often involve some element of the deception of one's self and others.

This is a phenomenon which has interested institutional theory (Meyer and Rowan, 1977; DiMaggio and Powell, 1991). One of the main points made is that ideas, ideals, and recipes for what should be done are being constantly developed, and some of them tend to have fairly widespread dissemination, which is often taken as evidence that the idea or recipe is useful and should be taken seriously. But more substantial evidence is often weak or non-existent. Ideas about how organizations should be governed, the right pedagogical methods, and how prisons and psychiatry should be organized are seldom unambiguous indications of what is best. They are often expressions of many different logics: for example, the spirit of the age, effective rhetoric by those who have developed new ideas and recipes and interest in fashion (Suddaby and Greenwood, 2001). The worry of being left behind or seen as slow on the uptake makes people and institutions inclined to follow the trend. This means that certain ideas and recipes may have a strong impact, even though it is difficult to specify what their benefits and viability are in practical applications—which are anyway often subject to local reinterpretation and adaptation, making what may work reasonable well in some context rather dysfunctional in others (Prasad et al., 2011).

Institutional theory claims that most organizations nonetheless adopt such ideas and recipes, at least at the formal structural level. They introduce, for example, techniques, practices, and structures, establish new departments, initiate projects and programmes, and employ certain terms. Such actions are implemented not because they have a proven positive effect on operations but in order to reduce cognitive uncertainty and/or establish legitimacy. People might, for example, be uncertain about what should be done. Is it essential to have a budget? Would quality circles lead to improvements? Is it a good idea to employ consultants? Would gender equality perhaps result in better managerial recruitment? It is not easy to disperse uncertainty. In the absence of self-confidence, time to think, and critical reflection, people tend to imitate others.

One advantage of doing what others do is that you gain legitimacy. If you do not have a gender equality policy, a training programme for 'leaders', strategic plans and visions, you may on the contrary appear to be out-of-date, irresponsible, sloppy, or unprofessional in some other respect. As a result, in order to avoid this and give the impression you are rational, ethical, up-to-date, or simply like everyone else, you adopt various well-established and new ideas and recipes, even though it is difficult to demonstrate any gains in efficiency or any other substantial advantages.

According to Meyer and Rowan (1977), such responses to what is generally defined as rational, sensible, and progressive tend to involve special structures, arrangements, and activities, which are readily presented and demonstrated, particularly in relation to the outside world. However, they are largely unrelated to productive operations, which might possibly be disturbed by the excessive impact of such new ideas and recipes for success. Hence, we find legitimated structures that reduce uncertainty in organizations and establish confidence in relation to the outside world. We also have work organizations and control mechanisms that are independent of such structures and that achieve productivity and efficiency. Institutional theory reiterates its argument by claiming that it is wise to keep these aspects apart, i.e., loosely coupled. In other words, organizations do some things to achieve results, and others to look good. As mentioned, this form of symbolic action is becoming increasingly important.[3]

Appearance then does not comply so well with the 'substance' of operations. Hypocrisy in which words and decisions differ from action is common, as Brunsson claims (2003). Organizations and politicians are faced with many different demands, and it is difficult to live up to all of them. Furthermore, the prerequisites change over time, and it is hard to be consistent. Expectations of compliance between words, decisions, and action are often unrealistic. The solution is a free-coupling of these elements: talk, decisions, and action may differ in order to satisfy different groups. Brunsson mentions the example of battery hens in Sweden. They were forbidden as the result of a political decision associated with the eightieth birthday of Astrid Lindgren, a famous author of children's books who was very popular in Sweden and a well-known animal lover. This political decision satisfied Astrid Lindgren's admirers and other animal lovers; however, at the same time, the government made many exemptions—the action—that satisfied chicken farmers and consumers who wanted cheap eggs. In other words, the decision and the action worked in different directions so that concern for hens and economic interests could be combined, at least at the illusory level.

The need for structures that provide legitimation is often justified in defensive terms. People want to do the same as others and make things look good, or at least acceptable, without necessarily seeming to be much better than everyone else. In other words, illusion tricks do not have to signal grandiosity, but may express some more modest meaning sufficient to make things legitimate, i.e., good enough rather than great enough. This goes hand-in-hand with a society possessing a strong awareness of images. Images have occupied the arena at the expense of more cautious representations of reality, and are setting their powerful stamp on ideas and attitudes.

Postmodernists, such as Baudrillard (1983), even consider that reality has come to the end of the road in today's society, replaced by hyper-reality. Other images of reality associated with pseudo-events and pseudo-structures circulate in the mass media and other contexts, whilst 'reality' is said to have

---

[3] All human action is in a sense symbolic. However, I am after something different here: actions with very little 'substance' or material referent, which are not clearly communicated or recognized as being 'purely' symbolic (like baptisms, weddings, and other ceremonies).

disappeared. Baudrillard is provocative, of course, but there is something in this, for example in contexts where brand names rule the roost. Maybe we can say that reality is in retreat, perhaps even threatened by extinction in some areas. This idea is reinforced by the demand for grandiosity.[4] The latter also reinforces the incoherence/hypocrisy identified by Brunsson and Meyer and Rowan.

As in the case of grandiosity, references to illusion tricks are neither new nor unique. For example, in 1787, Prince Potemkin mounted painted scenery along a road to spare the Russian Empress, Catherine the Great, the sight of an ugly and impoverished country. Potemkin was hardly the first person to gild the lily by making reality more attractive than it actually is. The illusion tricks to which I refer are not as blatant as Potemkin's and other similar creations.

The attention to illusion tricks is often more a question of responses to broad pressures for news and improvements created by an attractive and legitimate world. Illusion tricks do not necessarily lie about the world— they to a degree change and form it. They are making their mark with increasing force on the economy and working life and, in particular, they are permeating organizations and occupations. I want to point out the circumstances that are contributing to this—both external pressures and opportunities—as examples of such practices.

Relationships between the three elements

The three manifestations or aspects of contemporary development depicted in the above—the zero-sum game, grandiosity, and illusion tricks—can be described as trends, separate from each other. We can talk about the general transitions: (1) from non-positional goods to zero-sum games, (2) from most people and groups being concerned with survival and a not too uncomfortable life to being increasingly preoccupied with hype and grandiosity, and (3) from production and materiality to the display of images (illusion tricks) decoupled from basic practices. Each of these trends can be researched, and overall trends, variations, and exceptions, areas where these are strong, modest, weak, or even non-existing, can be identified and explored.

The major purpose of this book is, however, to show the links between the three. My aim is *not* to describe separate trends, but to show that these are manifestations or aspects of contemporary development and society. The

---

[4] The threatened nature of the real may lead to some efforts to preserve it from extinction. There is a lot of talk of authenticity, even in the most farfetched settings, such as branding, 'reality' TV, and leadership. 'Authentic leadership' is, for example, a vast field.

three aspects reinforce each other, often in vicious circles. With an economy characterized by positional goods and resulting zero-sum games, there is increased focus on and competition over grandiosity, and a proliferation of illusion tricks.

An ambition such as 'We must improve the status of...' is often voiced when some anxious and troubled writer or speaker wants to solve some problem in society. The status in question may involve the health care sector, primary education, librarians, or even the entire public sector. Status enhancement projects are common and often appear to be a question of labels and titles, or association with something regarded as eminent (for example, research) or that attracts media attention, and they are rarely linked with what the status-seekers know, can do, or achieve. Sometimes, the key factor is pay and public appreciation. The problem is that, by definition, status is a zero-sum game. Raising someone's status involves, per definition, lowering someone else's. In terms of status marking, it is relative pay that is crucial, not absolute pay. It is often not clear whose status is to be reduced, and sometimes the status of a small group may be enhanced without any immediate consequences for others. However, on the whole, attempts to improve status mean reduced status for someone else. This can be very clear: if, for example, teaching skills are to be given higher status in universities, then this might be equally formulated as a corresponding reduction in the status of research. And higher status for, e.g., nurses can affect other occupational groups, such as doctors and assistant nurses (I will return to this example in Chapter 8). Likewise, an improvement in the position of high school teachers through a significant wage increase will not do the trick if other occupations receive the same kind of increase.

The combination of positionally oriented consumption and the zero-sum game in line with economic growth exacerbates competition for the symbolism and the relative values that are at stake. In this context, individuals, groups, and institutions try to improve their positions at the expense of others, directly or indirectly. Politicians and other power-holders, who often have limited opportunities to provide additional dividends in the form of 'substantial satisfaction reforms', such as higher pay or independent and qualified working conditions, take initiatives in the symbolic field instead. Similarly, business and marketing operations focus on symbolic manipulation to a greater extent: useful products that meet basic needs take a more modest place in the market compared with products that have been successfully identified with status, identity, and self-esteem. The brand name rather than the product, becomes the key feature, and sometimes the product may become a kind of communication platform for the brand. The little Lacoste crocodile needs something to be sewn onto. Grandiosity, in other words, is encouraged by increased competition for positional advantages, and it leads to—and is reinforced by—greater propensity to initiate pseudo-events, develop pseudo-structures, and produce texts (documents) that convey an attractive and legitimating image of a group, an organization, or some other institution. The illusion trick gives a favourable or misleading impression that hides this deception.

The stiffer the competition for position and the more favourable impressions become, the more the individual's desire for grandiosity is fanned. Of course, one by-product may be improved performances and positive qualitative changes, as status may also be a positive driving force, but it means, above all, a greater propensity to carry out changes that give the impression of being more advanced, moral, modern, rational, innovative, original, or attractive in some other way. The level of ambition accelerates, and the pressure to make things look good increases. We create a need for the illusions with which we fool ourselves by harbouring, nourishing, and even augmenting such expectations. And we pay others to create them so that we can be deceived (Boorstin, 1961).

The incorporation into the groves of academia of occupations that were previously defined as largely practical, the purchase of the newest and most exciting gadgets, and the rapid adoption of the latest management trends are three examples in different spheres. Many more examples will be presented in the following chapters. Hence, we find a spiral development along the flowing lines:

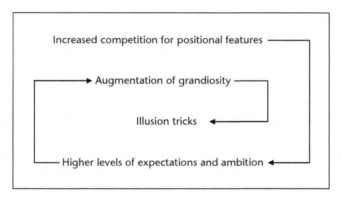

Figure 2. The interactive dynamics of positional goods, grandiosity, and illusion acts.

The idea here is that economic development leads to an emphasis on positional goods and relative standing. This is very much about status and the ambition to be ahead of others—or at least not be left behind. With escalating ambitions and expectations of above-average improvements, we get an explosion of signs on grandiosity—brands, titles, professionalization projects, and campaigns for visibility. These are in a sense 'unconstrained' and undisciplined by material restraints. Grandiosity, however, calls not just for what may be viewed as empty claims, but for backup in the form of structures, plans, signs of style, ads, well-prepared power points, and other physical, social, or textual representations that can be shown off. The prevalence of the latter means a crowded space for the trade in uplifting symbolism, intensifying competition. The spiral interplay between the three aspects (manifestations) of social dynamics is reinforced.

Forcing the pace of grandiosity and illusion tricks

I have already touched on the background to zero-sum game tendencies in the consumption area. Such tendencies also set the pace, to some extent, for grandiosity and the laying out of embellished smoke screens. But there is more to say about what generates and permits these phenomena. Once upon a time, most people were largely tied to a certain social position, and they lacked the material and symbolic means needed to change this situation or to signal something radically different. They were bound by poverty, parental background, class, gender, geography, and so on, but these factors have progressively become less important in an industrialized and post-industrial world, whose inhabitants now live in an open society that offers abundant opportunities in principle, and sometimes in practice, but above all in terms of expectations. Although it is true that there are many people, even in wealthy societies, who are not doing so well, particularly in times of financial crisis and recession, on the whole, the standard of living for the majority of the population is high and poverty is mainly relative. It can be very difficult to be clearly below average in income and material wealth but the general problem is hardly a lack of resources, but how these are distributed.

Status and position are not given factors, but are subject to conquest and struggle, or expectations that politicians, organizational leaders, and representatives of occupational groups will fix things. Diverse social trends spur on strong desires to move up positions, at both the individual and group levels. These trends include everything from economic and technological to cultural and identity-revising changes:

1. There is massive communication of images and ideals in areas such as education, careers, occupations, health, physical appearance, and (other forms of) consumption. The mass media, and in particular the screen media, are exerting a growing influence, and this means that rapid, superficial, and distant images are taking over from a deeper understanding of things that we know personally.

2. There are considerable choices and opportunities—there are resources and, in principle, little is determined in advance. Personal appearance can be improved—plastic surgery—and this also applies to some extent to the characteristics of one's children—by means of tests (possibly followed by abortion) and insemination by donors with the right characteristics.

3. People are aware that life is short and that the satisfaction achieved by being included in the continuity of a family is more limited as a result of divorce and the geographical separation of family members. There is a focus on 'me here and now' rather than on long-term and reassuring hopes about a 'better future for us all' or 'salvation after death'.[5]

4. There are strong hedonistic features in society, reinforced by the decline of religious belief in many affluent societies, the weakening of family ties, the dominance of a consumer culture, etc. We are on this earth to enjoy ourselves, and not to improve our characters by the sweat of our brows.

5. Societies based on social class and gender have weakened and disintegrated—this means that individuals have freed themselves to some extent from conventional ideas and limitations as to what they should and can do. Even if there are obviously certain gender rules and restrictions, they have become increasingly elastic—people can even change their sex.

6. There has been an initiation and demolition of identity-forming projects, resulting in the fragmentation of a sense of context and direction linked to a distinct self-image. This has weakened the 'internal' identity in favour of some 'external', staged source of identity.

Much of this is associated with, and partly a result of, economic growth and a change of emphasis in the economic system from production to creation of demand. This is because productivity developments mean that the bottleneck is now ensuring a demand for a surplus of products and services. In a 'persuasion' economy, production becomes less important than 'influence projects' that, in combination with other factors, tend to favour grandiosity and zero-sum games. McCloskey and Klamer (1995) estimate that about a quarter of the GDP in the United States is about persuasion, based on calculations of people in occupations with a high proportion of time spent at work trying to talk other people into something. They use a broad, perhaps too broad, definition of persuasion, also including non-commercial occupations (including social workers and judges), but it is still clear that persuasion—or 'sweet talk'—is a key component in the contemporary economy, and one steadily increasing in

---

[5] Cf. the death of master narratives, Lyotard (1984).

terms of percentage of work conducted as well as effects on people and society.

Much of the above covers trends that are reasonably well documented in the social sciences—even though there are strong tendencies to exaggerate the scope of the changes, their depth and speed. Social scientists refer to 'cultural liberation' (*kulturelle Freisetzung*) (Ziehe), 'detraditionalization' (Beck), and so on. Tradition and a culture that are passed on and are based on continuity and reproduction are losing ground, and thinking, ambitions, and life-projects are less predetermined. This opens up possibilities, but it also involves vulnerability and anxieties. Complying with established cultural patterns offers security and affinity, but it also implies ties and sluggishness. Encountering a more relaxed and changeable cultural universe offers freedom and opportunities, but there is a considerable risk that the 'self-identity' is not integrated and formed, but remains fragmented and vulnerable; an object of increasingly anxious identity work (Knights and Willmott 1989). A culture that offers continuity and a sense of direction is both a straightjacket and a safety net. The freeing of symbols and representations from material practices or 'substantial' social factors may be related to this liberation, disconnecting, or free-setting process (Boorstin, 1961; Ziehe and Stubenrauch, 1982). Post-modernists, in particular Baudrillard (1983), have been drawing attention to disconnections from a fixed, integrated social reality and continuous cultural (re-)production since the 1970s. The way companies and other social actors are increasingly focusing on their image, brands, and window displays has also been studied on a broad front and is relatively well documented (see Chapters 3 and 8). One interesting aspect is that 'reality' is losing ground. The material restrictions are becoming less obvious and the social forms more plastic. The representation sphere is increasingly taking over what it is supposed to refer to. The world—which is increasingly acquiring the character of a 'stage set society'—is failing to offer any clear resistance to various kinds of fantasies and wishful thinking. Personal observations and experiences carry little weight compared with everything transmitted and filtered via the mass media, but ironically social media may offer mini-versions of mass-media-filtered experiences. Of course Facebook, blogs, and other media can be used in an endless number of different ways, but large parts display similarities to the pseudo-events on which mass media focuses. The illusory (or pseudo-) structures, events, and other forms of representations often do not refer to much else than themselves, making anchoring or a sense of reality (beyond representations) a difficult project.

Consumer cultures—which are expanding from a purely commercial areas to also include the political, health care, and education spheres—give priority to the consumer, and requirements that consumer demands should be satisfied also impinge on tolerance for the rejection of our desires. Foley (2010) emphasizes the strong contemporary conviction that we are entitled to all the good things in life—and expect to get them too. Right-wing politicians and market forces seduce us with a consumption ideal, while the left-wing and the welfare state encourage us to demand rights without obligations.

> Seduced from the left by the righteousness of entitlement and from the right by the glamour of potential, it is easy to believe that fulfilment is not only a basic right but thoroughly deserved, and that attaining it requires no more thought, effort, or patience than an escalator ride to the next level of the shopping centre. (Foley, 2010: 41).

Ever more infantile and primitive desires are taking over. High and escalating expectations result in impatience with school education, working life, and consumption that fail to live up to these demands.

I will be returning to all these aspects—I have simply confined myself in this chapter to signalling some of the sources of inspiration for this book and its foundations in the social sciences, and indicating its overall frame of reference.

Summary and outline of the rest of the book

In this chapter, I have presented this book's general thesis and introduced some basic concepts as well as an overall framework for understanding some key aspects of affluent societies and affluent groups more generally. My major concept is grandiosity, but this needs to be understood in the context of an economy gradually moving from production in circumstances of scarcity to the zero-sum games that increasingly dominate consumption and other social institutions and practices, including education, organizations, and working life. Grandiosity also needs to be related to illusion tricks, for example, social arrangements giving grandiosity and other 'it-should-look-good' ambitions a strong visibility and backup, although often on ambiguous and shaky grounds. These are not 'pure' illusions, but they tend to present an orchestrated, improved image—typically different from what would be revealed by a careful inspection of conditions and practices the illusion tricks are supposed to represent.

These aspects or manifestations are interrelated and make increasingly strong imprints on contemporary society as a whole, dominating institutions and people's lives.

I will demonstrate this with respect to a number of key themes and institutions in the following chapters. My first theme is consumption. It is broadly realized that we, in the wealthier parts of the world, live in a consumer society. Consumerist ideals—immediate gratification, hedonism, and expectations that the world is there to satisfy our wishes—are crucial, not only in the specific domain of consumption, but also in other settings. A key aspect of consumption today is the increased focus on persuasion, desire, and wishes. At the same time, there seems to be an inability to bring increased satisfaction. The wish for more appears to know no limits, driving grandiosity upwards. This theme is addressed in Chapter 2 and, in particular, Chapter 3.

I then move on to higher education. In the so-called knowledge society, the most popular and most grandiose label for contemporary post-industrial society, expansion of higher education is common and viewed as both a key element in the qualification of labour and a key driver for positive economic development. Here knowledge and innovation are doing the trick—and routinized, non-qualified production is supposed to be carried out by others. A close look at higher education systems and institutions reveals a wealth of examples of grandiosity and illusion tricks. There is increased competition for position between universities and between graduates. The latter boost their CVs in the intensified struggles for the kind of attractive jobs that justify their academic qualifications.

This takes us on to working life, to organizations, management, and occupational groups. This is a broad and multifaceted sector and I choose four key themes to address (in Chapters 6–9): claims about rapid change and dynamics; the increased focus on window-dressing in order to produce an appealing organizational surface; the efforts to boost various occupational groups through professionalization projects; and the change—whether in organizational practice or in rhetoric—from management to leadership.

The following eight chapters (2–9) illuminate consumption, higher education, and working life/organizations. In all of them, I show how zero-sum games, grandiosity, and illusion tricks are key elements in developments and contemporary functioning.

The final two chapters integrate, develop, and summarize my overall approach. The triumph and emptiness of grandiosity is revealed. Its social and psychological costs are discussed.

2

Consumption—the shortcomings of affluence

My first main theme is consumption, which is the focus of this chapter and the next. However, since consumer culture also has a clear imprint on the other themes covered in this book—education, working life, and organizations—consumption orientations and logics make themselves felt throughout. Consumption development is strongly characterized by zero-sum games and the cultivation of grandiose notions and illusion tricks. And maybe such features are typically most marked in the consumption area (in its more restricted, traditional sense).

Consumption is about the satisfaction of needs, desires, and wishes, but of course also about the generation of those orientations. All this involves complicated construction processes. Given the enormous increase in consumption, at least in economically advanced countries, one would expect people to have become more and more satisfied. And perhaps feel saturation. But this is simply not the case. An interesting question is whether economic growth and increased consumption are satisfaction-creating projects? If they are not, and many indicators suggest they are only marginally so, the meaning of increased consumption in the world's most affluent societies and groups deserves exploration.

I start with a discussion of consumer culture, the increasing scope of consumption, and the apparently insatiable demand for additional goods and services, even in the richest countries. Subsequently, I examine some common views about consumption and consumers. The consumer may be regarded as everything from a heroic political figure to an undiscerning fool, from an active creator of meaning to a passive victim of market ideologies, fashion trends, and consumer manipulation. Next, I demonstrate that a massive increase in consumption is paralleled by a continual growth in demand, without any corresponding increase in satisfaction. The question then arises as to whether consumerism can be viewed as a major failure or at least a somewhat unsuccessful political and individual project. This chapter also addresses the significance and effectiveness of efforts to control consumers and consumption. The analysis of consumption continues in Chapter 3, addressing how consumption involves so many aspects and logics other than meeting needs, demands, and wishes, and can only, to a limited degree, be viewed as an ultimately satisfaction-raising enterprise.

Consumption and consumer culture

Consumption is obviously a broad, even gigantic, topic for discussion. Perhaps its scope is so wide that it is impossible to say anything sensible about it. Life calls for consumption. However, purchasing and consuming a litre of milk is, of course, quite different from buying and wearing a pair of gym shoes or a suit for formal occasions. And the decision faced by the breadwinner in a poor family who must choose between shoes for the children and a meal that fills everyone's stomach is radically different from that of a well-to-do citizen who cannot make up his/her mind which swimming pool to pick, or whether to replace the car this year or the next. Some consumption is strongly loaded with symbolic and cultural meaning, status considerations, and identity aspects, and scores high in terms of positionality (e.g., cars or clothing), while other forms of consumption are more private and comparatively free from social implications (e.g., toilet paper and carrots). The latter can be described as non-positional.[1] Some types of consumption have a negative impact on the environment, while others do not present an ecological problem. Some aspects of consumption are morally dubious—for example, fashion and status items that exacerbate peer-group pressures in the classroom and contribute to a sense of failure and outsider status for parents who are unable or unwilling to live up to steadily increasing norms and standards. This can also apply to the consumption of meat and fish, which is seldom ethically innocent. But even if some forms of consumption are fully justified and relatively unproblematic, this applies to a decreasing proportion of total consumption in an affluent society. More and more consumption tends to be socially and ecologically problematic, perhaps even destructive for the consuming individual. We need to consider the ethical nature of consumption; this book will do so in the context of grandiosity and social differentiation and their psychological effects.

---

[1] A reader of an early version of this text remarked, about the toilet paper example, that some of his guests had complained about his paper being too raw and too cheap. Of course, toilet paper is definitively part of a social and cultural context—in some groups, the practice of using toilet paper is unknown—and the socially conscious person may use the paper's softness, brand, and scent as a way of expressing identity and displaying a certain social level, at least when expecting guests. But still, the symbolism and positionality of toilet paper is, for most people, fairly limited, toilet paper is consumed in a private setting, and the satisfaction of the paper used is not directly related to other people's consumption of toilet paper.

There is no doubt about the rapid growth of consumption over the past century. In Great Britain, it is estimated that the working classes spent somewhere between a half and two-thirds of their income on food in the early twentieth century, whereas by the 1950s this figure had dropped to one-third. Today, expenditure on food represents only about one-tenth of income (Gabriel and Lang, 2006: 12). Hence, in the course of a couple of generations, the freeing of consumption resources for non-food products has now reached an almost unimaginable level—a level, of course, the vast majority of the world's population still regards as utopian. Estimates of the time devoted to shopping and the associated travelling indicate that this increased from about 40 to an average of 70 minutes a day between 1961 and the mid-1980s. It is interesting to note that this increase in shopping time corresponds to a reduction in working hours during the same period (Gabriel and Lang, 1995: 11, citing various studies).

Production per inhabitant in the more prosperous countries increased by an average of 2 per cent annually during the twentieth century, whereas consumption has doubled about every 35 years. Each generation has had about twice the material standard of living of their parents, and three to four times that of their grandparents when they were the same age (Jespersen, 1998). According to Jespersen, it would not be an exaggeration to say that the average person in a prosperous country has today a material standard of comfort that only royalty and plutocrats could have enjoyed a few generations ago. In the case of travel and mass-media consumption, for example, most people have much greater opportunities than royal families did in the nineteenth century.

Expressions such as 'post-scarcity' and the 'affluent society' have been applied to discussions of the modern consumer economy (Carter and Jackson, 1987; Galbraith, 1958). Consumption has multiplied in the richer parts of the world since Galbraith launched the latter expression. After the arrival of the affluent society, in countries such as the United States in the 1950s and in large parts of Western Europe in the 1960s, further affluence has spread. We may refer to many of today's nations as having a *post-affluent society*, and in many 'pre-affluent societies' there are significant post-affluent groups. There are also poor people in many post-affluent societies, but the small minority of people in wealthy countries mainly concerned with 'non-positional' goods is not the target of this book.

Post-affluence may be illustrated by the fact that billions kronor of food is thrown away every year in Sweden. Almost 25 per cent of all the food purchased is thrown away, most of it without good cause (*Svenska Dagbladet*, 24 April 2007).[2] A broader study estimates food waste of about 100 kg per

---

[2] A Swedish newspaper.

person in the industrialized world (FAO, 2011). Parts of this is, of course, difficult to avoid, but much of it is related to a very high level of wealth. Food is wasted due to quality standards that reject food items not perfect in shape or appearance. At the consumer level, insufficient purchase planning and food expiring 'best-before dates' also cause large amounts of waste, in conjunction with the careless attitude of those consumers who can afford to waste food (FAO, 2011). This is clear evidence of an enormous surplus.

Another indication of post-affluence is the very high amount of time and attention devoted to meaning-creation and attempts to establish an identity around the consumption of goods and services. In terms of values, desires, time, and self-awareness, people today are increasingly reliant on the steady supply of goods and services to make them feel good. Young people are socialized into a decidedly consumer orientation at an early age, particularly in highly commercial countries such as the United States (Schor, 2004).

In consumer culture, issues around consumption for the sake of survival and as a means to accomplish other goals have been replaced by the idea of consumption as a goal in itself. Consumption is set free from functional bonds and justifies itself by reference to its own ability to generate pleasure, Bauman (2001) writes. In consumer culture, desire is the key driver and rationale:

> The spiritus movens of consumer activity is not a set of articulated, let alone fixed, needs, but desire—a much more volatile and ephemeral, evasive and capricious, and essentially, non-referential phenomenon, a self-begotten and self-perpetuating motive that calls for no justification or apology either in terms of an objective or a cause. (13)

The appropriate individual is Homo Consumericus, who has adapted to and internalized the view that we have several fragmented and insecure self-images that need to be marketed by means similar to the traditional marketing of symbols. These self-images 'are to be constructed by the very acquisition and bricolage of those market and consumption symbols' (Bertilsson, 2009: 4).

Consumer culture is clearly closely connected to the three core aspects of this book. A large, increasing part of this culture circles around promises of grandiosity; around quality assurance markers such as brands, which are often uncertain and can, in many cases, be seen as illusion tricks; and around the relative standing of the consumer as compared to others. The grandiosity is expressed in direct sales messages, and in the way products and services are displayed, for example in shop windows, on packaging, and in the interiors of shops. Ads typically let the object on sale shine. Some commentators emphasize new forms of branding and advertising that are more sophisticated and work with, rather than trying to control, consumers (Arvidsson, 2006; Holt, 2002), but a few hours' observation of television commercials and 'lifestyle' magazine ads gives a clear impression of the strong, direct messages about products' glamour and superiority, as well as the promises of extraordinary qualities that will be bestowed on the happy consumer who owns and shows off the right product.

Relationships, work, knowledge, and actions are, according to some critics, losing ground in relation to materialistic values and consumption as sources of identity. As Bauman (1988) says, people of today find it hard to manage without adapting to the logic of the market. Of course, some form of consumption may always be social and collectively oriented, but a strong focus on material goods as a source of meaning may weaken social commitments. Much of the satisfaction of needs or wishes represented by the market involves the creation of a need or wish by the same market (i.e., its actors):

> New technical, social, psychological and existential skills of the consumers are such as to be practicable only in conjunction with marketable commodities; rationality comes to mean the ability to make the right purchasing decisions, while the craving for certainty is gratified by a conviction that the decisions made have been, indeed, right. (Bauman, 1988: 222)

It is, of course, not easy to achieve this rationality and sense of security. Aspects of irrationality, uncertainty, and confusion play a large part in the consumption sphere, and they are tending to increase in pace with ongoing increases in consumption.

The expansion of consumption and its mixed blessings

The consumer may be said to be in the place of honour in society. All societal institutions—including, as we shall see later, schools and universities, where the focus is on the student, not on learning—are increasingly voicing their customer and market orientation. Consumer choice is the hub around which society rotates. The consumer controls production, guides innovations, drives politics via increasingly sensitive politicians who administer 'political markets', and, it is said, determine the ecology by means of more or less environmentally destructive (or environmentally friendly) decisions and actions. A growing proportion of social control is more a matter of dancing to the tune of the consumer than a question of authority and morality: the consumer chooses, makes demands, and criticizes. This consumer orientation is internalized: satisfying customers (or quasi-customers such as patients or students) becomes a key source of self-realization and self-discipline for an increasing number of people in their professions or in other functions (for example, political decision-makers).

In his/her capacity as a central figure, the consumer is, however, highly controversial. Perhaps he/she is king, but is the monarch clever or stupid, directing actively or merely reacting passively? Is the consumer the incarnation of rationality: actively aware of his needs and wishes, capable of imposing efficiency and flexibility on various institutions as a result of his decisions in the marketplace and in quasi-markets? And can consumer choices overcome inefficiency and rigidity? Or is the consumer a typical example of amenability, a victim of power, manipulation, and limited rationality, permeated by illusions, wishful thinking, and the inability to acquire and process the information required to make a wise decision? Is the consumer ensnared in a complex web of dreams and wishful thinking with no sense of reality, driven to an ever-increasing and more intensively stressed consumption of products that do not result in greater satisfaction and that contribute to growing environmental pollution? Maybe the consumer finds it difficult to master this situation and cannot realize the political, ethical, and environmental consequences of his/her actions? These are, of course, difficult questions that cannot be readily answered, but I will try to shed some light on the various mechanisms and processes that create problems for consumers aiming to act in sensible and thoughtful ways.

According to the adherents of market economy, the consumer may be regarded as wisdom personified. For their opponents, the consumer is viewed as a pathetic victim. In other words, the consumer is either a force of rationality or a source of irrationality. So, consumption is very much a question of politics and morality. Initially, the very word itself had a negative overtone and was associated with destruction, exploitation, and depletion of resources. During the twentieth century, this term became more associated with satisfaction, enjoyment, and freedom. In democratic societies, the slogan of freedom has often been used synonymously with individual consumption. The new right wing and other sympathizers of the 'free market' have regarded consumers as 'the storm-troopers of freedom' (Gabriel and Lang, 2006: 16) On the other hand, the alternative slogan, solidarity, also means—ultimately—considerable individual consumption, but via income transfers and contributions to those with fewer consumption opportunities, combined with more production and 'consumption' under public sector auspices.

For its supporters, increased consumption is an improvement project that enriches and ameliorates life. Of course a high level of consumption may involve significant sources of satisfaction and personal development. Some people presumably enrich their lives through consumption and through acquiring possessions, even though the positive value may for many be overestimated. For sceptics, on the other hand, the problem lies either in the manipulation of consumers' desires and orientations or in the occurrence of unfortunate social dynamics such as status competition or following fashion. It is important to acknowledge here that as a well-paid academic with an interesting, free, and creative job—who gains status from intellectual accomplishments rather than conspicuous consumption—I need to be reflective about my own inclinations and my limited ability to understand other groups (see Miller, 2001, and Wilk, 2001, on this matter). However, this should not prevent the expression of critical views.

In any event, modern life is permeated by a powerful consumption orientation. Some researchers refer to 'hyper consumption' as 'a state of affairs in which every social experience is mediated by market mechanisms' (Gabriel, 2005: 21). Maybe they are exaggerating, but there is a strong pressure to comply with consumption ideals—even though one sometimes is supposed to deny or tone it down (Ulver-Sneistrup, 2008). If we do not have this consumerist orientation, we may appear to be deviants. Failure to keep up with fashion, refraining from buying innumerable objects for our children, not maintaining a standard of living that corresponds to our level of income and social position are met with raised eyebrows. A colleague from another country once asked what kind of car I had. When I replied that I did not have a car, my colleague reacted as if I had revealed some exotic sexual deviation or confessed to a serious crime. Likewise, my very old and simple mobile telephone is sometimes viewed as an expression of my idiosyncratic character. This is a minor issue for most people in the protected world of academia, but anyone looking for a regular career job would do well to demonstrate the right kind of consumption pattern: deviation from the norm can cost more than it's worth. (See, for example, Jackall, 1988, on the negative assessments of people in career jobs failing to live up to the proper dress norms in their companies.) Consumption permeates our social relationships, perceptions, and images. Whether we seek 'happiness, identity, beauty, love, masculinity, youth, marital bliss or anything else, there is a commodity somewhere that guarantees to provide it' (Gabriel and Lang, 2006: 17). In this sense, one cannot, with impunity, simply choose to refrain from being a consumer, that is to say, to minimize your purchases and consumption of goods and services in market transactions. We can say, inspired by Foucault (1977; 1980), that we are normalized as consumers, that is to say, we adopt the template of a natural, normal, and desirable person. This means that deviations from the norm involve feelings of insufficiency and discomfort and, as a result, the person concerned steers others and himself into the right degree of conformity. A consumer standard rules. This does not necessarily mean total streamlining—within certain frameworks, the template also allows for a display of individuality and creativity (Arvidsson, 2006). However, it does not contradict the possibility of a strong element of programming and conformity. Even if a consumption discourse does not necessarily prescribe, in detail, how people think and feel, it inscribes in individuals—

apart from a few deviants—the norm of being active participants in consumer culture and having strong consumerist orientations.

> Perhaps above all, consumer culture involves a search for meaning and life through consumption. At one time, and to a lesser degree today, people derived great meaning from work, family, community, religion, but all of these seem less important today as sources of meaning (and practice). Instead, meaning is increasingly likely to come from shopping or touring, both of which are likely to involve those visits to one or more of the cathedrals of consumption. (Ritzer, 2007: 168)

Normative consumerist forces operate on a broad front—not only in a strictly market context. 'Marketing is everything', according to enthusiasts such as marketing professor McKenna (1991). Apparently everything must market itself and everyone themselves. In Chapter 4, I touch on the headway made by a customer orientation in schools and higher education.

The consumption project—a major failure?

One might think that this powerful expansion of consumption would mean a high degree of satisfaction and a growing saturation of needs and desires for material objects—maybe even hypersaturation.

In the past, many economists and other social researchers and commentators assumed that economic growth would mean that most people, having become satisfied with their material standard of living, would put more emphasis on their spiritual and cultural development. Calm and harmony were expected to permeate our lives and we were expected to have more time for activities such as art, literature, the countryside, social contacts, and reflection. But this has hardly proved to be the case, at least not for those of working age. On the contrary, the pace of our lives seems to be increasing, and our existence is becoming more hectic. The question of higher incomes and the opportunities for consumption that result from this are of crucial importance, both for potentially elite groups and for ordinary people. More than 40 years ago, Burenstam Linder (1969) considered that interest in economic growth is itself growing at virtually the same pace as the increase in incomes. This increased interest in consumption possibilities applies to all groups in society, from politicians, union representatives, journalists, economists, and voters to ordinary consumers. This situation does not appear to have changed since 1969.

The strong interest in consumption is partly related to the emphasis on economic growth in order to keep unemployment down. In the past, we produced in order to have something to consume. Now we need to beef up consumption so that there is a demand for production and people can find employment. The means–ends logic has been reversed: from 'work to consume' to 'consume so that people can work'.

Sometimes, the focus on economic growth is justified in terms of poverty and sometimes by the need for additional resources for the old, the sick, or children. But such arguments are only of limited validity. If one of the main reasons for economic growth in Western countries is poverty in third-world countries, why are we so parsimonious about allocating more than 1 per cent of GDP to development assistance? And, as regards poverty in affluent countries—at least in welfare societies—this is largely a question of relative poverty: that is to say, some citizens are significantly below the average income level in a given country; therefore there is a considerable gap between their low income and the standard of living enjoyed by the majority. This is seldom due to actual needs as a result of lack of resources—the problem is rather an inability to participate in a normal pattern of consumption. Some people are considerably 'less rich' than others and, as a result, they experience frustration and a low level of self-esteem, and are probably looked down upon. While a difficult situation, it is hardly a problem directly linked to the need for economic growth—even if the material standard of living doubles, relatively poor/less rich people will still be in an unfavourable position. Such relative poverty (or lack of wealth) is an allocation problem and cannot be solved by economic growth.

It is often claimed that growth is needed to take care of an increasingly elderly population. There are several aspects here. One is the proportion of people active in the labour market. Given the notoriously high unemployment of young people and the high proportion in higher education, despite often limited interest and learning outcomes (see Chapters 4 and 5), it would not be too difficult to increase the number of adults working, while simultaneously reducing a great deal of the problems of the increased number of retired citizens. As regards care services, their quality and quantity are not directly related to economic growth. Higher productivity, which is responsible for the major part of economic growth, scarcely applies to the care sectors—more efficient technologies are not radically reducing the need for human labour in care facilities for the elderly (nor in schools, pre-schools, or even health care). Personnel costs are the main factor, and the employees in such services naturally demand pay increases in line with the society's economic growth. Thus, a 10 per cent increase in growth does not result in a 10 per cent increase in the volume of care services. A significant outcome is an increase in the consumption potential of the carers. Growth means that some services are delivered more efficiently by the use of technology, but it has no more than a moderate effect on labour-intensive public-sector services.

The decisive driving force behind the increasing interest in economic growth is probably, quite simply, a striving to raise material standards. People want higher and higher consumption, faster and faster increases in standards. This is hardly any revelation. What is surprising is simply people's unwillingness to admit the truth. The other motives customarily adduced are probably rationalizations, with no independent life of their own. (Burenstam Linder, 1969: 134)

Given the enormous interest in economic growth, which above all takes the form of increased material consumption, one might expect a considerable corresponding impact in terms of increased satisfaction. Although no one claims that improved material well-being solves all problems, one might expect that such a great increase in consumption over a few decades would result in a tangible increase in well-being and satisfaction. But this is hardly the case.

A considerable volume of research points rather unanimously to the conclusion that a general increase in economic well-being does not lead to any improvement in human happiness or satisfaction. (See overviews by Csikszentmihalyi, 1999; Kasser, 2002; Lane, 1991; and Pugno, 2009.) In the USA, the same percentage of people, for example, assessed themselves as 'very happy' over a 50-year period despite the fact that the material standard of living had more than doubled. Some nuances may be noted, however. People in rich countries report a somewhat higher level of satisfaction than those in poor societies, although this is particularly marked in relatively equal societies such as the Scandinavian welfare states. Perhaps dissatisfaction at having a clearly below average rating is greater than satisfaction at having an above-average rating. Studies of the relationship between income and satisfaction at an individual level showed no (or only a weak) correlation, with the exception of people who were clearly in the below-average category. In other words, having a low material standard of living, compared with the majority, is a source of dissatisfaction, whereas having an average, or slightly below or above average, standard of living is a poor indicator of satisfaction, even if people with a high income are slightly more satisfied than those with a low income. The fact that this is a relative phenomenon is illustrated by findings that suggest that higher income in a population as a whole does not lead to greater satisfaction (Easterlin, 2001). Of course, the measurement of satisfaction and happiness is difficult, and one can be very sceptical towards these investigations. Still, given the significance of the topic, the large amount of consistent findings, and the absence of counter-evidence, there are good reasons to take the results seriously—as an input to reflection and policy considerations—although not as unquestionable truths.

The important things in life are not money and consumption, but primarily friends and family, physical and mental health, working conditions, and a sense of doing and achieving something satisfying in and outside your work. Of course, these factors are not necessarily in direct opposition to consumption and they call for a certain degree of possession and use of material resources. However, an emphasis on material goods as the source of happiness might lead one to prioritize the materialistic aspects of life over those associated with 'the good life'. Csikszentmihalyi (1999) stresses, in particular, the inner satisfaction that results from creative and absorbing activities that are largely carried out for their own sake.

Higher income may be a source of greater satisfaction to the extent that it is regarded as a confirmation of the individual's capabilities, even though the key factor is perhaps skills and achievement. The perceived correlation between the latter and increased pay sometimes contributes to a feeling that pay increases are important. More money, however, does not seem to have any particularly positive effect. A study that traced a number of lottery winners after they had received their prizes showed that the winners did not feel increased satisfaction, rather the reverse (referred to in Csikszentmihalyi, 1999). (Undoubtedly, economic growth is quite crucial in poorer societies, and increased individual standards of living have resulted in a greater sense of well-being, but, as already indicated, this book's main focus is on post-affluent societies, which are characterized by a very high material standard of living.) It would be difficult to claim that dramatic economic growth and the almost inconceivable level of consumption from a global and historical perspective that characterizes the richest 10 per cent of the world's population—and this presumably includes almost all readers of this book—has resulted in any radical improvement in our lives in recent decades. Instead, it is more often the case that, overall, social indicators of well-being such as drug or alcohol abuse, suicide, criminality, and mental illness have pointed to a deterioration or stagnation in our lives in general (Csikszentmihalyi, 1999; Pugno, 2009). Psychological research indicates that individuals with a strong material-welfare orientation have a weaker sense of mental well-being than others. A strong interest in material things means that fundamentally these individuals are wasting their time in terms of mental well-being since they naturally focus more on satisfying materialistic needs and less on psychologically important ones (Kasser, 2002: 48).

Obviously, it is not easy to say anything about satisfaction with life in general, but I assume that many people would agree with Erich Fromm's (1976) assessment that the twentieth century might be regarded as a gigantic experiment as to whether greater material welfare/consumption designed for pleasure is the key to human happiness—and the answer is that it is not. A study of Americans' views on the changes in their consumption over a ten-year period indicated that they considered that they had experienced material setbacks, whereas objective indicators of consumption over the same period pointed in the opposite direction (Wachtel, 1983). In other words, there appears to be no correlation between the actual volume of consumption and the experience of satisfaction. Another study, cited in Lane (1991), showed that the amount of money (income or wealth) needed to maintain a given level of economic satisfaction over a fifteen-year period increased in an almost perfect correlation with the increased general level of material welfare, which is to say that more money was required than in the past to be equally satisfied with one's economic situation. Hence, the price of financial satisfaction increases in line with economic growth. In other words, people are stuck on an economic treadmill. Csikszentmihalyi (1999) cites two further studies. The first showed that the proportion of Americans who considered themselves to be 'very happy' was constant between 1960 and 1990, despite the fact that the standard of living doubled over that period. The second study indicated that people's views on the level of income required in order to be happy was about twice as high as their current level. People who were earning less than $30,000 considered that they needed $50,000 to realize their dreams, while those with an annual income of more than $100,000 thought that $250,000 would be called for. As soon as a lower level is achieved, the level of aspiration increases. The chief explanations typically offered are accustomization and social comparisons. Broadly speaking, the level of aspiration increases proportionally with increased income (Easterlin, 2001). No doubt, the massive efforts of advertising and other consumer propaganda designed to incite people to want more, help ensure that the level of expectation is increased even more, so that when you don't get more, you become dissatisfied. (More about this in the next chapter.)

Burenstam Linder (1969) wondered, almost half a century ago, whether we had entered a 'vulgarization of growth phase', or if we were well on the way to doing so. The benefits of further increases in the average level of income and consumption have declined considerably, while demands for improvements in material circumstances remain strong. Economic questions tend to dominate, in both politics and private life. And economic improvements have changed from being a means to an end to becoming an end in itself. In view of the doubling of growth and material standards since Burenstam Linder minted this concept, it may be fair to say that we are now some way into the 'vulgarization of growth phase'. Inspired by this idea, I will subsequently be referring to a 'vulgoeconomy' in which most needs and desires have already been satisfied, and the economy is mainly a matter of levering up and maintaining a high level of demand for goods and services that often involves social zero-sum games. I will develop this later. Braverman (1974) noted that 200 years after the Industrial Revolution, productivity is still regarded as a major problem, and frenetic efforts are being made to increase it. A passion for economic growth is more acute than ever before. Braverman considers that capitalists—and here we can add the average economist, politician, wage earner, and consumer—can say, like King Ahab in the Bible, that my means are sensible but my goals are insane.

Why is this the case? Why this ever-increasing interest in growth and higher consumption?

Controlling consumers—or the consumer as a cockroach

There is no doubt that consumers are exposed to a massive courtship launched by sales interests. The challenge in the vulgoeconomy is to create demand—production is seldom the bottleneck. We have an interesting paradox as regards consumer control. On the one hand, the consumer is king, and companies and other organizations are supposed to be at his beck and call. Customer reactions provide input to a crucial control system circling around the ideal of making the customer satisfied enough to be willing to come back and make further purchases. On the other hand, the consumer-king must also be controlled, and no resources are spared in this regard.

Consumer influence is a vast area. The consumer, full of desire, is not just there, but 'must be "produced", ever anew, and at high costs. Indeed, the production of consumer devours an intolerably large part of the costs of production, distribution, and trade' (Bauman, 2001: 13). Advertising expenditures are constantly increasing, typically faster than the growth rate in the global economy, although this varies with economic cycles and tends to go down during recession. As much as $280 billion was spent on advertising in the United States in 2007.[3] As a result of such extensive efforts, the risk that a particular campaign will drown in this plethora of information is increasing, which means that companies are spending more than ever to get their message across. Klein (2000: 9) cites an American advertising manager who says that 'Consumers are like roaches—you spray them and they get immune after a while'.

If we combine these metaphors, the overall picture becomes the 'cockroach king'—someone to respectfully submit to, but also someone who justifies increasing efforts to gain control. This double-bottomed characteristic—in which companies are controlled by, but also control, the market and consumers—involves all kinds of complicated attempts to build relationships in which traditional consumer influence is crucial, but is supplemented by efforts to achieve an effective reciprocity in which direct influences are preferably hidden.

---

[3] <http://www.galbithink.org/ad-spending.htm>

Such features may, for example, be seen in the way salespersons operate. Selling involves a combination of rational information and attempts to enchant with allusions to myths, such as the consumer as sovereign decision-maker. The salesperson exploits this ideal, while simultaneously undermining it through various tricks (Korczynski, 2005). Of course, as in all forms of persuasion the degree of success varies. The cockroach king–consumer can be unpredictable, and can sometimes even behave rationally, for example by comparing prices and postponing the purchase decision—something that many salespersons detest.

Here, the disciplines of marketing, design, and communication 'have played a vital role in the transmutation of goods and services into desires and needs and vice versa. In other words, symbolic expertise actively "makes up" consumers' (du Gay, 2000: 72). The forces producing the desire for goods stealthily convince the consumer that the want is natural and comes from 'within'. As Arvidsson (2006: 74) expresses it, 'the task of brand management is to create a number of resistances that makes it difficult or unlikely for consumers to experience their freedom, or indeed their goals, in ways different from those prescribed by the particular ambience (of the brand)'.

One indication of the strong influence of advertising is that American children know 200 brand names when they start school and can identify 300–400 by the age of 10 (Schor, 2004).

Shop windows and other ways of displaying attractive goods in a seductive manner are one form of stealth advertising. This applies to product placement in films and on TV, where a major share of revenue is generated from those products clearly depicted on the screen. When well-known actors in popular TV programmes wear a particular garment, this can have an impact on the demand.

But, of course, advertising—even in a broad sense—is only a small part of the consumer-influencing process. One variation is the establishment of special locations that function as consumption cathedrals in which a massive volume of buying and selling of goods and services takes place. Theme parks, cruise liners, casinos, tourist offices, sports arenas, airports, and shopping malls are examples of this phenomenon. People visit many of these places to enjoy themselves—but they are also shopping centres, more or less in disguise. If visitors to Disneyland think that the commerce ends when they have bought their tickets, they are quite wrong—there is an intertwined network of consumption involving overnight accommodation, restaurants, and gift shops to purchase anything imaginable (Bryman, 1999).

News is often consumption propaganda too, where items about films, records, books, fashion, technology, cultural arrangements, and so on are an intricate mixture of information and advertising.

Some sceptical consumption researchers employ the 'enchantment' concept to explain consumption and the attempts to control it. Enchantment involves the creation of pleasurable dreams and fantasies, endowing a product with an aura of magic. While some aspects of consumption are of an everyday nature and not particularly strongly loaded (buying milk, for example), wide areas of consumption are more amenable to these tactics, particularly in the case of high-status brands. What may be perceived as a fairly trivial product is presented as something remarkable, extraordinary, and grandiose—superior to all competing merchandise.

Enormous resources and efforts are undoubtedly devoted, both scientifically and via market surveys, to observing, monitoring, registering, predicting, and controlling consumer behaviour and to finding ways of exerting the right influence. 'In a desire to enrich the epistemology of the consumer, no stone is left unturned; no aspect of the consumer's inner life, decision-making process, and motivation is too odd, outlandish, or negligible to preclude extensive investigation' (Zwick and Cayla, 2010: 5). Today's consumer is subject to rigorous management, seduction, and control. Never before has every purchase been so carefully registered and every credit card transaction subjected to such detailed analysis (Gabriel and Lang, 2006: 4). Never before has marketing been so well-considered, ambitious, and aggressive, and personnel and resources employed so effectively in order to steer desire and get people to open their wallets—or rather to get out their credit cards and increase their debts.

Controlling consumers is nothing new, even though attempts at achieving control have escalated dramatically, in line with the problems faced by companies in selling their goods. Market segmentation—the identification and classification of the different customer groups that constitute the target group for a product or campaign—has been around for some time. This is not merely a question of identifying natural groupings, but is just as much motivated by a desire to divide up the world in order to establish a basis for attempts to control it. One result is that various categories of individuals are established, reinforced, and locked in place:

> Marked differentiations such as those of A and B films, or of stories in magazines in different price ranges, depend not so much on subject matter as on classifying, organizing, and labeling consumers. Something is provided for all so that none may escape; the distinctions are emphasized and extended. The public is catered for with a hierarchical range of mass-produced products of varying quality, thus advancing the rule of complete quantification. Everybody must behave (as if spontaneously) in accordance with his previously determined and indexed level, and choose the category of mass product turned out for his type. (Horkheimer and Adorno, 1947: 123)

This does not mean, of course, that the outcome of such attempts to gain control is fully in line with the intentions. Consumers are not so predictable or easy to control and many do not comply with the dictates of marketing regimes. This is partly because people think for themselves, and partly because the dynamics and turbulence resulting from all the various types of influence mean that the effects of various efforts may cancel each other out, resulting in immunity or cynicism, for example. Creativity, resistance, subcultures, values, and sources of norms that lie outside the sphere of consumption are, of course, a part of social life, restricting the grip of marketing and consumerism. Consumers can spot, at least partly, how companies try to control them. This means that marketers must renew their ideas and efforts to influence the customers. These new efforts, in time, eventually lose some of their effectiveness as people become aware of the new creative marketing techniques (Bertilsson, 2009; Holt, 2002). Some researchers stress the way in which individuals attach a radically different meaning to certain goods and services, a meaning that contrasts with that which the marketer is attempting to inculcate. The consumer is regarded as an active creator of meaning, as someone who gives objects a creative, even artistic touch, and who may adopt a rebellious attitude to attempts at steering and standardizing his/her responses (Arvidsson, 2006; Gabriel and Lang, 2006; Chapters 4, 6, and 8). Radical resistance to attempts at controling individuals is not particularly common, however. Although it can be observed in movements such as adbusters and those that celebrate the simple life, much of this 'resistance' takes place in the consumption sphere—where consumers may buy and consume goods and subsequently convey a meaning that differs from what the marketer is trying to communicate. But, in that case, the resistance project is defined and framed by consumption ideals. As Fleming and Spicer (2003) argue, ideology is not primarily expressed in people's awareness of and possible distance from what they are doing, but in their acts. So, if a person buys and displays a high-status brand product, this matters much more than whether he/she is aware of the mechanisms behind the product and does not buy the branding messages.

Corporate management and the shareholders are hardly interested in whether the consumers of Marlboro cigarettes embrace the macho message and ride out into the countryside on horseback, rounding up cattle and meeting up with other macho types, or whether they stick with their office jobs and a suburban life with their families between smokes. The key factor is whether the impact on their consumption is successful to the extent that the demand for the product is high. In other words, it doesn't matter if various groups of consumers interpret the advertising message or the product's 'soul' in different ways, as long as they stay within the market (Holt, 2002). A strong drift away from a positive 'core' meaning may, in the long run, undermine the position of a product, but often there is a variety of deviations in consumer responses and reinterpretations of nuances of meanings. It is the 'overall meaning', often associated with status, recognition, and a sense of security, rather than any precise, fine-tuned meaning, associated with any unique brand quality, that typically is the key element. Uncertainty reduction is a quite different motive from brand love (or fetishism).

At least, overall, we may say that the aggregated consumption persuasion is effective in the sense that it helps to ensure that people give priority to their consumption. One may refer to incarceration in a consumption cage in which freedom—in the form of a choice between taking a substantial cut in salary and consumption—does not strike many people as a realistic alternative. Freedom becomes consumption, while lack of freedom is the absence of consumption opportunities. The costs of 'consumption-dependent freedom' in the form of the felt necessity of having a well-paid job, long working hours, etc., are regarded as a negligible reduction of freedom. Individuals lock themselves and others in a high-consumption existence and, ironically, this is often referred to as 'freedom'. The effects of marketing are seen not merely, or even primarily, in the fact that individuals buy the specific things that are promoted, but just as much, or more, by the establishment of people as consumers, making them strongly oriented towards, and dependent on, a high and ever growing level of consumption. Primitive urges are triggered here and demand gratification. As Foley (2010) puts it, the ad woos the id (the desire) and the ad-driven id of the consumerist subject goes wild: 'The contemporary id is rampant and in no mood to be tamed. Never have so many wanted so much so badly. Never has the id been so flattered and so indulged. This is the golden age of the id' (21). Doubling the level of consumption exercises no control over the desire to consume, rather the contrary. As Wachtel's (1983) study (reported earlier) suggests, an actual increase in consumption may go hand in hand with experiencing a lower standard of living.

Summary

In this chapter I have illuminated the significance and nature of contemporary consumption. Given that Galbraith (1958) quite reasonably described wealthy countries as becoming affluent societies in the 1950s, and given that people in these countries enjoy today a material standard of living which is, on average, about three times as high as it was then, we can conceptualize most of the Western world and some segments of many other countries as post-affluent societies. Of course, within these, there are poor people, and within 'pre-affluent', developing societies there are often post-affluent groups, for example, in India and China even very large ones.

Under conditions of post-affluence, the critical sector for most companies is not production—there is a significant overproduction of merchandise and services—but demand; specifically, how to achieve sufficient demand. Any sense of need has, in post-affluent society, been given up in favour of desires and wishes. These are the effective stimulants needed to keep the acceleration of consumer demand in line with increased production and consumer offer. Marketing then becomes key and enormous resources and talents are invested in trying to convince people that they need the products and/or will become much happier and appear more impressive in the eyes of themselves and others if they purchase and use these products. That is, people take on the strong belief that consumerism is a major route to happiness. This is the core of what I will refer to as the *economy of persuasion*. Its logic is not restricted to the capitalist market, but infiltrates all sectors of society, as will be demonstrated in later chapters.

In this economy, a wealth of, perhaps rather odd, habits have been produced. Vast quantities of food are thrown away, for the most part unnecessarily. We find phenomena such as Scandinavians importing bottled water from France, while Central Europeans demand the same liquid from Norway. The distance between the origin and the place of consumption signals a sense of this being authentic and especially valuable as it is obviously worth transporting over such a long distance. In many cases, local tap water is of equally high quality and as healthy as bottled water, but this does not destroy the market for the latter. The creation of the bottled water market, also in regions where there is no need for the product, is not accomplished without costs and efforts—indicating the strength of this economy of persuasion. The term *vulgoeconomy* captures some of the many excesses that characterize consumer culture: grandiosity, waste, overemphasis on consumption as the means to happiness.

The demand for higher income and material standard of living, as well as the abundance of messages suggesting that happiness is supposedly accomplished through consumerism, would indicate a strong correlation between increased material well-being and happiness (satisfaction, subjective well-being). However, there are strong indications that 'economic welfare is a very small part and often a very poor indicator of human welfare' (Scitovsky, 1976: 145). The grandiose world created by design, product placement, advertising, and other consumption-promoting tactics does not seem to deliver what it promises, at least not at the overall level of increasing human well-being and creating good lives. We need to understand this, and the next chapter addresses this theme at greater length.

3

Explaining the consumption paradox—why aren't people (more) satisfied?

Given an average of 2 per cent economic growth and a doubling of the material standard of living every 30–35 years, one would assume that most people would be more than satisfied by now, experience saturation, and not be particularly interested in greater consumption. However, this is hardly the case. Few, except a handful of 'green' activists portrayed as naïve and development-hostile, doubt the value of growth and increased consumption. Economic growth is broadly viewed as a self-evidently rational and positive objective, and any stagnation, or a mere 1 per cent growth, is viewed as problematic. This is partly a matter of securing employment, of course, but equally if not more important is the increase of consumption. Why is there no satiation? Why these continual complaints that many groups in society are not getting sufficient increases in pay or grants to have a satisfactory material standard of living?

Such questions are addressed in a review of a number of theories and themes that cast doubt on the great consumption project: Why does higher consumption, on the whole, not lead to greater satisfaction in life? Among other things, I touch on the need problem, the difficulty of making wise decisions, and the role played by consumption propaganda in forming and, perhaps, distorting the priorities in life and driving up expectations and claims. All these create considerable ambiguity and uncertainty around wants and consumption as a way of meeting these. I also address the significance of fashion and brands, making consumer satisfaction temporal and contingent upon living up to rising standards for what is acceptable. Finally, I discuss the time aspect and how people with increased consumption possibilities run into time constraints. One could talk here about the time limits of growth. I will also be returning to this book's principal thesis about the social limits of growth and the problem of much consumption in post-affluent societies being of a positional character and leading to zero-sum games about benefits and satisfaction.

The mysteries of needs and problems of priority

The concept of 'need' is tricky. It is certainly true that we need food, water, oxygen, warmth, and sensory stimulation. In most cases, people also have social needs and, for the most part, a need for some form of activity (there are very few hermits and people who are totally apathetic and not interested in human contact). But on the whole, what are regarded as needs are basically social constructions, that is to say they are not an objective part of some natural law but are instead the consequences of social ideas and institutions that form individuals and their self-awareness. Previously, some psychologists and sociologists referred to 'false needs', which is a problematic concept in many ways. It is often misleading and elitist, to make a distinction between genuine and false needs.

In the marketing area, 'need' usually means what people feel they want to have or, even more to the point, what they are prepared to pay for. The problem is that this point of departure neglects the various ways—conscious and systematic—in which needs and their expressions in the form of wants are formed. This involves equating various types of needs—reducing needs to what people can be persuaded/manipulated to purchase—while questions concerning what is important and of value for a good life and meeting wider needs are neglected.

Even if there is good reason to be cautious about expressions such as 'false needs' or even to stay away from any discussion of needs, it may be crucial to investigate the processes and mechanisms that help shape desires and orientations, and whether they achieve well-being (Kasser, 2002).

While the relationship between needs (desires) and the object employed to satisfy such needs has been relatively stable in previous cultural traditions, need categories in modern society are characterized by a high degree of changeability and unpredictability. No definite meaning is attached to goods these days; they function as fluid symbols, to which various kinds of unstable meanings may be ascribed (Leiss, 1983; Sahlins, 1976). One may, in this context, refer to an 'overproduction of signs and reproduction of images and simulations lead to a loss of stable meaning, and an aestheticization of reality in which the masses become fascinated by the endless flow of bizarre juxtapositions which takes the viewer beyond stable sense' (Featherstone, 1991: 15). Marketing contributes significantly to this decoupling of symbols and references, a separation of goods from every form of intrinsic relationship with function or need.

> When goods become rapidly changing collections of characteristics, the individual's judgements about the suitability of particular objects for particular needs are destabilized. Characteristics are distributed and redistributed across previously distinct categories of needs, experiences, and objects. For example, the taste of menthol in a cigarette is said to be 'like' the advent of springtime and the purchase of a certain type of automobile 'like' gaining a new personality. Thus the expression of need itself is progressively fragmented into smaller and smaller bits, which are then recombined in response to market cues into patterns that are temporary, fluid, and unstable.... Under these circumstances the sense of satisfaction and well-being becomes steadily more ambiguous and confused. (Leiss, 1978: 98–9)

The consumption sphere abounds with examples of the use of background images that are linked with the product, but actually have no relationship with it. Cars and cigarettes are shown against the background of untouched countryside, while a bottle of wine is displayed in a farmhouse full of old handmade furniture. Apparently, the number of different and arbitrary meanings that can be attached to various objects is almost infinite.

Some commentators argue that objects today have a completely arbitrary and fluid relationship to various meanings. Absolut Vodka is an interesting example. According to the manufacturer, the 'core values for the brand are Absolut clarity, simplicity and perfection'. You can experience these qualities simply by looking at the bottle. The clarity and simplicity are emphasized by the absence of a label, while the perfection is clearly linked to 'rinsing the bottle with something absolutely pure' prior to filling it with vodka (according to the Absolut Story advertising brochure, 2004: 17). Notwithstanding the alleged core values, it might be said that Absolut's market strategy is to minimize the importance of the product by stressing 'a blank bottle-shaped space that could be filled with whatever content a particular audience most wanted from its brands: intellectual in *Harper's*, futuristic in *Wired*, alternative in *Spin*, loud and proud in *Out* and "Absolut Centrefold" in *Playboy*' (Klein, 2000: 17). The average consumer hardly realizes that clarity, simplicity, and perfection is what you are expressing when you consume the liquid in question—in most cases clarity and perfection are probably not the outcome of vodka drinking. And simplicity may not appeal to someone who has allowed her- or himself to be impressed by all the advertising—some of which alludes to cultural aspects—and has paid a rather high price for the product. There are no specific links between the alcohol product and 'the core values'—apart from a price which signals the status that many people associate with high prices, heavy advertising, and attractive packaging.

Baudrillard considers that the whole secret lies purely in a successful differentiation that makes a product look different, rather than in some conveyed value or meaning. Repetition and persuasion make the product appear special and evoke a response. But 'this is undoubtedly the most impoverished of languages; full of signification and empty of meaning. It is a language of signals. And "loyalty" to a brand name is nothing more than the conditioned reflex of a controlled affect' (Baudrillard, quoted in Gabriel and Lang, 2006: 59). Thus, (iconic) brand enthusiasts are compared to Pavlov's dogs in this context. While the latter started to drool at the sound of Pavlov's bell before their food was served, Baudrillard imagines consumers' increased production of saliva at the sight of the brand, following intensive exposure to sales efforts in which some arbitrarily positive aspect—sex, elegance, youth, beauty, status, or whatever—becomes strongly associated with the brand. As with Pavlov's bell, the brand is the inculcated link between the object and the conditioned response.

But for marketers and other consumer enthusiasts, brands are supposed to have deeper qualities, meanings, and values. And for some people, some particular product may have a distinct and strongly loaded value, sometimes referred to as iconic objects or brands. For some people, for example, Harley Davidson motorcycles or Nike shoes have an almost sacral meaning; they may be a part of an 'extended self' (Belk, 1988). Such objects may have a deep, unique personal meaning or score high on grandiosity.

Generally speaking, the fluidity of product symbolism, the increasing complexity of the product world, and arbitrariness and ambiguity in relation to meaning and value create a sense of uncertainty and anxiety about identity themes in relation to material objects and consumption. This contributes to a propensity for people to look for status, identity confirmation, self-esteem, and so on in material objects. The increasing decoupling or liberation of goods in relation to certain values or needs means that the specific good in question becomes less effective as a source of satisfaction. Compensation for this decline in effectiveness or precision takes the form of greater quantity. To use a military metaphor, one might say that the consumer is forced to switch from precision bombing to block-buster tactics that require greater resources to achieve results. And here lies an important explanation of the perceived need for growth.

Thus, many influences on consumption may be assumed to make it more difficult for consumers to think through, clarify, and stabilize their possible wishes and orientations. Marketing involves establishing myths and smoke screens, and not merely the mystification of the relationship of products to specific values. Marketing may also be regarded as aggregated consumption propaganda in the sense that only the positive potential of consumption is stressed. The good life is equated with a life permeated by consumption.

A market society tends 'to give priority to those items that are directly price indexed, whereas life satisfaction is more closely linked to areas of life which are, if at all, only indirectly price indexed' (Lane, 1978: 808). Life is increasingly linked with:

> market mechanisms in order to monitor and evaluate social relations. It means, in particular, a monetization and commodification of social relations. In this world, marketing can tell us the 'price of everything, but the value of nothing!' Anything can be marketed. It does not have to be the more obvious goods and services; it can be 'good causes', 'political parties', 'ideas'. The whole world is a market and we are consumers in a gigantic candy-store. Just sit back and enjoy it! (Morgan, 1992: 143–4)

When mental energy is invested in material objectives, there is less focus on, and interest in, other objectives, objectives more crucial for achieving well-being (Kasser, 2002).

Difficult and systematically distorted choices

A related aspect of the question of the inability of steadily growing consumption to increase the level of satisfaction is the problem of making good decisions in the consumption sphere. 'Rationality' is complex; here it refers to being reasonably well informed, thinking through preferences and goals, critically assessing pros and cons of different alternatives, and making decisions likely to lead to outcomes that are satisfying (pleasurable experiences, making the neighbours envious). In practice, time and the ability to gather information and process it are limited. People tend to look for confirmation of preconceived ideas rather than having an open mind and applying critical evaluation. In the consumer area, a lack of knowledge and information, an increasing lack of time, and the presence of powerful forces that directly impinge on the ability to make wise decisions may all be noted.

Marketing has interested itself in, and tried to steer, the consumer's unconscious for a great many years. In the United States, the difficulties of getting demand to keep up with the prodigious level of supply resulting from productivity increases in manufacturing industry were making themselves felt as early as the 1950s. Psychological expertise was mobilized on a grand scale and a plethora of techniques and tricks started to be used to manipulate consumers (Packard, 1981).

Marketing may be regarded as a mixture of rationality distortion and assistance in coming to a decision:

> [I]n an extremely complex, noisy, almost insanely competitive world when there is much that is so familiar to choose from, where choice based solely on rational

factors is now almost impossible in most fields, brands make choice easier. Brands are the device we use to differentiate between otherwise almost indistinguishable competitors. Without clear branding, in some fields we literally could not tell one product or service from another. (Olins, 2000: 61)

But even without this profusion of 'rationality-distorting' aspects of marketing, there are still major problems in achieving soundly based and sensible decisions in consumption questions (Gabriel and Lang, 2006). One problem is that people are often not particularly rational even when not exposed to 'attempts at rationality distortion'. Studies indicate that many people who stubbornly prefer a certain product cannot distinguish it from other products in a blind test, and they justify their refusal to buy a given product by saying they do not like the taste, even though they have never tried it (Packard, 1981). But, in addition to certain fundamental problems with acting rationally, there is a high degree of control in consumer behaviour, adding to the problem of engaging in 'rational' consumption. Burenstam Linder (1969) points out that greater consumption means that there is less time per product and consumption decision. On average, as incomes increase people devote less and less time to each decision. Likewise, the number of impulse purchases and other spontaneous consumer actions increases. There is a growing propensity to rely on advertising, brand names, and other time-saving clues.

A decline in the quality of decisions made means that the value and satisfaction with what is consumed is decreasing, on average. Naturally, this may be more than compensated by an increase in the volume of consumption. But some of the potential increase in satisfaction associated with higher consumption is probably lost due to poorer opportunities to make proper decisions. Here, lack of time and marketers' attempts to reduce consumer rationality and independence are working in the same direction. In the light of the consumer's time constraints, the advertising will become more of an information surrogate. It may, for example, suggest that a product is good because it is well known, and of course it is largely known because it features in advertising. This applies in particular to well-known brands. If you know the brand and believe it represents good quality, this has the effect of reducing uncertainty and hence replaces more rational but also more time-consuming behaviour. However, in view of the consumer's limited opportunities to study the product's characteristics in more detail, this may be sufficiently 'rational'. Decision anxiety is reduced and time is used more efficiently, in some sense. It allows you to buy much more and/or devote your time to other things than to thoughtful—and typically time-consuming—purchasing decision processes. But there is often a high price to be paid for the sense of security provided by a well-known brand. You pay for all the investments in promoting the brand—the cost of uncertainty reduction may be much higher than that of the product itself (production costs).

Consumption and dissatisfaction

Consumer culture also involves a significant element of dissatisfaction. Consumption is not just a matter of a small plus; something also happens on the debit side. The substantial influence apparatus involved in increasing consumption largely involves the creation of dissatisfaction. An American advertising agency has described this as:

> What makes this country great is the creation of wants and desires, the creation of dissatisfaction with the old and outmoded. (cited in Packard, 1981: 24–5)

In the past, the main idea of advertising was to demonstrate and exaggerate certain advantages of a product. But the modern advertising industry is not content with such a modest goal:

> Now it manufactures a product of its own: the consumer, perpetually unsatisfied, restless, anxious, and bored. Advertising serves not so much to advertise products as to promote consumption as a way of life. It 'educated' the masses into an unappeasable appetite not only for goods but for new experiences and personal fulfilment. It upholds consumption as the answer to the age-old discontents of loneliness, sickness, weariness, lack of sexual satisfaction; at the same time it creates new forms of discontent peculiar to the modern age. (Lasch, 1978: 72)

Hence, interest in consumption is largely a question of dissatisfaction with the products, services, and your general standard of living. If you are completely satisfied with your car, your clothes, your golf clubs, or your skin, you have no reason to consider further purchases. Dissatisfaction is a key motivational force. No doubt you may 'spontaneously' get tired of something in the course of time, but the strong propensity to do so in a consumption society can hardly avoid being influenced by powerful 'dissatisfaction-producing' forces that point to the advantages of new products and fashions—and hence the deficiencies of everything that is out of date. Hence, the discrepancy between what you have and what you might have, and what this could offer in the form of improved personal appearance, higher status, greater self-esteem, and a more enjoyable life, are emphasized in advertisements, window displays, and other forms of sales influence. In a study, women expressed less satisfaction with their appearance than a control group, after they looked at advertisements showing very attractive models (cited in Kasser, 2002). Some advertising focuses directly on stigmatizing behaviour or traits, such as commercials showing people in a line at a deli not using a credit card when paying for lunch, fumbling with cash, and making others, all using the right credit card, irritated (Heath and Heath, 2008). Consumption influencers are often in the frustration business, in some sense.

Some of these effects are achieved via the individual's immediate environment, where increased consumption/higher standards of living create dissatisfaction with his/her own situation. After you have seen your neighbour's £50,000 fitted kitchen, your own looks inadequate. And if you feel personally inspired (feel yourself pressurized) to get an even more expensive kitchen, maybe this dissatisfaction can be fielded back to your neighbour. This is often a matter of social dynamics outside the direct control of marketers, but sales promotion often hints at motives such as superiority/inferiority to others. I recently read an ad for an attractive apartment in a major city, stating: 'make your friends and relatives envious'.

One crucial aspect of the possible establishment of the 'wrong' priorities is consumption-oriented social competition. Already, back in the late nineteenth century, Veblen maintained that a high proportion of consumption was governed by the social competition motive. He considered that enormous values were wasted without increasing well-being. The scope for such status-enhancing was considerable, even in 1900, and was reinforced by advertising as 'an organized fabrication of popular convictions', according to Veblen (cited in Söderberg, 2002: 208). Veblen's successors have stressed that consumption by the rich serves as a benchmark and results in a spiral of steadily rising status consumption which, by definition, does not lead to satisfaction, except for a small minority who manage much better than average. But, as we have seen previously, this is not a source of lasting joy for them either, even though resources to keep ahead of other groups give them a certain permanent advantage.

In the case of really poor people, consumption of luxury and status products is typically a marginal to non-existent phenomenon, but sometimes occurs at the expense of more needs-oriented goods. During the eighteenth century, major groups were consuming tobacco, coffee, sugar, and silk despite an economy that was not expanding significantly, often at the expense of food and other basic needs (Söderberg, 2002). Perhaps this suggests that the 'need' to give life a gilt edge is deeply rooted, or perhaps it says something about tendencies to imitate others and the attractions of status. But although such propensities may be observed in different societies and epochs, and are by no means novel phenomena, they are greatly strengthened in contemporary society and thinking. With the democratization of consumption and the option available also to the relatively poor in the post-affluent societies of spending money on other things than pure survival, status concerns become more broadly salient. Here relative poverty is not, as for previous generations, a broadly shared, given condition but a source of personal failure and shame (Sennett, 1977). Perhaps the characteristic feature of our own age is the focus on giving a golden shimmer to many aspects of our lives via consumption. With the triumph of grandiosity in consumer society, the need to shine and impress is foregrounded. This desire is the motivating force behind our interest in economic growth. The tendency to put a golden touch on life with different symbols of grandiosity is strong, and has a considerable impact, particularly in the consumption sphere.

At this stage, it might be objected that purchase and utilization transform this dissatisfaction into increased satisfaction, and possibly compensate (and even overcompensate) for this feeling of dissatisfaction. This may sometimes be the case. The 'net effect' would then lead beyond a simple zero-sum outcome. Technical developments, etc., can clearly achieve various improvements that genuinely result in increased satisfaction. You may be very satisfied with your material objects and regard, with an air of lofty calm, all efforts to tempt you with the message that you would be much more attractive, more popular, more successful, or happier with a holiday to B with travel agency X, with car Y, or with shampoo Z. But you can never be quite certain about this. The feeling that maybe you made a mistake or missed some opportunity is encouraged by the many messages about alternative superior consumption objects and consumption experience.

Here the interplay between grandiosity and zero-sum games is central. As there is a wealth of signals indicating improvements in consumption offers and the actual consumption strongly imprints our lives—by marketers and/or through people around you—the promises to improve appearance and increase status and envy also means that feelings of inferiority and uncertainty and anxieties around the lack of grandiosity become set in motion. This sometimes triggers actions, communicating these reactions to others. The zero-sum games continue. Satisfaction is only temporary. Soon the balance and the rest will be disrupted. One dynamic force that effectively prevents people from becoming relaxed and content but keeps them on their toes is fashion.

Fashion

Fashion means shifting attention and positive assessment in favour of something that is appreciated for its novelty value. Fashion has been a relevant factor for many centuries, particularly for those who are well off. As a result of dramatic increases in productivity and consumption, fashions have changed more rapidly, covering wider areas and eventually affecting the entire population in affluent societies. Even people who are not particularly interested in fashion are well advised to keep up with the trends, and this applies to all areas, not merely consumer goods. One example is social science, where we are more likely to adopt new trends since this may benefit our careers and make it easier to find something credible to say. (Big ears and quick footwork—being attentive and responsive to what is 'new'—can compensate for a lack of inspiration and originality.) As explained in Chapter 6, organizations are also often fashion-sensitive. But fashion is clearly a particularly dominant feature of the consumer area. Lack of sensitivity to fashion is one source of social failure.

Celebration of novelty value also has a negative side. New products may be fine, but this also implies that the 'non-new' is inferior. One tactic employed by car salesmen is to make people feel ashamed if they are driving a car that is more than two years old (Packard, 1981). It is commonly felt that it is best to keep up with your time and preferably be ahead of it—being behind the times is always regarded as something negative. This is based on the assumption that there are constant improvements as time passes, and that keeping up is a positive characteristic.

Fashion is not, however, merely a question of the masses allowing themselves to be bullied by commercial interests into accepting what is 'in' and smart, or what is 'out' and hopeless. Fashion also involves a social dynamism, as Simmel pointed out in the late nineteenth century, an analysis that is still relevant. Simmel (1904) stressed the importance of imitation and social competition in understanding fashion. Fashion involves a change that covers a social group. The change, in breaking with precedent, involves differentiation and deviation from the masses. This applies especially to those who are quickest to adopt the new fashion, which has tended to be the upper classes due to their financial resources, cultural skills, and awareness of trends. According to Simmel, fashion is closely linked to class distinctions, which has the double advantage that those who follow the fashions are well established in a circle of like-minded people emphasizing their special position and superiority in relation to others, i.e., those following behind in the fashion stakes. In this sense, fashion is not unlike other social distinction phenomena such as social classes, professions, and organizational levels.

Simmel considered that fashion was exclusively a matter of social logic. There is rarely any objective, aesthetic, or other good reason for explaining why one fashion replaces another. It is seldom a question of progress or improvement, and this social logic follows a given pattern. Fashion changes social forms, aesthetic judgements, the whole style of human expression. But, as already said, this primarily applies to the upper classes. As soon as the lower classes start to copy them and approach the demarcation line which the upper classes have drawn up, and hence disturb the homogeneity of their affinity, the upper classes change their style and adopt a new one which, in its turn, differentiates the propertied classes form the masses, and then the whole game starts all over again. As early as the 1730s, Carl von Linné was able to note how consumption habits developed and changed as certain groups tried to copy each other and differentiate themselves from others:

Tobacco, which was first smoked in Stockholm, was abandoned when the peasants also took up smoking. They took snuff instead, but the peasants also learnt that trick; until 1734 when they started smoking again when the rabble went over to snuff. But the rabble eats bread too, so one should cut that out as well. (Linné, quoted by Söderberg, 2002: 203)

This observation illustrates the way in which imitation and distinguishing aspects are linked. Habits developed by the upper classes were adopted by other groups and, as a result, lost their positive meaning for the former. The distinctive value of such consumption then disappeared or was reduced. When a fashion spreads, it is simultaneously on the way out. Success and decline are closely linked. The value of fashion in distinctive terms is greatest in the early phases, but it deteriorates as the fashion spreads and is adopted by a wider circle.

Fashion is clearly not a new phenomenon, but the dynamics of fashion have become more accentuated and the speed of change accelerates. Production of surpluses, increased emphasis on sales, and greater competition and uncertainty about social standing means that attempts by those with the greatest resources and the best positions to surge ahead of the slower mass of the population are intensified, while the masses have been catching up at an increasing rate. Increasing consumption opportunities for less wealthy classes and access to the mass media dilute this competition. The establishment of young people as a major, powerful consumer group, in particular, is contributing to this dynamic process. Attempts at surging ahead and catching-up follow each other in an ever-increasing tempo.

This swallows up considerable resources—on the one hand, fashionable objects are expensive and, on the other hand, items that were previously in fashion lose their value rapidly. Since the satisfaction value of fashion is largely a matter of social positioning—and not aesthetic development or better product quality—it has the character of a zero-sum game. Thus, a high proportion of economic growth is devoted to this game, while some of the additional growth is expended on the destruction of value which is an intrinsic feature of fashion. This partly explains why economic growth and a parallel increase in the level of consumption do not seem to result in any greater degree of (lasting) higher satisfaction or contentment. There may be initial feelings of satisfaction, but this is fleeting and does partly amount to having socially accepted products and avoiding losing in zero-sum games.

The triumphal brand bandwagon

Another aspect of saturation and dissatisfaction is due to the increasing dominance of products with well-known and expensive brand names. The core activity in marketing is typically a massive investment in making a brand or company name known, enhancing its reputation and achieving standardized and positive thoughts and expectations in this area.

Expensive, often iconic brands—which are the main object of my interest in this context—rarely offer a 'substance dividend' in relation to their price. Highly expensive watches and sports shoes do not usually represent any great advance on the time-keeping or running capability provided by cheaper alternatives.

As time passes, the market is flooded with similar mass-produced products. Since such products cannot be distinguished from one another, the solution is to persuade consumers to bestow different meanings and overtones that are relatively detached from the products themselves. The similarities are hidden by massive marketing of ideas about the differences, thus avoiding intensive competition concerning quality and price. Already in the 1950s, manufacturers and marketers were launching 'personalities' for their products. In 1956, a leading proponent of 'image creation' explained that:

> 'Basically, what you are trying to do is create an illogical situation. You want the customer to fall in love with your product and have a profound brand loyalty when actually content may be very similar to hundreds of competing brands'. To create this illogical loyalty, he said, the first task 'is one of creating some differentiation in the mind—some individualization for the product which has a long list of competitors very close to it in content'. (Packard 1981: 46)

Today most people probably take the existence and naturalness of brands for granted, but this branding of contemporary society, economy, and people can be seen as quite peculiar:

> Brands that from the beginning were a tool used to mark cattle to signify and distinguish ownership are thus, ironically nowadays happily and often un-reflectively used by people to mark themselves in search for distinction. (Bertilsson, 2009: 2)

Sometimes this does not involve exactly the same product—small variations or improvements may be added, based on the same platform, and these are then strongly amplified in communication with the general public. This is known as 'gold plating', and it is very common. Sennett (2006) describes this as follows: 'To sell a basically standardized thing, the seller will magnify the value of minor differences quickly and easily engineered, so that the surface is what counts. The brand must seem to the consumer more than the thing itself' (144). This is often, Sennett claims, a question of a 10 per cent difference in the content and 100 per cent difference in price, for example when comparing a Skoda and an Audi. Naturally, a brand may emphasize some distinctive feature or essential quality that is communicated in a manner that does justice to the good/service in question; the consumer's attitude is then based on a competent assessment and a sense of reality. (This may sometimes be established by a blind test.) But, more often, the impression of an illusion trick is the dominant feature. Here, one could talk about a grandiosity price. If Sennett is correct, one could say that the Audi buyer pays a 90 per cent grandiosity premium price compared to the Skoda buyer.

Interest in brands has expanded to encompass not only certain products but also the economy, and even our culture as a whole. When the real enthusiasts of brand jargon get going, almost everything seems to be a question of brand names.

There were a couple of deaths at a children's hospital in Sweden a few years ago that might possibly have been avoided. A daily newspaper wondered whether this might harm the hospital's brand image and interviewed a 'brand expert' about this, who replied that damage of this nature could result. Another 'expert' claimed that a successful intervention by the nation's security police would improve its 'brand'. It is increasingly common that institutions might be regarded as brands, and why not every individual person? Personal branding is increasingly common (Lair et al., 2005). A marketing textbook encourages the reader to regard him/herself as a brand: 'Let someone you know describe your core identity and extended identity' (Uggla, 2001: 112).

People are regarded as complying with the same logic as the sale of goods:

> If we then equate human identity and brand-name identity, we tend to regard people from a competition perspective, rather like cars that are to be positioned and sold in the market place. (Uggla, 2001: 175)

Without any particularly obvious traces of irony, the author goes on to refer to the resultant possibilities for personal development:

> At the same time, the strategic discussion of brand identity may provide inspiration for people who feel they want to develop further but do not have a concrete plan of action. They may have got stuck in one or more position traps (= being overidentified with a certain characteristic), and a stronger and more nuanced identity may be the solution. (Uggla, 2001: 175)

Re-branding as an emancipation project? Making yourself free through reification? One important aspect of attempts to influence consumer attitudes is to animate the product—give it human characteristics of a desirable calibre. Marketers and some consumers even talk of products having personalities. At the same time, the idea is that consumers are given attributes associated with what they consume. You could say that they are 'productified'. Here we find a further characteristic of the vulgoeconomy—the interweaving of individual identity with a brand-marked world of products, animated by objects and turning souls into objects. The somewhat odd idea or fantasy is that all the engineered grandiosity of the product (brand), created by billions of investments, will somehow sprinkle on and boost the image and the identity of the person.

The escalation of the visibility of logotypes in certain areas has meant that 'Logos have grown so dominant that they have essentially transformed the clothing on which they appear into empty carriers for the brand they represent. The metaphorical alligator, in other words, has risen up and swallowed the literal shirt' (Klein, 2000: 28). The parallel with the illusion trick's competitive obviation of what representation is supposed to stand for and what it denotes is obvious in this case.

Brand names are invading the mass media. Sponsored media projects involve the appearance of the right products everywhere, without being subtitled as a 'commercial'. Sport journalists, sportsmen, and other celebrities wear clothing with brand markings. TV programmes display products, and are in return given exposure in catalogues and other mass-media materials issued by the company concerned. Klein considers that, following a trend that has continued for almost a century, there is a tendency for a complete welding together of advertising and art, brand names and culture. Artists advertise themselves by producing and participating in advertising.

The music industry, in particular, has become interwoven with brand initiatives by firms that sell clothing, for example. The company name and the pop group enter into a symbiosis in which they indulge in mutual selling of each other. Music videos and pop concerts provide opportunities for the modelling of branded products, and assiduous featuring in various commercials is one way for musicians and actors to promote themselves. According to Klein, who provides countless examples (in her Chapter 2), the artists sometimes become minor figures in such contexts:

> The brand is the event's manufacture; the artists are its filler, a reversal in the power dynamic that makes any discussion of the need to protect unmarketed artistic space appear hopelessly naïve. (Klein, 2000: 48)

It is clearly difficult to withstand the advantage of a superior level denoted by the feeling that you are special at the same time as you are safely located within the framework of a reasonably hidden conformism. As Foley (2010) puts it:

> Consumer culture is aware of the universal hunger for differentials and has provided an artificial form of exclusivity in the brand. The genius of branding has been to disguise the undesirable conformity of consumption as its highly desirable opposite, distinction. So conformity is the result of everyone striving for distinction in the same way. (60)

For the most part, specific examples of brand worship are not particularly problematic, but in the case of children and young people this may take more serious forms. Under her 'Logo terror' heading, Naomi Klein describes how a girl in her school class:

> used to make her rounds up and down the rows of desks turning the collars on our sweaters and polo shirts. It wasn't enough for her to see an alligator or a leaping horseman—it could have been a knockoff. She wanted to see the label behind the logo. We were only eight years old but the reign of logo terror had begun. (Klein, 2000: 27)

Brand symbols have the same function as if the price ticket was still there. Everyone knows what excess price the wearer was prepared to pay for dressing in style and avoid social sanctions. The high price for the right product can perhaps be seen as a reasonable price for the avoidance of embarrassment and shame.

Obviously, many consumers regard goods and services with well-known logotypes and a high price as worth the money—even if some primarily pay in order to avoid being shamed by Naomi's little fellow student and others who are keen to see that norms are maintained. This increasing brand-name orientation means, however, that a proportion of economic growth is devoted to paying the excessive prices involved. The negative side of the establishment of powerful high-status brands is that those who fail to live up to this ideal appear, more clearly, to belong to a B category.

Cultivating grandiosity is a key element underlying most of the management of certain (celebrated) brands. This is the object of influence and a key aspect of 'value creation', to use modern business jargon. But a second grandiose meaning is also involved in branding. Often references to a 'brand' seem to be little more than an opinion or impression about something. Brand is then a stylish synonym for reputation, image, and impression. Brand talk may in itself be seen as an example of grandiosity—an effort to make something well known and fairly trivial sounding exotic, smart, and remarkable.

The time problem

The limited ability of growing consumption to achieve greater satisfaction or saturation can also be related to the time-economic dimension (Burenstam Linder, 1969). Consumption takes time. Buying, maintenance, and consumption/utilization all take time, and consumption time is becoming increasingly product intensive. No one gets much of a kick out of a summer cottage, a boat, a tennis racket, or a pair of shoes that are not used. No doubt a sense of ownership and the display of some possession to an admiring group of neighbours may be significant sources of satisfaction but, in the main, enjoying consumer goods is time-consuming.

And time is in short supply, at least for people in paid employment. Higher productivity implies that the economic return required per unit of time is also increasing. Economic growth leads to time stress. Even if leisure/consumption time is not openly or clearly priced, individuals will consciously or unconsciously put a kind of 'shadow price' ticket on their consumption time. 'Time is money'. And this price rises in line with productivity in work life and with incomes. The feeling that leisure time is being used inefficiently is becoming increasingly tangible. In addition, all consumption goods call for maintenance time—the house must be cleaned, repaired, repainted, and so on, and the car must be looked after—and also time to enjoy the object concerned. The more consumption goods you own, the more maintenance time they require (even if some products such as washing machines also save time), and the more competition there is between such goods in terms of time to enjoy them. Each new product calls for more purchasing, maintenance, and utilization time.

> In the economic land of dreams that many see as the end result of a long process of growth, the inherent thrift of nature would be overcome. It is only by a sort of optical illusion that one can imagine this meanness on nature's part being eliminated in a material Utopia. In an economic heaven, the problem of time will be particularly pressing. We will find there an infinite volume of consumption goods, which pleasure-hungry angels will feverishly try to exploit during the limited time at their disposal per day. (Burenstam Linder, 1969: 13)

The need to rationalize our use of time means that purchases are made with less and less time devoted to each product. Even though the total shopping time is increasing significantly, the time allowed for each purchasing decision is declining. Purchasing rationality is curtailed but, given the consumer's total life situation, this may be sensible. More purchasing decisions of dubious quality may be preferable to better decisions that take too much time. Burenstam Linder gives the example of 'your money back if you are not completely satisfied' promise that is often made by retailers, with little risk, since customers seldom take the time to return products, even if they are dissatisfied. The higher their incomes, the fewer goods will be returned.

A lower quality of consumer decisions is often followed by lower maintenance of the goods themselves. The time devoted per product to maintenance is becoming more expensive and is in increasingly short supply as consumption rises. Manufacturers have adapted to this situation to some extent by producing goods with a shorter life cycle. But since consumers do not think they can afford to spend much time and energy on maintenance per product, and since higher productivity is making goods cheaper and lower expectations of durability pave the way for further cost reductions, we are moving towards a 'use and discard' consumer economy. This makes sense from a time-economics perspective. But once again, limited product durability means that higher growth and consumption result in a smaller increase in satisfaction than might have been expected.

Consumption is accelerating to increase the time pay-off. But there is a risk that higher incomes may mean that the 'return' on consumption time is reduced. Activities that call for skill, discipline, patience, and practice suffer from attempts to save time. But goods can be a source of stress too. Someone who acquires a swimming pool and then finds that it requires a considerable amount of time for maintenance may not use it as much. And the accumulation of things that you don't have time to use may result in a bad conscience and stress. The consumer class of our era—the harried leisure class, as Burenstam Linder calls it—suffers from time stress, largely generated by the volume of consumption.

This time constraint also undermines the romantic idea of many consumption enthusiasts emphasizing the consumer as a creative person, governed not by marketing regimes, but as someone high on sovereignty, expressing his/her own unique identity through complex acts of expression. The so-called postmodern consumer is engaged in a

> never-ending project to create an individuated identity through consumption. This project requires absorbing an ever-expanding supply of fashions, cultural texts, tourist experiences, cuisines, mass cultural icons, and the like. As a result, we are in the midst of a widespread inflation in the symbolic work required to achieve what is perceived as real sovereignty. (Holt, 2002: 87)

But the time is seldom available for all this—'it is simply too taxing to constantly reassemble the knowledge and skills required to significantly rework commodity meanings when they proliferate so rapidly' (Holt, 2002: 87). In the end, the creative and sovereign consumer tends to follow the templates offered by marketers, as Holt puts it: 'Consumers want to author their lives, but they increasingly are looking for ghost-writers to help them out' (Holt, 2002: 87).

Burenstam Linder (1969) concludes that, irrespective of desires to improve the material standard of living, the increasing shortage of time will mean that consumption goods will contribute a declining increment to this standard. Hence the possibilities of enjoying greater consumption will become fewer and fewer, due to increasing lack of time. The idea of sovereignty heavily increases the burden of the already 'harried leisure class'.

Greater consumption—limited satisfaction

Although dramatic increases in consumption in a post-affluent society do not seem to have resulted in greater satisfaction, there are still renewed demands for further economic growth and increased consumption, perhaps even more than ever. The number of individuals in the United States who feel they are 'very happy' has, for example, been constant over a 40-year period while, at the same time, average incomes have more than doubled. On the other hand, in parallel with this, the proportion of the population that considers it is very important to 'be very well off financially' has increased from 40 per cent in the late 1960s to 70 per cent in the late 1990s, triggering the comment that 'society's value-making machine is an efficient one' (Kasser, 2002: 104). Of course, all data of this nature are unreliable and we certainly can't see them as providing us with the final truth but, in the absence of better information, it is probably wise to take them seriously.

As can be seen above, a number of mechanisms contribute to leakage in the transfer of goods and services from economic growth's generous production machine to utilization and enjoyment in the consumption sphere. This includes the mystifications of needs, the 'wrong' priorities, difficult and systematically distorted choices, and the time problem. One might also say that the efficiency quotient of consumption is not particularly impressive. The potential for rationalizing production is not paralleled by similar successes and improvements in the consumption sphere. Greater consumption opportunities are only converted into greater consumer satisfaction to a limited extent.

Another aspect of consumption is the high cost of its marketing. In the case of high-status brands, consumers pay the major proportion of consumption costs in the form of costs for being controlled—achieving the conditioning that makes them instinctively put their hand on their credit cards when they catch sight of the right logo, even if they do not actually drool. Some of the economic growth is devoted to paying these costs. This drives up the desire for higher incomes and more expensive consumption.

But perhaps the most crucial aspect is—once again—the social limits of growth. An ever-increasing part of total consumption is positional, that is to say that your perceived satisfaction depends on your level of consumption in comparison with that of others. Applying Bourdieu's (1984) terminology, we might refer to the distinction value of consumption. The point is that this value results from consumption's capacity to denote a positive, special characteristic in comparison with some other inferior form of consumption associated with other social groups—which are defined negatively in one way or another.

Social standards and cultural guidelines for what is a normal and acceptable consumption field are also being raised on a continuous basis. Hence expectations are going up and negative deviations from what is expected present more of a problem. And this is part of a cultural context that has little to do with individual needs and wishes, but with a social logic that depends on economic growth and an ongoing increase in expectations about what is normal and may be anticipated. Ambition levels are raised, and a superior future is anticipated. Once again, the grandiosity concept illustrates this.

Consumption—between grandiosity and emptiness

A high proportion of modern consumption involves associating oneself with and communicating ideal images of oneself and one's life. But the communication of these glorified ideal pictures is rarely subject to some simple logic. One key aspect, as already mentioned, is the production of uncertainty, doubt and dissatisfaction:

> Strictly considered, however, modern advertising seeks to promote not so much self-indulgence as self-doubt. It seeks to create needs, not to fulfil them; to generate new anxieties instead of allaying old ones.
>
> By surrounding the consumer with images of the good life, and by associating them with the glamour of celebrity and success, mass culture encourages the ordinary man to cultivate extraordinary tastes, to identify himself with the privileged minority against the rest, and to join them, in his fantasies, in a life of exquisite comfort and sensual refinement. Yet the propaganda of commodities simultaneously makes him acutely unhappy with his lot. By fostering grandiose aspirations, it also fosters self-denigration and self-contempt. (Lasch, 1978: 181)

A consumption culture may, however, be related to the narcissism theme in a more direct manner. Mass consumption and the social mechanisms that it supports appeal directly to grandiose ideas, fantasies, and desires. A great deal of modern consumption—from cosmetics and personal hygiene products to sports equipment and clothing—encourages what psychoanalysts refer to as the grandiose self: omnipotence fantasies, attractiveness, and exhibitionism. This also applies to attempts to associate narcissistic desires with, in themselves, completely unglamorous products, like underwear. One example might be when sports celebrities advertise instant coffee, underwear, and other products and allow the glow of their superhuman achievements, heroism, and exalted idol status to colour the image of the products in question. At the same time, these celebrities also become or can reproduce themselves (prolong their lives) as superstars, partly due to their active exposure in an advertising and branding context. Retired sports people often seem to have a second career as a brand name.

A consumer culture produces ideals and hopes that are some way from everyday reality. They inflate expectations, hopes, and demands, and not only realistic aspiration for marginal changes and success in social contexts—status, popularity, and sexual contacts—but also more primitive fantasies and unconscious desires. The grandiose self-denotes a defensive reaction to feelings of the disintegration of the self, emptiness, and depression. Here there is a psychological parallel with more socially oriented grandiosity concepts which are my main interest in this book.

Identity creation or identity-undermining projects

The importance of consumption in creating or expressing identity is frequently emphasized, and this gives the consumer project a positive meaning. Expression, experimenting, and communication issues around who you think you are or would like to be are relevant features of this. One key aspect is that identity is not regarded as given but is seen as a more open project, and consumption provides some opportunities. There are also additional aesthetic and creative possibilities that should not be underestimated, even though they fall outside the scope of this book.

The intimate relationship between consumption and the formation of identity has been clearly established for some time. Klein (2000) stresses that, for those born in the 1970s or later, their generation's identity 'had largely been a pre-packaged good and for whom the search for self had always been shaped by marketing hype' (96). Commercial organizations have taken over a major proportion of the socialization that parents, churches, the neighbourhood, and the school previously represented (Schor, 2004). During the 1990s, the focus of marketing on groups of young people was reinforced.

> This was not a time for selling Tide and Snuggle to housewives—it was a time for beaming MTV, Nike, Hilfiger, Microsoft, Netscape and *Wired* to global teens and their overgrown imitators. Their parents might have gone bargain basement, but kids, it turned out, were still willing to pay up to fit in. Through this process, peer pressure emerged as a powerful market force, making the keeping-up-with-the-Joneses consumerism of their suburban parents pale by comparison. As clothing retailer Elise Decoteau said of her teen shoppers, 'They run in packs. If you sell to one, you sell to everyone in their class and everyone in their school'. (Klein, 2000: 68)

Being part of a group and experiencing oneself as being basically similar, but perhaps not too similar, to others is key for some, perhaps especially young people. Occasionally, there may be brand communities, that is, people sharing a strong interest in a brand and developing community feelings around that (Arvidsson, 2006) but few brands have such a potential (Bertilsson, 2009). And presumably few people are fixated on a specific product making up the theme for long conversations.

There exists some research claiming that possessions are part of an 'extended self', that is, a merger between 'my' and 'what is mine', implying the centrality of consumption for identity (Belk, 1988). The extended self may, however, be stretched so far that it becomes rather thin and does not touch upon key themes in terms of identity.

For some people—particularly marketers and other consumption enthusiasts—the actual act of consumption is the core feature of identity projects. You buy the ingredients for an identity, or stage, and express such an identity via given objects—from houses and furniture to clothing, hair shampoo, and cigarettes. But the question of identity is more complicated than this. Gabriel and Lang (2006) claim that to the extent that identity constitutes a 'problem' or a 'project', the solution or the response must include not only an image (which can be purchased) but also meaning and value (90). Some products and forms of consumption may have some potential here, but most probably do not. A home you have worked very hard to make aesthetically pleasing and personal is quite different from buying the most recent and impressive car that you get rid of when a newer model is available. Identity is more than a question of manipulating self-images via objects and superficial representations—it also involves personal life stories, attention, value, feelings, and respect. Consumption-based identities (or identity claims) often involve fragmentation, uncertainty, superficiality, and vulnerability—resulting from the lack of substance or deeper meaning in the project itself.

> As a result, the individual is subject to an increasingly rapid spiral process, even more distraught but also more inclined to try to adjust his late-modern fluid identity by means of new consumption directed by the media, advertising and 'life-style magazines'. (Ragneklint, 2009: 184)

As far as postmodernists such as Baudrillard are concerned, consumption is scarcely an identity project since the products and their message are meaningless. They constitute mere designations that only refer to themselves and hence lack the 'depth of meaning' and the symbolism required for identity creation. One might, perhaps, refer to pseudo-identification. Simply using an empty and arbitrary symbol—that is, a brand—as a basis for self-definition does not get us very far.

Consumption often has a weak or uncertain relationship to identity issues. Sometimes, consumption may instead be distorting and confusing rather than staging and communicating identity. People who drive around in city centres in macho 4WDs may indulge in fantasies about being able to master nature and demonstrate their prowess. People try to compensate for their boring office jobs and suburban existences by wearing T-shirts with revolutionary icons or buying products that shout 'authenticity' in comparison with an ecologically correct countryside. From an identity viewpoint, this is all rather arbitrary, contradictory, and in a sense meaningless. Meaning calls for some integration, coherence, and 'richness' in terms of affections and symbol-processing in order to work. Identity expressions need to hang together with at least some other parts of existence in order to work. It is often an open question whether the consumption projects express, confuse, or are very weakly linked to identity.

Status is a key theme in this context. It may be argued that a high level of consumption involves living up to socially determined norms and that the status motive is the crucial factor. Identity and status are often closely linked, while identity projects normally try to hide the status aspect by stressing special characteristics, individuality, creativity, aesthetics, taste, and so on. Being very status-oriented has low status and may undermine self-esteem. The ideal is typically to try to secure high status—and denying and concealing that this is in any way a motive. In a study on home furnishings and furniture, Ulver-Sneistrup (2008) demonstrates that the status theme is crucial as regards purchases and display, but that this tends to be denied or toned down in favour of aspects that are more socially acceptable, such as personal good taste and preferences, attitudes, etc. The identity theme is merged with both a desire to appear to be free from status motives and a desire to live up to standards that denote high status. Thus, at the same time, people both confirm and deny status as a motive force.

Thus, consumption is not independent of identity aspects, and if there is no consumption of any kind, identity is probably a question of some ascetic nudist or hermit. But emphasizing consumption as a way of creating identity probably often means a shaky project.

Gilded squalor

A very high proportion of manufacturing activities have been outsourced to factories in the third world, factories with cheap labour, a wretched environment, and tough conditions of work, often on a tax-free basis. This is where the physical attributes for brand names are mass produced at very low costs, before they are sold at high prices to consumers in affluent countries. When visiting the Cavite Export Processing Zone in the Philippines, which is a centre for this kind of manufacturing, Klein (2000) noted that almost all the global brands that are so heavily exposed in a public context elsewhere had a very low profile here. Top brands products such as Nike jogging shoes, Gap pyjamas, and IBM computer screens were manufactured here. But there were no signs or logos to indicate this on the factory's frontage. Competing brands were not separated, but were often produced side by side in the same plants and by the same workers. Klein saw a mountain of Nike shoes, but otherwise nothing to indicate that they were produced here. The location is unremarkable, not worth a fancy logo, Klein remarks, and observes:

> Windowless workshops made of plastic and aluminium siding are crammed in next to each other, only feet apart. Racks of time cards bake in the sun, making sure the maximum amount of work is extracted from each worker, the maximum number of working hours extracted from each day. The streets in the zone are eerily empty, and open doors—the ventilation system for most factories—reveal lines of young women hunched in silence over clamouring machines. (Klein, 2000: 203–4)

Klein quotes an influential copywriter who was active in the 1920s who warned his colleagues in a famous pronouncement: 'if you market a product, never visit the factory where it is made...Don't look when people are working...when you know the truth about something, the real underlying truth, it is very difficult to write the superficial fluff that has to sell it' (Klein, 2000: 409–10).

There are, of course, many squalid backdrops to consumption. One of the most important is clearly environmental pollution—since my focus in this book is on social factors, and the ecological disasters coming from economic growth and post-affluent consumption are well known, I only mention ecological problems here. Although many of the themes treated in this book do not offer such dramatic contrasts in terms of a glittering surface and a sordid underlying reality as Klein's example of high-status shoes and production in a Third World country, or grandiose images of life made into perfection through iconic products and enormous waste and pollution, on the other hand the gold colours hiding something grey or black tends to be a consistent theme in a society characterized by grandiosity, where parallel value creation and value destruction as well as increased satisfaction at the expense of someone else's dissatisfaction are hard to avoid.

Summary

In what I refer to as post-affluent society, a high material standard of living for the great majority is combined with strong demands and expectations of an increased level of consumption. Doubling material standards in comparison with the previous generation does not seem to have resulted in any greater degree of satisfaction or satiation. Research indicates that greater consumption in affluent countries is not a source of greater average happiness, even though individuals with high incomes often report greater satisfaction with their lives than those living below average. The key element here is not consumption per se, but scoring higher than other people. It is the relative standing of consumption that primarily matters, as noted by the social limits to growth thesis claims about the increased significance of positional goods.

The mystery implicit in the contrast between people in a post-affluent society focusing on increased consumption and the limited return in the form of greater satisfaction and satiation tendencies are explained in the three main themes in this book.

A consumption society is permeated by *grandiose* fantasies about the achievement of satisfactory, attractive, and continuous improvements in life as a result of consumption. Massive propaganda for price-indexed objects and activities is based on ideals that encourage claims and expectations for the realization of an elegant and pleasurable life. Many of the imperfections of life and individual shortcomings, it is promised, can be solved by consumption. But consumer culture often fails to deliver the promised satisfaction and even undermines it. The consumption culture generates narcissism—an unstable sense of self and intensive attempts to regulate, stabilize, and improve a self-esteem permeated and frustrated by fantasies about superiority and perfection. According to psychoanalysts, narcissism involves a vacillation between a somewhat exaggerated self-image and its opposite in the form of emptiness and sham (Kohut, 1971, 1977; Lasch, 1978). Consumption fills this emptiness for a time, and improves self-esteem. But this is part of the problem, and not the solution. Cultivation of grandiose ideas, promoted by the consumption ideal, combined with expectations that almost certainly collide with an imperfect world and experiences of the hollowness of the blown-up sense of self reinforce narcissistic sensitivity and vulnerability. What appears to be the solution is therefore often counterproductive.

There is a massive plethora of *illusion tricks* in the goods and services area. Goods and services are largely sold in the form of arbitrary links between objects and values/meanings that are totally independent of the product in question. Mystification in the relationship between things and value/meaning makes it difficult to match needs/desires with specific objects. The overtones sometimes ascribed to strong brands are the result of intensive conditioning rather than an emerging symbolism associated with meaning. The world of consumption propaganda is partly a world of illusions, e.g., gold plating. High-status goods, in particular, may often be regarded as illusion tricks, surrogates, or representations with a dubious and misleading relationship with substantial values. Quality features more succinctly in communications media than in the objects to which they refer. This escalation of socio-psychological tricks by branders, marketers, etc. is partly an outcome of an increasingly 'post-affluenza' society. Branders and marketers must target more and more objects and respond partly to their audiences becoming more suspicious and used to the tricks, which calls for new creative illusions tricks (Holt, 2002). But still, there is a heavy bombardment of rather straightforward advertising, showing a beautiful model exhibiting the product or the latter portrayed in an unlikely context (like a car in a fantastic landscape not destroyed by roads).

Increased growth means that consumption is acquiring an increasingly *positional* character—with less focus on individual needs and more on your status in relation to others. The consumption project is becoming increasingly demarcated by the social boundaries of growth, and these limits are being drawn increasingly tighter around people. The scope and the turnover rate of consumption with a high distinction value have escalated. Goods rapidly become outdated, lose their value, and may be discarded. This is hardly a question of sustainable satisfaction—dissatisfaction is always waiting round the corner. The cost of social positioning is high and this may explain why many people find it difficult to make ends meet.

The relational (positional) nature of many goods and services makes changes in satisfaction virtually a zero-sum game—you have to hang in there and preferably do better than others if you are to be satisfied, and you cannot fall behind without landing in an unfavourable position.

4

Higher education—triumph of the knowledge-intensive society?

'BE SOMETHING GREAT' and 'FAST TRACK TO TOP JOBS' were two head-lines in advertisements for education that caught my eye some time ago. The specific message was that a specific school was offering a route to success and a brilliant career. In other words, education paves the way for success in life. With the passing of time, this has become a well-established truth. There are no other options—unless you have exceptional talents in the arts, sports, or the entertainment context.

Fantasies and hopes for an outstanding career are encouraged on a broad front. The higher education sector has developed rapidly, even exploded, in recent decades and so have promises of a fantastic career resulting from a degree of the right kind and at the right place. In one UK university, the business school building is plastered with large posters claiming that 'We create world-class minds'. And a Swedish university, located in a remote part of the country and with difficulties in recruiting faculty members and students, advertises heavily, claiming 'research and education in world class'. If an institution is not 'world class' it is often described in terms of 'excellence'. At my own university a few years ago, I saw a poster headed 'Do you want to be President or Group CEO?' for a course in commercial law specially designed for people who expect to reach the top in the near future. Since the target group consists of students, and most of them will probably have to bide their time for a decade or two before they can put 'President' or 'Group CEO' on their business cards, we may conclude that the department in question has realized the value of a long-term approach, and is assuming that many students have a high estimation of their potential. Perhaps education institutions support such more or less realistic self-images and career aspirations. If the department in question succeeds in recruiting a large number of students, it is perhaps primarily the less realistic self-images that will be reinforced.

At a more collective level, education is now also considered to pave the way for national greatness. It is a key political ambition in many countries to become a leading knowledge-intensive nation, to win the unofficial world education championships and—as a result—to lead, and continue to lead, the world in economic terms. 'College for all' is a common ideal in the United States (Arum and Roksa, 2011).

This is partly related to the belief that the contemporary economy calls for a close to universal high level of knowledge and use of intellectual capacities. It is commonly claimed that:

> workers' cognitive and social capabilities are elements of the forces of production and, over the long term and in broad aggregate, the pressure of competition forces firms and societies to upgrade those capabilities. The development of capitalism thus tends to create a working class that is increasingly sophisticated. (Adler, 2002: 392)

In EU policy texts, for example, the various grandiose qualities of excellent universities, the knowledge society, and economy are closely linked, and the expansion of the former is assumed to be a self-evident engine for the latter: 'The "excellence" of universities is construed as a necessary condition for success in becoming a "knowledge society" and KBE (knowledge based economy) (notice that these arguably distinct concepts and objectives are semantically merged)' (Fairclough and Wodak, 2008: 132). This sounds really positive, but may exaggerate contemporary working life's demand for well-educated people who will use a lot of brainpower at work. Rather than a wealth of qualified jobs, there are even in post-industrial societies very many routinized, low- or medium-qualification jobs. This will be explored.

In light of the possibility that the knowledge-intensive society may not really live up to expectations, this chapter examines the strong faith in education, in particular higher education, as a motor for growth and other objectives. The ideology of educational fundamentalism is critically explored, as is what takes place in terms of education within the overall university umbrella. Furthermore, I discuss to what extent a highly educated, at least on paper, labour force can find employment in line with what academic degrees may lead them to suspect. The zero-sum games that increasingly characterize higher education are also discussed, where the large number of graduates leads to lowered merit value, and many people face increasing competition for positions in a labour market that seldom fully lives up to expectations.

I should perhaps warn the reader that I am rather critical of contemporary higher education and current trends. My scepticism towards the expansion of higher education is not grounded in a belief that only the very best should go to university, but in concerns that almost mindless quantitative expansion may lead to serious quality problems. I am concerned that higher education is increasingly becoming a matter of positionality, where values such as critical reflection, cognitive development, and ability to communicate well in text and speech are losing import in favour of efforts to improve credentials in order to access attractive jobs. As Collins (2002) writes, 'credential inflation processes will continue, indeed at even higher pressure. First; with few good jobs, there is extremely high competition for access to them, hence driving up educational requirements to very high levels. Second: the educational system comes to play an important role in dealing with the displaced part of the labour force...the warehousing also keeps up the supply of educational credentials, reinforcing the first process' (27).

Educational fundamentalism

Education has very strong positive connotations in modern society. Being negative to education in public debate is hardly feasible. This also applies to 'competence', learning, quality, knowledge, science, and common sense. This complex of qualities is often presented as 'competence development', to which it is hard to make objections. The rhetorical overtones in this term are overwhelming. You might be sceptical about 'participation in a course', but competence and development sound admirable and, if you combine these words, the results are irresistible. I am, of course, not opposed to education (which is usually what is implied by 'competence development'), at least when it leads to greater knowledge and improved intellectual abilities. But there is a wealth of evangelic beliefs in higher education as a way of increasing economic growth, making the population intelligent, and solving all kinds of problems. The good society—the knowledge society—is supposed to be accomplished by expanding the university sector and persuading more and more young people into an ever-widening spectrum of education. They should be taught, it is claimed, by academics with a PhD who need to do research in order to be good teachers. There are good reasons for being critical of what may be referred to as *educational fundamentalism*.

This is an ideology that expresses a strong belief—and often a naïve blind faith—in the opportunities and positive results offered by education. There has been an explosive increase in the number of educational institutions that have been promoted to university status. Most of them have expanded significantly over the years, and there is a considerable inflow of students into what is defined as university education. In the United States, college enrolment has more than doubled since 1970. Some elite institutions are overwhelmed by the large number of applicants, but many admit any applicant with a high school diploma. In the UK, the number of graduates more than tripled between 1990 and 2010.

Promising higher education for half the population—as is the case in many countries—and proclaiming that this is essential in a knowledge-intensive society, kindles fantasies and ambitions which, in most instances, are unlikely to be fulfilled. It also leads to serious quality problems. Expansion of higher education is virtually a zero-sum game, at least with regard to subsequent opportunities to obtain qualified and well-paid jobs. Perhaps extension of higher education to the masses involves a further zero-sum element in the sense that quality reductions may mean that teaching and the rewards of degrees in terms of employment possibilities and conditions do not necessarily increase simply because more people are studying longer. Cutbacks in resources per student, considerable variations in motivation and study ability, a focus on student satisfaction and a corresponding allocation of resources to making students happy rather than to teaching, a shortage of good teachers, and strong pressures for a reduction in academic standards suggest that an increase in quantity may be counteracted by a deterioration in quality. We risk winding up in a situation where never before have so many studied for so long and learnt so little—on a per study-year and degree basis. We are probably already there.

Educational fundamentalism, which is currently a widespread phenomenon, is characterized by the following basic assumptions and the resultant policies and practices:

- Education is something good, and its consequences should be described in positive terms.

- Education and its expansion are crucial for economic growth. Greater investment in higher education has a clear payoff in terms of economic growth.

- There are also clear benefits from the individual viewpoint from investments in education.

- You can't get too much education—the more education the better. The higher the proportion of the population that can be classified as well-educated, the better the society.

- Human beings can be formed—education institutions create the right kind of people.

- The ability to perform at work is primarily achieved as a result of education.

- Certain people may be defined as poorly educated. We should ensure that they can benefit from initiatives to remedy this negative situation.

- Education is the solution to a great many problems, from unemployment to international competitive capability.
- As much education as possible must be upgraded/relabelled as higher education.

Educational fundamentalism is heavily imbued with grandiosity, including the promotion of all kinds of vocational training institutions to become universities; efforts to make education more impressive by marrying it with research; and the association of an expanded higher education with the knowledge society, where advanced symbol-processing is performed by creative and intelligent people whose capacity has been boosted by the universities' function as spearheads for this beautiful new world. This is an international trend, and countries turning higher education into export big business (especially the United States, the UK, and Australia) are marketing the great transformative powers of turning consumers of such education into 'tomorrow's world citizens', on whom the following subjectivities are conferred:

> Ambitious...they see themselves as the future elite...The prize is to be movers and shakers when they return to their country...They know that an education in an English-speaking country is a passport to intellectual citizenship of the world. (British Council, 1999, cited in Sidhu, 2006: 130)

A knowledge-intensive society has the great advantage of ideological impact—no one can really advocate the opposite standpoint: an ignorance society. The idea of the rise of 'the creative class' is also highly ideologically appealing. It gives a further boost to the hope that we live in a fantastic society where the creative class makes up 30 per cent of the US work force (Florida, 2001). 'Creative class' is loosely and widely defined to include teachers, engineers, and others not necessarily working creatively in any particular distinct or advanced sense. Few people doubt that the simplest forms of mass production have been outsourced from many advanced economies and that the number of jobs calling for, or facilitated by, higher education is probably increasing. And although the number of jobs with low educational requirements has declined in many Western countries, they still represent a substantial share of the labour market, and this includes societies in which people are most intensively trying to convince others (and perhaps themselves) that their nation is truly a 'knowledge economy' or a 'creative economy'. Educational attainment has changed at a faster rate than the job structure, with as a result of increasing over-education in jobs with low educational requirements (Åberg, 2002, 2003; Sweet and Meiksins, 2008; Wolf, 2004). A full-blooded education fundamentalist prefers to forget the considerable and continuing need for less qualified labour, even in advanced economies. While other countries may have lower wages and can compete in mass-produced goods, the advanced nations are playing in a higher division—in the attractive knowledge-intensive league—where talents and innovations are the decisive factor. Western know-how and intelligence are contrasted with quick and cheap hands and feet in the low-income countries. So goes the reasoning in most Western countries.

Education is something of a mega project, with ambitions to be a 'world leader'. Sometimes one feels that the education enthusiasts are thinking in terms of winning first prize in an imaginary world championship in education. The formula for success in this context is large numbers in long education programmes, although having universities in the ranking lists for the world's '100 best universities' is also an important competitive arena, permitting claims of causal effects and correlations with a knowledge economy and innovation. It is frequently alleged that increased education is accompanied by a high economic return, more effective forms of democratic government, better quality of life, greater environmental awareness, less crime, and better health (Swedish Official Report SOU, 1996: 164). More higher education, it is claimed, builds an optimal society. Many argue that a large and expanding higher education sector is absolutely crucial in a globalized competitive economy.

Educational fundamentalism does not necessarily imply fanaticism, even if it is based on ideology, provides cocksure descriptions of the state of the world, indicates ideals and directions, and involves little critical and nuanced thinking. On the whole, there is much extremely simplistic and naïve thinking on the part of politicians, economists, educators, and major groups in society about the do-good effects of an expanding higher education sector (Wolf, 2004).

Education as an investment and creator of growth

It is often claimed that education is a sound investment, for society, companies, and individuals. On the one hand, increased education presumably leads to better professional qualifications and, on the other hand, individuals improve their ability to orient themselves and acquire and process information, and also their capacity for independent thought. It appears likely that, over time, an increase in (professionally relevant) education has been accompanied, at least in some cases, by better economic results and other positive outcomes.

At the same time, it is almost impossible to find simple causal and universal effects. The link between education and productivity is often presented as a causal relationship, almost a natural law. More investment in higher education means greater economic prosperity. Such observations are often rather simplistic—for example, that wealthy countries have more higher education than poor countries and people with a longer education have a higher income than others. But this does not say much. Correlation is of course not the same as a cause–effect relation.

As Wolf (2004) points out, wealthy countries also have more motorways, hospitals, and symphony orchestras. Some very wealthy countries, like Switzerland, have much less investment in higher education than somewhat less economically successful countries. Some developing countries that have devoted considerable resources to higher education also have low levels of economic output, and have sometimes also been inclined to 'expand state bureaucracy in order to create jobs for otherwise unemployed graduates from their expanding universities' (Wolf, 2004: 322). It may well be the case that wealthy countries also create a large number of jobs that are not necessarily particularly productive (lawyers, consultants, bureaucrats) in order to respond to the massive explosion of higher education. There is no easy way to establish a causal relationship between increased investment in higher education and economic growth, but nonetheless many policy-makers and others stick to the idea of an imputed relationship between education and the economy, 'for which the empirical evidence is, in fact, extremely weak' (Wolf, 2004: 316).

It is not very realistic to treat education as a homogenous product and measure it in terms of study years, or to regard it as a homogenous input into the economy with simple, constant returns. The potential impact of education depends on its quality and its composition. More years in education and more degrees do not necessarily imply an increase in human capital (work-related skills). Sometimes, appropriate expertise may be achieved in other equally good or better ways, for example on-the-job training. In addition, if education is to be economically relevant, there must be an alignment between the technological level of a society, the labour market, the jobs available, and the possible learning and qualifications acquired as a result of higher education. As we will see, both the qualification effect and the matching between the huge number of graduates and the labour market are, to say the least, debatable in most Western countries.

Longer education is generally viewed as increasing the income of individuals. In most, if not all countries, people with a higher degree tend to earn more than those with a shorter education. Education is then viewed as a good investment for young people. The logic here cannot, of course, be translated at a societal level, although this is sometimes the case. As people with higher education tend to have a lower unemployment rate and are doing better, some policy-makers suggest that, with more higher education, many more people will get better jobs, earn more, and reduce the risk of unemployment. But the point is, of course, that those with credentials better than those of others are doing better—this is a positional matter. Turning a very large part of the population into scientists, lawyers, and physicians would only lead to a drop in the earnings, job conditions, and a steady rise in unemployment for those with such an educational background. Irrespective of increases in the average length of education, there will always be one half that is better off than the other half in terms of educational credentials, whether this is the result of having a higher degree, better grades, more vocationally oriented education, or studying at an institution with a better reputation.

Higher education and the associated payoff are often regarded as indicating an increase in the human capital or ability of the person concerned. Pay is regarded as a proxy for the productive capacity and contribution of such a person. There are several complications here and the correlation between longer education and high income (and generally access to more prestigious and attractive jobs) may be explained by the signal factor of the education or its value as a credential. Education as a signal system means that the ability— intelligence, reliability, work morale—of the individual is indicated by their educational status. It is not the learning or the qualifications acquired that matter, but rather the completion of an education as a proxy for intellectual capacity. The correlation between educational level and income then masks the causal effect of intelligence and diligence and also class background that lead to a higher income—or simply the more or less well-founded belief of employers that formal credentials give a strong indication of ability. An extreme view would say that schooling, in itself, does not really matter; rather, it functions like a gigantic test and sorting mechanism. Employers choose and reward those with a longer or better education than others, because the employers believe they are better. If the higher education sorting mechanism works, then there is a signal value of a degree (in general or from a specific institution). Hardly anyone believes that education solely concerns such factors, but there are good reasons for regarding the signalling aspect as an important factor in why higher education pays off and, within the overall higher education sector, why a degree from an elite institution is better rewarded than a degree from somewhere else, and, within a non-elite category, why graduates from an institution with a high ranking generally score much better than those from an institution further down the greasy rankings pole.

A related reason for the payoff from longer education and, in particular, from high-status institutions may be that employers seldom know in detail how their employees are performing in many jobs, and may well be influenced by an employee's educational level and affiliation in perceptions of performance, pay negotiations, and decisions. A person with an MBA or a degree from a high-status institution may, in the absence of reliable indicators of what people are actually doing and accomplishing, be thought to perform better than others. Expectations play an important part in this. In addition, higher education institutions may be good at cultivating people's capacity of impression management, in the form of the right kind of talk and self-confident manners. In some jobs sweet talking may be a crucial skill, but in many, rhetoric is not a key element in work, but can conceal an ability (or lack thereof) to actually contribute. Pay does not necessarily say as much about ability and job contributions as it does about an individual's capacity to communicate an impression of deserving a high wage.

Another key aspect underlying higher pay for people with a degree relates to the expansion of a credentials society, in which qualifications are increasingly used to prevent people from getting certain jobs, while giving the green light to others (Collins, 2002). Education is thus an entrance ticket to one sector of the labour market while those outside are locked out, thus giving rise to pay differentiation. This can mean that education may not, in itself, lead to particularly valuable skills and capacities, but there is still a payoff for the individual.

If we move on from the advantages of higher education from the individual's viewpoint to examine the potential advantages of a well-functioning education system from the viewpoint of employers and the overall economy, there are a few additional aspects that should be taken into account.

A successful education system involves more than simply ensuring that an increasing number of students become somewhat cleverer. There is also the question of whether a degree and grades give employers—and also students—information about knowledge and personal capacity. Good information of this type reduces the cost of recruitment, selection, and employment; minimizes the cost of in-house training and wrong placements; and increases efficiency by putting the right person in the right position. It also gives the individual indications of his/her ability and an appropriate choice of occupation. If an education programme provides little information of this nature, due to the reduced quality of education, this leads to considerable additional costs and problems. Both the employer and the student are left in the lurch, and employment decisions will be made at random. If programmes and grades give little indication of knowledge and skills, their signal value will be reduced. Employing someone with a given degree may be a pure gamble. For employers eager to recruit good people, careful testing, despite its imperfections, may be more reliable than degrees and characters.

Expansion of 'non-university' university education

Many universities now have courses and programmes with a distinctively 'light-weight' flavour. This trend may be traditionally less pronounced in Europe—where vocational training has been viewed as the major road to employment for the majority—than in the United States, where colleges and universities have been more all-embracing and less distinct, but I think we can talk about a general, perhaps global 'de-universitification' of universities. One often-used expression is the McUniversity, where some ingredients of McDonaldization—standardization, efficiency, routinization, etc.—have been incorporated (Ritzer, 2004).

A Google search in November 2011 for 'bizarre university courses' got many hits. Some top scorers include psychology of exceptional human experiences (ghost busting) at Coventry University, surf science at Plymouth University (as well as some Australian institutions), and the Harry Potter and the Age of Illusion module, available as part of the BA in Education Studies at Durham University (the latter doesn't teach spells or Quidditch). Entertainment-focused topics are not alien to contemporary higher education.

In many universities in the United States, Australia, and other places, there are courses on 'food and beverage management'. One such course at the University of Queensland 'underlines the strategic importance of the department within organizations'.[1] Another example is the 'Spa-program' in Sweden, which does not, as you might think, involve some leisure occupation for tired or hedonistic teachers and students, but rather a full, three-year academic programme. At the time of writing, this was offered at two universities, with the participation of several faculties:

This programme is cross-disciplinary and contains courses from different faculty areas. The emphasis is on physical activity, diet, relaxation and recovery, and also massage. (translated from Umeå University website[2])

And some people say that cross-disciplinary studies are difficult! These two spa universities are showing the way.

My thoughts turn to Tom Lehrer, the brilliant pianist and satirist, whose creative zest had a serious setback when Henry Kissinger was awarded the Nobel Peace Prize. Like Lehrer, I sometimes feel that a surrealistic world makes irony impossible. You think you are being heavily ironic, only to discover that the Nobel Prize Committee and many, perhaps most, universities and others make it all fall flat on its face. Once upon a time, it is said, reality surpassed fiction. Now it is outdoing satire as well. Some contemporary universities may score higher as comic theatres than as sites for intellectual qualification.

---

[1] On being a food and beverage manager: 'A typical day might include checking to make sure you have sufficient staff and products, and making sure that your staff has regular breaks throughout the day. You'll also need to hold key staff meetings every week'. Education and training: 'Some have no formal training while others will have a two-year diploma in food and beverage management or even a bachelors or Master's degree in hospitality management.' 'There are nearly 1000 colleges and universities which offer a four-year program in restaurant or hospitality management'. Please see 'Food and Beverage Manager' <careers.stateuniversity.com/pages/cveg8ta2e7/Food-and-Beverage-Manager.html> (accessed 23 November 2011).

[2] <http://www.umu.se>.

The need for a highly educated labour force

Nobody denies that a large number of highly educated people are of the utmost importance to contemporary societies. But the great majority of jobs, even in advanced economies, hardly call for the use of intellectual skills corresponding to what a university degree was once supposed to represent.

In contrast with the idea that the knowledge-intensive society has arrived, or is in the offing, and that there is a very considerable need for a highly qualified labour force, one may make some simple observations concerning the kind of jobs that actually exist. If we take industries and occupations such as hotels and restaurants, transportation, tourism, security guard duties, waste disposal and street cleaning, retailing, care of the elderly, and artisan occupations (hairdressers, electricians, car mechanics, carpenters, and so on), they are hardly characterized by stringent demands for a protracted period of training and education. And if we look at a major sector such as health care, which is often described as professional and which obviously requires well-educated personnel, we also find that a high proportion of the tasks involved hardly require a high level of theoretical knowledge. Transport services, the mass production/distribution of food, washing dishes, washing and bathing patients, cleaning, routine administration, and feeding and taking care of the personal hygiene of patients probably do not call for many years of professional training.

This is not to say that such jobs do not require a considerable amount of occupational skills—but this does not correspond to a higher education requirement. Some people may think that these are marginal occupations that only employ a small and declining fraction of the population. But in the United States, the occupations that have expanded most in absolute terms during recent decades include retail sales, nursing, cashiers, general office staff, truck drivers, waiters, children's nurses, cleaning personnel, and systems analysts (studies cited in Sohlman, 1996: 26; see also Reskin and Padavic, 1994). Personal services and personal assistance in the home showed the fastest growth, followed by computer services. Most of these jobs, with the possible exception of computer services, do not necessarily require a long and qualified education. More than likely, the number of occupations matched by qualified education has increased and is still increasing, even if the rate of increase may have declined during the 1990s (according to Åberg, 2002). But this increase is much less than that promised by the education enthusiasts.

Although the number of jobs in manufacturing in the United States has decreased in relative numbers over the decades, there were as many jobs in the early 2000s as there were in 1970. One of the expanding areas is the 'mega delivery sector' (transportation, retail, etc.), mainly made up of routinized, low-skill work. Sweet and Meiksins (2008) note that 'there is a tendency to assume that the declining importance of manufacturing in the US economy means that mass production is on the wane. It is not. Indeed, what has happened is that mass production has been widely integrated into other sectors, including the rapidly growing service sector' (29–30). It is interesting to note that in the United States, in 2005, 3 million people were employed in computer and mathematical occupations and almost 11 million in food preparation and catering-related occupations (Bureau of Labour Statistics, 2006). Or as Sweet and Meiksins (2008: 24) put it, for every successful computer programmer who works for a company like Microsoft, there are three poorly paid workers labouring on hamburger assembly lines for firms like McDonald's. Ideas of the knowledge-society and the strong need for a highly educated workforce appear quite grandiose in relation to a labour market that hardly seems to be crying out for employees with academic degrees.

While working on this chapter, I received a phone call from one of the many telemarketers who want to sell me something. This is a large occupational group, at least in Sweden. I put aside my manuscript, muffled my irritation, and listened patiently to a well-rehearsed sales script. I was more interested in interviewing the seller, Oskar, about his work. I mentioned that I was writing about work and education and wondered if I could have his views on this subject. It was not hard to get Oskar started, despite—or perhaps due to—this break in his normal routines: my initiative opened up a flow of emotions.

'Education!' Oskar exclaimed, 'I could say a lot about education.' He said that he had studied a wide range of subjects over a long period, but that no value whatsoever was placed on this when he applied for jobs. The managers in the company where he was employed had no education, but this did not keep them from earning a lot of money. Oskar sounded resigned. This topic clearly interested him. I asked him about his job and what education or training was required. 'You get one day's training', he said. 'I can do it in my sleep. I feel like a robot every day.'

One day's training is more than other telephone salespersons get. Ten minutes' instruction and one hour's listening-in was the rule in another company (SDS, 5 June 2004). Thirteen minutes' introduction is considered sufficient for certain jobs in fast-food chains (Reskin and Padavic, 1994). One may wonder how important training is in many occupations in the 'human service sector', compared with personal characteristics such as suitability, morale, and interest in the job.

There is sometimes a serious shortage of personnel in a number of artisan occupations and in practical health care services in certain countries, and young people tend to reject such training programmes. In Sweden, where economic crises and high unemployment in the early 1990s triggered a rapid expansion of higher education, there was, for example, a protracted shortage of trained car mechanics (SDS, 3 November 2003). There has also been an acute shortage of level-two nurses and nursing assistants. According to the Swedish Board of Health and Welfare, almost half a million vacancies will have to be filled over the next 12 years, while places in the nursing programme remain vacant. In Stockholm, only twenty young people opted for this programme as their first choice in 2002 (DN, 30 November 2003).

But even in the case of jobs held by people with a long academic education, we may wonder how crucial this kind of education really is. In jobs that call for medical or scientific training this is presumably a crucial factor, but it is less clearly required in many other fields. A study of psychologists and architects suggested that such professionals rarely used the specific knowledge and techniques to which they had been exposed in the course of their education, although their education presumably contributed, at a more general level, to their capacity for thinking and solving problems (Svensson, 1990). Similarly, a formal education is not regarded as a decisive factor in the advertising industry (Alvesson and Köping, 1993). Studies of consulting firms and managerial functions indicate that people involved in such activities tend to regard further education as of relatively limited importance for 'competence development' and learning (Fosstenlökken et al., 2003; Wenglén, 2005).

Managers usually say that their employees learn on the job, not in training programmes. Such programmes are mainly useful for the contacts they provide, it is claimed. Most managers say that employees develop their skills and expertise through varied and challenging assignments and the ongoing interaction with colleagues, customers, and clients. My interviews with IT company managers also suggest a playing-down of the importance of a formal education. 'Do you need to have studied in higher education to be an IT consultant?' I asked. 'No', said one senior manager, a graduate engineer, adding that other people may be just as good. He said that they recruited plenty of young graduates with many strange degrees, as well as people straight out of school. 'It is just as important to have people who are autodidacts or have the right personality as people with the right education', he said. At one successful IT consulting firm, the crucial importance of personal characteristics was stressed, while education-related knowledge was played down (Alvesson, 1995). They argued: you can always give people the know-how, but it is hard to influence someone's personality.

A former senior executive with a highly qualified academic background says:

> The fact that we nowadays recruit graduates to such an extent is, for the most part, because we are interested in their ability rather than their theoretical knowledge. In this day and age, most of the people with ability go on to study at university.

This is a kind of catch-22. But there is something that the universities provide that we are interested in, and that is the ability to analyse various types of problems and to question half-baked ideas in a critical spirit. (Personal correspondence)

All these remarks do not mean that I deny that it is an absolute necessity for contemporary societies, and in particular for advanced economies, that a number of people receive a university education. The importance of research and education in developing people who can think critically, reason deeply, and communicate effectively in writing and speech—traditional objectives of higher education—needs to be emphasized. But this does not legitimize either educational fundamentalism or the naïve view that expansion of higher education necessarily results in such learning outcomes and/or its universal relevance and significance for the entire labour market and the economy. Unfortunately, such outcomes seem to be decreasingly produced in higher education institutions. Rapid expansion of higher education seems to go hand in hand with the decline of intellectual qualification.

Cynicism or stupidity: the problem of a lack of correctives for grandiosity

It is hard to say to what extent many politicians and other supporters of education fundamentalism and the expansion of higher education are trapped by their own rhetoric and by verbose fantasies and wishful thinking about the beneficial effects of higher education, or to what extent they are simply being cynical. One problem in this area is the grandiosity implications and positive connotations of higher education. Wolf (2004) writes: 'Everyone believes education is a good thing, and there are no interest groups who will visibly be harmed by expansion, or will mobilize in opposition' (330). In addition, there is seldom any obvious evidence of success or failure, so correcting the stupidity mechanism calls for more intellectual work than is easily demonstrated in public debate.

Apart from the hope that increased higher education means economic growth, it has the great advantage of being a means of reducing unemployment, at least during the time people are studying. Any possibility of keeping people occupied is a valuable factor for politicians and governments hardpressed to create jobs and reduce unemployment. Pushing unemployment into the future (when graduates will face an overcrowded labour market) or down the hierarchy (to those with a shorter education) does not really solve the problem, for which perhaps there is no solution, given the technological developments and the perhaps questionable norm that a working week be close to 40 hours. Described by Collins (2002) as a hidden welfare system, higher education thus functions as a warehouse or a parking garage for young people. In this context, one can imagine a combination of cynicism and naïvety on the part of many politicians and policy-makers—a mixture of smart manoeuvring and of hope that the formula of the economy-boosting effects of more higher education will reduce unemployment by keeping people occupied, possibly facilitating economic growth and hence creating more jobs.

Zero-sum games

Two kinds of tendencies for the occurrence of zero-sum games should be noted:

1. Greater numbers often mean a deterioration in learning and in completion of studies due to the wide variation in student ability and motivation and, in many educational programmes, the very large classes, where students are processed in 'McDonaldized' ways (standardized modules, multiple choice exams, etc.).
2. Greater numbers reduce the value of education in the labour market, thus pushing people into more advanced forms of education in order to improve their credentials, before they face a labour market with large numbers of job applicants with pumped-up CVs.

Problems of wide variation

One of the major problems in higher education is the extremely wide range of possible subjects of study and interest in studying. An increasing proportion of students have inadequate prior knowledge, have no particular aptitude for studies, and are only mildly interested (Arum and Roksa, 2011). Some may be studying because they do not have a job, because everybody else is studying, or because they have been ensnared by the education-fundamentalist message that you have nothing to contribute to a knowledge-intensive society unless you have a proper education. Perhaps the strongest motive is simply to avoid winding up at the back of the queue for a reasonable kind of job—a long education, at least for some, is the entry ticket to the upper levels of the labour market. From another perspective, one could say that, for some, it is a way out of the many routine jobs available which a higher proportion as a result of the raising of expectations, hopes, and demands, are eager to avoid.

The wide variation in student abilities and interests makes it difficult to provide a satisfactory university education. At the international level, because there are so many students, the situation is far from ideal:

The greatest problem today in university teaching is the demands and expectations of the outside world—and also extreme variations in the student mass, that is to say their prerequisites, motivation and requirements. This makes omnipotent demands on university teachers and, in view of the way these demands are defined, it is impossible to live up to them. (Handal, 2003: 18)

Another commentator observes that 'many students never really internalize the new demands and standards of university work. Instead they drift from course to course, looking for entertainment and easy grades' (Grafton, 2011).

There are indications that there has been considerable deterioration in many areas. At the Lund University Institute of Technology (Lund is an old university ranked among the top 50–100 in the world), the mathematical knowledge of first-year engineering students has been tested since 1997. While the proportion of students assessed as 'weak' has doubled, the proportion adjudged as 'excellent' dropped by a third between 1997 and 2005 (SDS, 1 December 2005). Most teachers in the humanities also note a deterioration in the student input. According to Arum and Roksa (2011), a very large number of students entering a higher education programme in the United States are not prepared for it. Arum and Roksa cite a survey according to which 40 per cent of college faculty agree with the statement: 'Most of the students I teach lack the basic skills for college level work' (86). Irrespective of who is to be blamed for this—poor high schools, poor counselling, limited resources for colleges, bad students, or bad teachers—it is clear that higher education often does not function as intended. The gap between the ideal and the reality is huge, in many cases.

One may wonder how much the weaker or less motivated portion of those embarking on a university education expect to get out of their years of study, in terms of opportunities in the labour market. This applies to both learning (including intellectual development) and the return on years of study in terms of job assignments and pay. To some extent, this problem might be handled by establishing a range of institutions and programmes for weak students, and strong differentiation of higher education institutions. Of course, many countries have strong hierarchical quality differentiation within the sector, but this does not necessarily mean that students are homogenous within an institution. Most face the problem of the great diversity in student ability and interest. In addition, the creation, in the context of traditional university ideals, of low-quality institutions with unfavourable reputations may lead to limited learning for better or ambitious students and credentials worth very little.

Inflation of grades and an increasingly widespread consumer orientation—in which satisfied and confirmed students constitute a benchmark—also result in poor and unreliable feedback that reinforces rather than corrects exaggerated self-images in which students regard themselves as clever and destined for high-status jobs.

Devaluation of merit value

It is frequently proposed that an improvement in educational levels solves all kinds of problems. In a special pleading for more resources for schools, the chairmen of two large union organizations—whose members are expected to benefit from such arguments—say that 'we know that people with the lowest level of education are overrepresented as regards unemployment, ill-health and criminality' (Preisz and Nordh, SDS, 3 June 2003). It is also claimed—based on research—that if two people have the same education but different levels of basic knowledge, those with better knowledge will have a better income, with the passing of time. This is a standard argument, and it is probably correct: people who have better than average qualifications receive a better than average return.

But if we cannot imagine that everyone is to have the same level of education and basic knowledge—an ambition that is probably unattainable—then some people will always wind up in second place. Even if we could reduce the differences in knowledge and education, people in a less advantageous position will be underdogs compared to those classed as average or superior. To the extent that basic knowledge determines pay and the risk of unemployment, they will be in an inferior position in these respects as well.

General increases in the length of education lead to inflation and zero-sum games, as far as effects on the labour market are concerned. As Collins writes,

> credential inflation processes will continue, indeed at even higher pressure. First; with few good jobs, there is extremely high competition for access to them, hence driving up educational requirements for very high levels. Second: the educational system comes to play an important role in dealing with the displaced part of the labour force ... the warehousing also keeps up the supply of educational credentials, reinforcing the first process. (2002: 27)

As regards attractive employment opportunities, relative rather than absolute education is of primary interest, that is to say the individual's educational qualifications compared to those of others. Since most people, for individual, rational reasons, increase their investment in education in order to be successful as candidates for attractive jobs, they resemble a group in which everyone is standing on their toes in order to get a better view (Hirsch, 1976). Everyone is forced to devote an increasingly longer period of their lives to their education, without any particular improvement in the average person's chances of getting an attractive job.

As a result of the massive expansion of higher education, we live in an 'era of educational hyperinflation' (Collins, 2002: 26). Here the overall value of such an education is declining, and the importance of a degree from the right institution is the crucial factor. This can be seen particularly clearly in the United States where some institutions are seen as the best in the world, while the university and college system as a whole is subject to heavy criticism (e.g., Menand, 2011; Piereson, 2011). There is intense competition over the positional goods involved in higher education that provide access to social prestige and incomes. The rapid development of a global commercial mass market for education, headed by US, UK, and Australian universities, means that rankings are becoming more important (Marginson, 2006). The hierarchy of these rankings 'is steeper in some nations than others, and more powerfully felt in some places than others, but always exists' (3).

The social boundaries for growth in education—problems in reducing class inequality

While the impact of expanded higher education on growth is ambiguous, it is clear that with increasing wealth there is an extension and increased focus on education. Wolf (2004) notes that 'growth creates education. As families obtain extra income, the overwhelming majority seek good schools for their children, press them to obtain qualifications and crowd them into expanded institutions at ever higher levels' (323). The acceptance rate at Harvard was 85 per cent in 1940 (mainly reflecting that sons of fathers who had gone to Harvard and could afford the fees were sent there). The corresponding figure in 2010 was 6 per cent (Menand, 2011). It is becoming risky not to have an academic degree from a reasonably highly ranked institution, and the investment in higher education as a positional good—valued in terms of how it relates to the qualifications of others—is increased, with a heavy augmentation of fees for the more attractive university places in countries with market prices (Hotson, 2011).

In the case of those who are not awarded degrees by top universities or are not in exclusive programmes (such as medicine or veterinary science), mass education does not necessarily have a leverage effect in the labour market. The measure of justice that may prevail in differentiation and ranking based on level of education may be replaced by other, more arbitrary sorting mechanisms. This presents problems for people who have embarked on 'class journeys' or for immigrants who wish to demonstrate their abilities via the education system. This means, paradoxically, that an expansion of education that is partially justified in terms of better opportunities for underprivileged groups, may make it more difficult for them to demonstrate their ability in the education system. Of course, problems of differentiation and disadvantage for those with an underprivileged background are not new. But when university education was relatively limited and when the qualification element more or less guaranteed a certain degree of knowledge and ability—at least a higher degree of work effort (as mentioned, Arum and Roksa, 2011, report a significant reduction in hours of study per week since the 1960s)—those with the wrong background could 'prove' their value through a degree. Today, a degree from most non-elite universities has an uncertain value as a qualification indicator, making it difficult to use education as a reliable route to a class journey. This is partly a matter of mass education and partly a matter of low demands and uncertain learning in much education.

One ambition in many countries is to increase the number of students with a working-class background by means of an expansion of higher education. But this is not at all the same thing as access to attractive, well-paid, and influential jobs. Those who clearly learn a great deal at universities often come from highly educated families and attend highly selective colleges and universities. If we look at the distribution of social background in the various higher education institutions and their unemployment figures, the picture is clear: local higher education institutions and new universities have a relatively high proportion of students with a working-class background—and they also have high unemployment figures. Fewer students with a working-class background tend to study at universities or other higher education institution with a high status and a high admission points requirement. This also applies in a country such as Sweden, with free higher education and very strong equality ambitions. In the Stockholm School of Economics—private, fairly small, and well resourced due to support from business, and broadly seen as a leading institution in its field—5 per cent of its student body come from a working-class background, while in other universities and leading medical and engineering schools, the proportion is 16–24 per cent. The average in higher education in Sweden is 37 per cent. There is also a tendency for institutions with a high proportion of students with a working-class background to subsequently have a higher percentage of graduate unemployment a few years later (SDS, 29 May 2002; DN, 4 October 2002).

The impact of class background in this form is a classic phenomenon. Although the proportion of students with a working-class background has increased as years have passed, this has involved the less prestigious programmes and institutions. If we look at professional degree programmes, we find that the children of highly educated parents are mainly found in the medical, dentistry, law, and graduate engineering programmes, while people with a working-class background participate to a greater extent in pre-school teacher, recreation instructor, and nursing programmes (Swedish National Agency for Higher Education, 2002). In other words, there is considerable social stratification. Without beating about the bush, we might say that, in the past, working-class children attended elementary school before proceeding to low-paid, low-status jobs, while today they have higher education (and student loan debts) before they get a similar job. (When I refer to low-status, this applies to the category of programmes that have wound up in the higher education sector.) Maybe we can speak of a *higher education proletariat.*

In their study of intellectual development during higher education years in the United States, Arum and Roksa (2011) found that students from the upper classes learned significantly, while those from disadvantaged groups, especially Afro-Americans, did not. They concluded that 'individual learning is characterized by persistent and/or growing inequality' (30). One could say that people enter higher education unequal and leave (more) unequal. This mainly reflects deeper and broader social structures and dynamics and the exact role of higher education institutions is difficult to specify. One element is that students with well-educated parents are better prepared, and study more effectively. A very long history of attempts to create equality via education has persistently met with failure—the pattern has been the same over the years (Arum and Roksa, 2011; Collins, 2002; Hansen, 2002). Higher education apparently does not function as a successful equalizer.

In this sense, one might perhaps refer to the expansion of higher education as a new class trap, brilliantly (but maybe unintentionally) laid by those who claim they want to eliminate class divisions. On paper, it gives the impression of achieving class equality, and overall statistics and, to some extent, degree certificates appear to confirm this. This would be in line with the ideology of educational fundamentalism: higher education for as many as possible is a good thing. But here we see the problem of grandiosity: impressive talk indicating remarkable achievement of the good society with strong signs of a well-educated population living in a knowledge society. The grandiose talk about a large and expanding university sector, including indications of how much competence is being developed, stand in contrast to the actual learning, labour-market prospects, and standards of living of many graduates. The actual labour market situation offers a less grandiose story, as do debts of study loans. If the reader wants me to suggest a solution to the problem of inequality, I can only say 'no bid'. It is clear that reforms in higher education have only had limited success (Arum and Roksa, 2011; Hansen, 2002).

Summary

Education fundamentalism has been on the war path for some time, and its triumphal progress is continuing. A rather simplistic view of the necessity or desirability of a university education for half the population is becoming widely accepted. One may refer to the fetishizing of 'competence' and a 'knowledge-intensive society' (Salomonsson, 2005). What we have here is a classic example of grandiosity, based on international competition problems, a downturn in the manufacturing industry and major employment problems in many post-industrial, advanced economies. It is hard to argue with the two pillars and rationales for educational fundamentalism—economic growth (and thereby reduced unemployment) and a reduction in inequality. At least before we seriously consider the (often limited) qualification acquired, the increasing mismatch between formal educational level and labour market and, in particular, the social limits to growth must be taken seriously.

The expansion of higher education can be linked to an ambition to repair a tarnished national reputation in countries in retreat by becoming 'a leading knowledge-intensive nation'. In former colonialist countries, such as the UK, the idea of 'educating the others is presented as a national investment to consolidate neo-colonial power, with the state using the glamour of advertising and public relations to spin and soften its hard-hedged political and economic rationales' (Sidhu, 2006: 136). Via higher education based in the UK, students are promised 'intellectual citizenship of the world' (British Council, 1999, cited in Sidhu, 2006: 130). This sounds impressive, of course—once again, a prime example of grandiose claims—but the quality slippage is often huge and the wave of academic degrees with little or no quality assurance means that 'education credentials are increasingly viewed by both universities and their clients as tradable goods, just like any other commodity' (Sidhu, 2006: 144).

In other post-industrial societies too, people are desperately looking for something new onto which they can pin international competition and employment. 'Knowledge'—research and education—appears to be the solution. One idea seems to be that while all the fine people in Western countries concentrate on knowledge projects, people in other countries are taking over manufacturing and services that do not call for the intellectual refinement and advanced know-how which people in wealthy nations like to see themselves as capable of producing.

There is no reason to question the need for important and growing sectors of industry to compete at an international level, and with a knowledge-intensive focus. Telecoms, pharmaceuticals, and biotechnology are clearly key industries, and health care and IT call for well-qualified staff. However, there are no grounds for doubting that major areas of working life—

even in advanced economies—will not require a protracted theoretical education within the foreseeable future. It is clear that, on the whole, working life cannot offer as many qualified jobs as the education system and the proponents of a 'knowledge-intensive society' would have us believe.

One grandiose dream in many countries with decreasing economies in agriculture and industry is to lead the world in higher education. The grandiosity in the 'higher education for half the population for a knowledge-intensive life' project appeals to politicians and others who want to present a politically attractive message, the average citizen who is normalized as someone who is looking for education options and possibly expects job opportunities in line with a higher education, and education coordinators who draw in people 'who want to be something great'.

Of course, the intrinsic value of knowledge and intellectual stimulation is not primarily a matter of positionality, but education in relationship to the labour market has a strong positional element: with expansion, the intensification of zero-sum games follows. The demand for higher education is complying with the logic of the zero-sum game to an increasing extent. For some people, this is a question of whether you are genuinely interested in and have an aptitude for higher education. These people appear to be in the minority. You have to study for an increasingly extended period to qualify for most occupations if you are not to fall behind. This involves avoiding a 'low education' status, that is to say below average. A key driver for many is to escape from the bottom and locate themselves in terms of above-average formal qualifications. To the extent that an increasingly strong instrumental orientation characterizes higher education, the zero-sum game is becoming an increasingly prominent feature of higher education. We get a society and labour markets full of CV boosting. Higher education is more and more a question of positional goods. And since higher education is becoming increasingly uncertain, perhaps even meaningless as evidence of skills and expertise, and there is growing competition for attractive jobs, students are forced to view education in more tactical terms, while institutions respond with grade inflation. What is to be done to ensure that you wind up in the diminishing proportion of graduates who can expect to get a job more or less in line with their education—or even get a job at all?

I should perhaps remind the reader (and myself for that matter) that in this book I am primarily addressing the positional aspects of higher education and its expansion. There are, of course, also non-positional aspects of knowledge acquisition and intellectual development. Critical thinking, a capacity for abstract reasoning and reflection, and the ability to communicate are traditional ideals of education, and these clearly go beyond improving one's position for status purposes and job prospects in competition with, and at the expense of, others. With the expansion of higher education and increased competition for jobs and a general intensification of the positional goods qualities of educational credentials and the general decrease in quality, higher education as an arena for cultivating intellectual development as an intrinsic value has lost much of its significance.

5

Higher education—an image-boosting business?

In this chapter, I continue to address higher education. A key question is the role and function of higher education, especially the universities, in contemporary society. Is it primarily a vehicle for the improvement of knowledge and intellectual qualifications? Or is it about other issues? As hinted at in Chapter 4, there seems to be a lot of variation and a lot of shakiness concerning learning and improvement of cognitive capacities for all or the vast majority of students. A second key question is what the signifier 'university' means (in the context of education). Does it mean anything particular or is it just a label intended to trigger positive responses and then work as an umbrella for all kinds of activities? This raises the question as to what extent the entire sector in itself, rather than merely certain arrangements within higher education institutions, can be viewed as an illusion (i.e., not accomplishing what it increasingly claims that it represents and achieves). Higher education is perhaps better at producing degrees, documentation for CVs, and keeping young people out of unemployment for a few years than producing knowledge and people who are good at critical and abstract thinking, seeing patterns, and analysing problems. A third key question concerns the benefits of higher education for individuals. Do people, on the whole, gain from higher education and, if so, in what ways?

This chapter is rather broad in scope. It starts with critically examining to what extent higher education—here, meaning primarily university education—leads to qualifications and whether an academic degree offers a clear message about the graduate's ability. These questions are related to, and trigger further consideration of, inflation tendencies in the entire educational sector, but in particular in universities. One potentially significant and problematic outcome of the inflation is over-education; i.e., the number of graduates strongly exceeds the number of jobs for which their formal education and degrees indicate they are qualified. A heavily expanded, and often dominating, area of education is business and management studies. I give this sector some extra attention in the chapter, as it is my own sector. Thus, this chapter draws not only upon published work, but also on my long experience and work at many universities in several countries in combination with numerous informal conversations with colleagues all over the world.

I also address the issue of power, both in the conventional sense of powerful interests, which form and provide higher education and formal qualifications with legitimacy, and in the more Foucauldian sense of norms and ideals. The latter produce regulated ways of being, including the normalization of education as *the way* of being, and making other routes to qualifications socially problematic. The dominating norms of education call for critical scrutiny instead of just being taken for granted and reproduced.

Does education guarantee qualifications?

It is commonly assumed that education almost automatically leads to a greater ability to think and act in working life and in society as a whole. Education is believed to solely or mainly have positive effects for individuals and society. But it cannot be assumed that, simply because people have taken a course or acquired a degree, they have become much more knowledgeable and developed their analytical capacity or their ability to express themselves, or whatever else is involved.

Limited learning and cognitive development

In *Academically Adrift* (2011), Arum and Roksa followed 2,200 US students over their college years, using tests designed to investigate critical thinking, analytical reasoning, problem solving, and writing. The study indicates that some 45 per cent of students in the sample had made no effective progress in critical thinking, complex reasoning, and writing in their first two years and 37 per cent did not improve after four years—the periods covered by the study. According to Arum and Roksa (2011: 36), 'an astounding proportion of students are progressing through higher education today without measurable gains in general skills'. Such skills are what higher education institutions broadly emphasize as their major contribution, making contemporary US higher education appear to be rather unsuccessful.

The students who score the lowest and improve the least are the business students.

Traditional subjects and methods seem to retain their educational value. Nowadays, the liberal arts attract a far smaller proportion of students than they did two generations ago. Still, those majoring in the liberal arts fields—humanities and social sciences, natural sciences, and mathematics—outperformed those studying business, communications, and other new, practically oriented majors.

A study of an MBA (Master of Business Administration) programme in Britain is also somewhat depressing. An MBA is further education at university level for students who have graduated in a subject and have subsequent work experience. This programme stressed—in the usual way—the practical applications of the course contents. In a subsequent follow-up five years later, none of the participants could point to having used any specific part of the programme in practice, although they thought they had gained something in the form of a general understanding of the area (a bird's-eye view), and improved self-confidence and social contacts. No doubt, they had some benefits that they could not report in concrete terms, but nonetheless this study suggests a meagre outcome in terms of practical consequences (Sturdy et al., 2006). This example indicates that education programmes do not necessarily result in a tangible improvement in the acquisition of knowledge.

One could, of course, also emphasize that higher education means a broader outlook and an improved capacity to participate in society, including a democratic commitment. This is possible, but once again it cannot be assumed. According to the Swedish National Agency for Higher Education's Student Mirror, students in Sweden consider, for example, that higher education does not contribute to any greater extent to an involvement in societal development (DN, 2 September 2002). Perhaps, democracy is no longer benefitting from further increases in higher education?

The problem of a flabby education system and a consumer orientation

Part of the quality problem is due to a *low level of requirements* in many subjects and at many higher education institutions. (Obviously, there are enormous variations, but this is not an appropriate forum for a detailed examination of different subject areas, institutions, and countries.) For the most part, the only/crucial form of evaluation is student assessments, which are more an expression of student satisfaction, rather than a reflection of the quality of the education provided. The incentive for teachers may be to use less-demanding course contents or to be less strict or demanding in assessments of student performances. If the students are paying substantial fees, there is an additional pressure to ensure that the customers are satisfied and to avoid reducing the market by failing students with weak results. In some countries, resources are allocated in accordance with the passing of exams and awarding of degrees, which also means a negative influence on quality. Institutions, programmes, and courses that have low standards achieve a high student completion rate and are rewarded accordingly. Courses that have a reputation for being demanding may also be less appealing to students and lead to fewer applicants.

It can be supposed that many institutions want to maintain high standards in order to improve their reputation with employers and ambitious students. But if we take into account students' overall input, low standards have considerably greater impact. On the whole, the tendency is a reduction in standards (SDS, 9 December 2005).

Another problem is student *motivation*. Many commentators stress the low level of motivation and the limited study input for many students (Menand, 2011; Piereson, 2011). According to Arum and Roksa (2011), many students come to university with no particular interest in their courses, and no sense of how these might prepare them for future careers.

Many students spend modest time studying. In the United States, the average time spent on studies in higher education was reported to be as low as 12–13 hours per week. (This is in addition to spending, on average, 15 hours per week in class.) In 1961, the average was 25 hours per week. Even at the elite University of California, students report that, on average, they spend 'twelve hours [a week] socializing with friends, eleven hours using computers for fun, six hours watching television, six hours exercising, five hours on hobbies'—and 13 hours a week studying. In Sweden, the numbers are similar. Only 32 per cent of the total number of students devoted more than 30 hours a week to their studies (time in class and self-study combined) (Franke and Jacobsson, DN, 2 September 2002). Other studies give a similar picture. Study time averages closer to half-time than full-time. This can be seen in a message convening a seminar, issued by a director of undergraduate studies at one institution:

> In many evaluations from our students in recent years, we have been criticized for having too few teaching sessions, or 'contact opportunities' as they are now called. At the same time, students say that they are spending an average of 20–30 hours a week (in the best case) on their studies. Furthermore, many students appear to consider that it is the teacher's fault if the individual student does not receive a top grade (distinction) in his/her examination. To use a current term in Swedish, we are increasingly expected to act as 'curling teachers' for our students. Many students seem to be mainly interested (in the best case) in what will come up (or not come up) in the next exam.

This is probably not an entirely new phenomenon, but the director of studies, like many others, feels that there have been changes over the years.

A colleague in Canada, with considerable ambitions as a teacher and with personal charisma that should have had an impact on student enthusiasm, says that she has almost given up trying to create a commitment to her subject (business studies). The classroom was permeated by silence and indifference until she reluctantly introduced grading based on classroom participation. Then the hands went up everywhere. When she asked her students why they had chosen this subject, she received two responses: either 'To earn as much money as possible' or 'Don't know'. These two answers are hardly representative of business students only, but seem to illustrate two major problems with contemporary students more broadly. One is the instrumental and opportunistic attitude amongst many to higher education, while the other is that many students are 'drifting through college without a clear sense of purpose' (Arum and Roksa, 2011: 34).

Clearly, many students have a high degree of commitment, as least in the classic university subjects, but modest motivation is hardly a marginal phenomenon.

Limited requirements and a low degree of motivation are to some extent linked to a market- and consumer-oriented higher education field, reflecting, on the one hand, a greater consumption focus and, on the other, a greater public provision of services. The market approach is more widespread (Barnett, 2004; Weymans, 2010), while the idea that one is to be regarded as a customer, even in supposedly strictly non-commercial contexts, has become increasingly common (du Gay and Salaman, 1992). This has resulted in a high level of expectations, while simultaneously contributing to the erosion of work and study morality. (There are other pieces to this puzzle, such as funding shortages, students working part-time, research-focused teachers viewing teaching as something to minimize, and very large and anonymous institutions, but I'm not going to go into all of this.) In a consumer culture, market fundamentalists sometimes believe that consumer satisfaction drives quality, but this may lead to a less-demanding workload, fairly easy course content, entertainment in class, and generous grading, plus the allocation of resources by universities to non-educational arrangements (sports, counselling, career advice).

Higher grades an illusion trick?

Even though Arum and Roksa's (2011) study indicated that more than half the students showed improvement during their time in college, it cannot be assumed that education automatically confers learning, qualification, and greater wisdom. If we look at higher education in a broader perspective, the picture is rather depressing. The Swedish National Agency for Higher Education's Student Mirror suggests that 'increased specialization, fragmentation and a utility focus seem to be the dominant characteristics of higher education today, and a self-interested professional and career approach seems to characterize many students' attitudes'. The broader purpose of education, which should lead to well-informed, reflective, and critically thinking citizens, is thereby not really accomplished.

What the university offers is often perhaps not guaranteed improved intellectual skills or knowledge but rather credentials: a diploma that signals employability and basic work discipline, but that often has uncertain information value.

American universities 'attract ferocious criticism' (Grafton, 2011), especially for their strong focus on entertainment and keeping students happy, giving 'bizarre courses', and employing low-cost part-time teachers and postgraduate students for a large part of the teaching, thus ensuring that the professors' teaching time is reduced so that they can produce research articles that make it possible to maintain or improve ranking positions (Arum and Roksa, 2011; Menand, 2011; Piereson, 2011). One line of criticism focuses on the assumption that students are 'customers', that increasing costs are being devoted to marketing and producing a good customer experience for students, as a result of an emphasis on facilities and generally having a nice time rather than focusing too much on studies and learning (Hotson, 2011). Most of this criticism is also current in other countries with a large higher education sector.

All this means that we may be justified in regarding significant parts of contemporary higher education systems as a gigantic illusory arrangement. We live in a knowledge society, elite groups like to claim, thereby boosting their status and self-esteem and improving hope and pride for themselves and their groups. The expanded higher education sector can be seen as an arrangement of doubtful substance, but high on symbolic and signal value. It is a legitimizing structure that gives some credibility to the knowledge society's claims and protects such claims from careful scrutiny.

It is, of course, important not to exaggerate in this context. It would be ridiculous not to acknowledge the significance and value of much of the research and education that is leading to knowledge development and increased qualifications. This is still a key characteristic of much university activity. But to the extent we can rely on Arum and Roksa's (2011) study, then about 40 per cent of US students do not really learn much, and that might indicate that the illusion element might be of this order. My point here is, of course, not to claim that it is really possible to clearly separate illusion and substance, but to argue that higher education claiming to be a competence-raising institution can, like many other things, be understood as partly an illusion arrangement. This view offers a counterpoint to predominant claims about a knowledge society and the necessity and value of the expansion of higher education.

Illusory arrangements and actions in higher education institutions

One classic solution of the problem of a decline in substance is to focus on image reinforcement, that is to say special procedures, activities, and labelling that give a positive picture of operations. Higher education *as* an illusion is then backed up by illusions *within* the higher education institutions. What follows are examples of illusion tricks within the higher education sector: the turning of all (or many) higher education institutions into universities, and the way that business schools try to improve their position through branding efforts.

Inflation in the universities

Inflation in the university title is an international trend. In some countries, including the UK and Australia, a large number of polytechnics became universities during the 1980s. One problem is that polytechnics typically focus on vocational training and have a weak research function. This re-labelling may therefore be seen as a smoke screen since it gives polytechnics a misleading image and identity. To some extent, the character of vocationally oriented alternatives are disguised under a university label. This also complicates the status of certain practical vocational programmes expected to exhibit some clearly academic ingredients. To the extent that the latter may be regarded as particularly advanced in theoretical terms, based on twelve years of previous schooling and teachers with research training and scientific foundations, the incorporation of all kinds of programmes under the mantle of 'university' may be virtually regarded as an illusion trick. The idea is that all universities are supposed to be based on or linked with research. (Otherwise the university label falls flat.) This is costly and resources are often taken from teaching. It also means an upgrading of academic aspects in relationship to vocational knowledge, often a mixed blessing for people being educated to take up semi-professional jobs, like nursing, many forms of engineering, and 'non-professional' jobs like beverage management. Higher status is sometimes achieved at the price of a risk of deterioration in content. What are key features of higher education are of limited relevance for vocational training and of limited interest for many students.

The problem of inflation means that the value of being a university is reduced, status is lost, and the sector as a whole loses attractiveness and influence. Whether this is good or bad, the point must be taken into consideration, along with the risk of an imbalance between the different types of qualification routes and content in education, practical or vocational elements being marginalized. These issues are less significant when practical education is marketed under a university brand, providing a possibly misleading image and making it possible for politicians and others to show favourable statistics on university graduates indicating how progressive and successful the country is.

Manipulation of the image—branding business schools

Management education has expanded heavily and is now the largest part of higher education at many universities. In the UK, the number of business schools has increased from two to fifty over a couple of decades. (Part of this is a result of management departments re-labelling themselves as business schools, which sounds more commercially and vocationally viable, and an interest in imitating those with a strong market position, i.e., the first movers established as business schools several decades ago.) They are all competing for favourable positions in the various ongoing ranking exercises.

At many places, this bizarre logic is as follows: in order for an institution to look good, it recruits top researchers, pays them a great deal of money with a minimal teaching load, and hires part-time, cheap people to teach as much as possible. This may lead to a good ranking, as research output is central here. This makes it possible to recruit good students and charge high fees which are used to pay the star research-academics whom they rarely see and who often teach courses more adapted to their research projects than to student needs or interests. All this indicates questionable value for money in terms of educational quality, but due to the ranking effect and the value of the positional good acquired—a CV that enables one to move further up in the job applicant queue compared to those who attended institutions with an inferior ranking—there may nonetheless be some payoff. Of course, there is some substance associated with these arrangements. Some excellent researchers may be good and inspiring teachers—especially for intellectually interested students—and the overall logic means that fellow students may be good (and rich!), which is good for learning and network building. Elite universities and colleges are particularly important for the 'coalescence of privileged identities, group boundaries and social networks' (Stevens et al., 2008: 132). Access to a valuable network is another positional good derived from higher education—going to a good school allows one to establish a career-building network of contacts that is clearly more valuable than that formed by people going to colleges with—from a career point of view—inferior networks.

My broad familiarity with business schools across Europe provides many insights into how common it is to apply illusory arrangements.

In many schools, there are 'Centres of Excellence', areas where, one might assume, research and potential education would be of exceptionally high quality. However, the meaning of 'excellence' in a school I once monitored was that these were areas in which research plus teaching took place. Hence, 'excellence' only meant that the 'centres' were somewhat better (or less poor) than other areas in the school. The motive for the excellence centres seemed mainly to be to adapt to the demands of an accreditation committee wanting to have a research strategy. This often looks good on paper, but may be best decoupled from practice.

Another school had a Master's programme tailored to people who were unemployed, or not getting what they regarded as a sufficiently good job. The programme involved organizing internships for students, the idea being that this created some job-relevant training as well as contacts with employers, leading to higher job prospects. Not much wider education was involved; a report was requested, but the main point was that the students got their diploma and contacts that facilitated employment without much education. The Master's programme was basically a disguised job placement agency. This can be a minor feature of higher education, but turning it into a major point—indeed, the business rationale for the arrangement—is another matter.

Another institution, one with an excellent reputation since it was part of a top university, spent about a third of its teaching resources on preparing the students for job applications and, in particular, job interviews. This meant that the graduates were very skilled in impressing management and could negotiate a high salary. As official rankings are partly based on the graduates' pay relatively soon after they qualify, this made it easier for the school to come out as a leader in this field. Students willing to pay high fees could be recruited, since they could see that this was a 'good' education with a clear pay-off. When asked about this, the dean could not see anything wrong with this strategy and resource allocation.

One business school prepared for a ranking based on an assessment of the research performed by removing some low-performing faculty from the website and temporarily moving others to units where their low research output was expected to do least harm.

Generally, many places appear to downplay ambitions to contribute to good knowledge and mainly hire researchers capable of producing a high output of articles, boosting the ranking and status of the school, even if these are not necessarily regarded as the best in terms of producing innovative, interesting, and valuable knowledge—the latter being more risky, time-consuming, and therefore, to some extent, at odds with a high level of productivity (Alvesson and Sandberg, 2013).

One important trend is the increased focus on accreditation. With the massive expansion of management education and the growth in the number of business schools, a market for accreditation has emerged. The idea of accreditation is that the better schools can use it in order to distinguish themselves from the rest. It is difficult to know whether this really works, but getting the accreditation involves three significant costs:

1. The financial cost of paying the accreditation institute and of doing the necessary internal work (e.g., producing the required documents);
2. The increased bureaucracy and standardization of operations required to satisfy the institute that the 'right' modes of operating are in place (this presumably reduces creativity and originality); and
3. The moral costs of faking when developing illusion tricks so that everything looks good in the eyes of the accreditation committee.

These are all significant quality-lowering ingredients but, apparently, most business schools consider them worth paying. It is so important to distinguish oneself from all the other, non-accredited institutions and not be seen as secondary to those with accreditation.

European business schools are, of course, not unique in partly sacrificing their original purpose and integrity for the benefit of scoring well in the rankings, thereby maximizing their visibility and status. In many places around the world, including the United States, the ratio of teaching and administrative staff has changed significantly, and there are many posts that focus exclusively on facilitating students' careers, for example, 'Credential Specialist and Vice President for Student Success' (Piereson, 2011). Much of this is directly focused on improving the student's options in zero-sum games in the labour market.

All this focus on ranking and careers may be fine from the viewpoint of the students, who instrumentally benefit from this, but it means an intensifying of zero-sum games, since manipulating in order to improve rankings, boosting the students' CVs, and preparing for job interviews only mean that someone may get a better place than others in the job applicants' queue. All this contributes nothing to what higher education is supposed to accomplish: people who can contribute via their intellectual skills and knowledge to their lives, jobs, and society as a whole, as good citizens. It only means that positional goods competition takes a purely 'non-productive' turn, aiming to maximize self-interest. When rankings and credentials are based on 'true' performances, which are contingent upon the number of resources that have been used for teaching, salaries tend to be a better reflection of capacity. A degree from a specific institution then provides considerable information about the knowledge and intellectual quality of a graduate and fulfils a productive and valuable role. Position competition based on 'true quality' is often valuable. Ambitious rankings that do not look at easily manipulated and misleading criteria, but at gained qualifications, can be a productive force that improves teaching. But there are plenty of examples of clear deviations from this, leading to pure zero-sum games.

Over-education

There is, however, a problem with 'over-education', that is to say if the supply of (on paper) well-educated people does not comply with the demand, and individual persons can only get jobs that are well below their level of education. The 'over-education' phenomenon is controversial but common (Wolf, 2004). Although the individual concerned may have some degree of education that is required in formal terms, this education is not utilized in the actual job in question. Sennett (1998) gives an example of a bakery in which computer skills were required for employment, but employees were only allowed to do routine work and to press buttons; and if something went wrong, they were instructed to request expert assistance.

There is even increased unemployment among those with a doctoral degree. In Sweden, both in 2004 and 2010, about 5 per cent of those with a PhD were unemployed (SDS, 20 August 2010), this proportion being particularly high in the natural sciences. 'There is a major transition to doctoral studies in the natural sciences. For some, this is one way to postpone unemployment: many students who do not get a job decide to study for a doctoral degree in order to obtain further qualifications. And subsequently they don't get a job after their PhD either', according to the chairman of their association (translated from Universitetsläraren no. 15, 2004: 4).

More than 100,000 PhDs were awarded in the United States between 2005 and 2007, and 15,800 new assistant professorships were created. Many of the 85 per cent who did not get a job in higher education probably obtained relevant positions in R&D-based firms, as consultants or as analysts in the government sector. But 'many of these redundant PhDs wind up driving taxicabs or managing restaurants', while many are 'recruited back to campus to teach courses for a fraction of what tenured professors are paid' (Piereson, 2011).

How prevalent is over-education? It is impossible to say as the statistics are unreliable—and the distinction of matched versus overeducated in relationship to jobs is highly ambiguous. The labour market situation is also constantly changing. Jobs are elastic; sometimes a qualified person can change the work situation. Nevertheless, the research gives some input for assessing the situation. Different studies indicate figures ranging from 9 to 42 per cent, depending on definitions and measurement methods, according to Oscarsson and Grannas (2002). Most UK studies indicate that 30 per cent of all graduates are overeducated (Chevalier and Lindley, 2009). An investigation in the UK estimated that 6.5 million jobs (26 per cent of the total) required no qualifications, but that only 2.9 million people in the labour market had no qualifications, indicating a very large surplus of people with qualifications exceeding what their jobs demanded. In every category calling for qualifications there is a clear surplus of people with the required level of qualifications (cited in Wolf, 2004). Possibly there is a tendency to exaggerate education requirements and underestimate over-education. Employers and others are inclined to give the impression that the employment they offer is not so simple and routine-oriented but actually calls for skills and training. This ensures some measure of status and self-esteem and facilitates recruitment.

At the same time, we are faced with a trend for higher demands on education, driven by ambitions of becoming 'something great', and widespread references to a knowledge-intensive society and the expansion of higher education mean that many people have unrealistic expectations and demands in working life. Some research suggests a negative correlation between the level of education and job satisfaction. A study of American and Japanese workers found, for example, a negative correlation between the level of education and job satisfaction and organizational commitment for both national groups (Lincoln and Kalleberg, 1985). This was despite the fact that those with higher education probably had better working conditions than their colleagues. Other research indicates that who were regarded as under-educated in relation to their work on the whole expressed greater satisfaction with their jobs than those who were over-educated (Oscarsson and Grannas, 2002). This suggests either that formal education was not necessary for the work concerned and/or that people who received such employment, despite their lack of education, were personally suitable and that this compensated for deficiencies in education. The over-qualified were the most dissatisfied group, probably reflecting that jobs did not live up to their expectations. In addition, according to Åberg (2002), they had less pay than those with an inferior education in jobs with low educational requirements.

Over-education is, of course, not only negative. There is, for example, a learning and information acquisition ability that means that well-educated personnel can sometimes increase their capacity and make contributions greater than normally required in such job situations. When people study something they are genuinely interested in, this is, of course, valuable for them and, to a degree, for society.

Some might object to the idea of over-education, arguing that because students study so little on average (at least in many countries) and because the range of acquired pre-university knowledge, interest, and ability is so great, higher education only achieves a modest degree of improvement in many cases (Arum and Roksa, 2011). To the extent that the 'never have so many studied so long and learnt so little' paradox applies (per individual/ years of study), the discrepancy between a large number of 'highly educated' persons and the jobs that await them is not so great. The problem of over-education becomes, in a sense, less acute if it does not imply over-qualification. There may be a good match between some jobs requiring limited qualifications and the fairly high proportion of graduates that have learned little from their academic education. But this does not imply harmony between education and the labour market. Also, among those that actually learn quite a lot from their university studies, many will have problems finding a matching job. A discrepancy develops between perceived knowledge/abilities and actual working life, making it difficult to develop realistic expectations in this area. The grandiose overtones in reference to education and a knowledge-intensive society counteract this kind of realism. If you have an academic degree, even if it does not say much, you don't expect to have to drive a taxi, be a personal assistant, or perform a routine administrative job.

In order to provide a better match between an individual's qualifications and the labour market, we need (1) an education that means and guarantees real qualification and gives clear feedback to students (rather than letting students pass despite modest or even low effort and ability), and (2) a more varied qualification system where some go to university while others undergo a more practically oriented education and/or apprenticeship. A problem with the latter is that it is not so glamorous and tends to be represented as inferior to universities.

Knowledge—a source of problems?

Although recognized as capable of being used for wrongful purposes, 'knowledge' has almost always been seen as something valuable. 'Normal', socially sanctioned uses of knowledge can also be seen as a source for solving problems, in particular when the 'knowledge sector' is heavily expanding.

Without wishing to denigrate the concept of knowledge, nonetheless, it should be pointed out that it is not only good, guaranteed, and objective. Many forms of knowledge are, of course, positive, or are mainly used in helpful and/or harmless ways. But the knowledge embodied in various programmes of education is also selective, provisional, frequently uncertain, and often subject to discussion and criticism. There are competing schools of thought in many areas as regards what is good and true knowledge. Knowledge is always part of a social and political context and, as a result, is loaded with values (although this applies more to the social sciences and the humanities than to the natural sciences). This value-loading applies to all kinds of knowledge and knowledge products—including this book and the references noted herein. Much knowledge (i.e., claims to knowledge) stands on shaky ground and the intensive rhetoric behind the knowledge claims of an increasing number of 'experts' and organizations needs to be considered (Alvesson, 2004).

It is also important to assess the truth-creating results of knowledge. Several studies indicate, for example, that (political) economists become more selfish as a result of their studies focusing on theories based on assumptions of rationality and the maximization of self-interest as the key to human nature (Frank et al., 1993). Among university academics, economists in the United States, for example, give less money to charity than their colleagues in the science and arts faculties, despite being better paid. More broadly, economic language, when influential, may lead to unfortunate effects. For example, organizational arrangements that stem from the expectation that people are opportunistic and motivated by material incentives lead employers to focus on these (Ferraro et al., 2005).

An increasing proliferation of lawyers means more legal problems (Collins, 1990). This does not mean, of course, that the world would be less problematical without all these lawyers and all this legal knowledge, merely that problems might be formulated and solved in other ways. The point here is that the number of holders of such legal knowledge gives rise to and generates legal issues, promoting a 'legalizing' of society—for example in the form of 'ambulance chasers' (lawyers looking for a legal conflict to initiate and profit from). Clearly, regulation and legal clauses are needed in all societies, but they often lead to an emphasis on formalities and hinder effective work. Hence, an increase in the number of representatives of legal knowledge, for example in the public sector, may be a mixed blessing.

Knowledge in what are known as the 'assistance professions'—consultants, psychotherapist, social welfare advisers, psychiatrists, and so on—may involve a clientization of the groups who are to be helped—they are recreated as people in need of assistance (e.g., Lasch, 1978; Johansson, 1997). This leads to a therapeutic sensitivity—a sensitivity to frustrations, violations, and imperfect job environments, resulting in an increased use of psychiatric diagnosis, and the medicalization of more and more aspects of human life (Foley, 2010).

Within medicine, a surplus of physicians can potentially lead to questionable changes of criteria for treatment. Plastic surgeons in large numbers will lead to face-lifting and larger breasts being more the norm, making those not capable or willing to 'improve' their looks through surgery risking appearing less attractive in comparison. Obesity has become a target for the surgeon's knife rather than being solved with healthier food and exercise.

In the corporate strategy area, critics claim that there is a tendency for knowledge to generate a propensity to act 'strategically'; as a result, companies spend more time on assembling portfolios by buying and selling companies than on investing in the long-term internal development of companies (Mintzberg, 1990; Sveningsson, 1999). The acquisition of such portfolios may lead to short-term profits, but possibly also to long-term problems. Strategic knowledge is successful, in the sense that it has impact, but whether it pays off is less certain. Research into corporate mergers—a typical area for strategic knowledge—indicates, for example, that they fail more often than succeed (Berggren, 2002; Kleppesto, 1993). With the heavy expansion of business schools and management departments there follows an increased and expanded use of management knowledge through which life becomes targeted for management and the organization:

> All areas of life—work, play, consumption, civil discourse, sex—are becoming more 'organized', that is subject to the dictates of regimes of instrumental rationality, whether originating from government, management, or craft standards. It is a measure of the pervasiveness of this ideology that it is difficult to describe in public discourse how 'becoming more organized' can be anything other than a good thing. (Batteau, 2001: 731)

The question of the value and use of the contents of knowledge is complex, of course. I do not intend to claim that economic psychotherapeutic, and business management knowledge guiding practice only, or primarily, present problems. I merely point out that the knowledge concept should be subject to critical discussion in terms of its origin and consequences, which are seldom simple and unambiguous if we take everyone's interests into account. Foucault (1980) may be right in thinking that all knowledge is dangerous since it tends to produce a world in line with its pronouncements. It would be naïve to think that knowledge only involves the depiction and solution of problems. Knowledge creates particular versions of the world and its problems.

The expansion of higher education means a considerable increase in the number of people trying to find a labour market for the knowledge they have acquired. Our society is then flooded with people eager not only to meet existing spontaneous demands for communication, management, law, psychotherapy, counselling, health and life style improvement, etc., but also to create such demands. Many people and organizations are promoting demands which they then can claim they are able to meet. More and more people are encountering intensive persuasion about the need for improvements and changes as part of advice and counselling. In management consultancy firms, for example, senior people are mainly engaged in marketing and selling, since this is the decisive sector in one of the many businesses today in which 'needs' and demands are more an outcome of successful construction efforts than a spontaneous occurrence. The persuasion of potential clients of the need for consultancy service is crucial. Promises of spectacular gains may sometimes be positive, but often the outcome is ambiguous and many initiatives of change never lead anywhere, partly because top management is persuaded to start too many change projects and falls too easily for the latest fashion offering a new, seemingly very profitable recipe for better management (Jackall, 1988). I will address this further in Chapter 6.

The professional education complex

Politicians, policy-makers, and others interested in offering simple solutions often emphasize expanded higher education as the route to economic growth and reducing inequality. But schools, teachers, unions, the middle classes, education researchers, municipalities, higher education institutions, course arrangers, consultants, and education publishers also tend to independently propound the crucial importance of education. More specifically, there is an extensive commercial 'competence development industry' focusing on all possible groups, with promises of improvements in all possible respects (Salomonsson, 2005). These are often in the grandiosity-boosting business, emphasizing promising careers rather than useful skills. And almost whatever the problem, education is the solution! This is a familiar formula. It is easy and cheap—often too easy and too cheap. And it often amounts to an illusion trick: 'competence development' does not always have a clear impact on ability or work input.

Education as a source of disciplinary power

Conventionally speaking, power is regarded as the ability of certain actors to enforce their will, and persuade other actors to behave in a given manner against their will. Hence, power is the ability to force someone else to obey or forego their own interests and wishes. In recent research into the exercise of power, however, there is an emphasis on the way power operates in forming ideals, identities, and desires (Clegg, 1989; Lukes, 1978). Power functions via the voluntary adoption and subordination of a certain way of being. In its modern form, power is disciplinary—it shapes the individual rather than forcing him/her to do things in a given way. Power is persuasive, sometimes even helpful—the subject is moulded by means of advice, information, and predetermined standards of what is right, rational, necessary, and natural (Foucault, 1976, 1980, 1982). Power creates specific effects, particularly by ordering and forming the individual. This is achieved, for example, by indicating standards and norms for how the individual should be. Human improvement—an extensive and expanding industry—is not an innocent occupation. Based on Foucault, we can see how the formation of individuals focused on schooling occurs. Such formation is the opposite of openness and freedom of choice in the school context. Deviation from an interest in schooling is countered by stigmatization and clientization. Education indicates normality, that is to say it specifies guidelines for what is natural and right. In this normalization, individuals adopt and subordinate themselves to the predominant standards for how people should be, think, and feel. One of the driving forces is to avoid things socially defined as failure, and the outcome is falling into line and becoming 'interested' in being educated. Failure to acquire such an orientation and a lack of success in education lead to feelings of guilt and shame. However, this interest in education is not—as a normalized person would like to believe—an expression of the individual's own genuine wishes, but is best understood in terms of social processes and the regulatory effects of power.

There is often some scepticism regarding the value of education institutions in sectors of the business world not based on bureaucracy and staff careers, and where an entrepreneurial spirit is claimed to be the key factor. Successful self-made entrepreneurs may, for example, claim that academic studies lead to decision-making anxiety and produce bureaucratic administrators rather than entrepreneurially minded businesspersons (Berglund, 2002). But even if university education is met by increasing suspicion and its significance is downplayed, it is still viewed as necessary for most people aiming for a qualified job.

Higher education then functions as a broad norm and, within this norm, there is a carefully differentiated system of distinctions regulating status, normality, and self-esteem, offering possibilities but also constraining templates for being that are associated with its power effect as a normalizing discourse.

Education fundamentalism and the marginalization of people

One of the problems with education fundamentalism is that major parts of the labour market are closed to people who do not have at least 12–15 years of school education. Even if a rather high proportion of jobs do not call for a protracted period of education, mandatory school attendance and social norms assume that increasing numbers of young people will be obliged to extend their school education. The absence of a longer period of school education is interpreted as maladjustment and a stigma. Employers suspect that people who do not have a normal education are untrustworthy and undisciplined and lack 'competence'. To employ people who only have a basic education may also harm the organization's image in a society where knowledge-intensiveness is the norm.

Reform enthusiasts may claim that people with insufficient schooling cannot do the job, and should be persuaded to embark on additional education. But in this case, expansion of the education system is just as much the problem as the solution. Expansion is an ongoing phenomenon and with it the raising of the bar. Formal education has monopolized what is regarded as legitimate entry to many, if not most, jobs apart from those with the lowest status.

Some young people regard practical skills without some form of 'theoretical' merits as having no value. According to a young woman who participated in a study of young people and unemployment, 'Even cleaning jobs require training, although this is crazy, everyone can do cleaning... this is something that people know how to do' (SDS, 22 October 2000).

In other words, education fundamentalism involves marginalization for those who are not adapted to a school system. Alternative forms of qualification such as apprenticeships, which would probably suit many individuals and types of activities, are excluded or marginalized. Hence, education fundamentalism is a source of the problem that is defined as inadequate education, and simultaneously promises a solution for virtually all kinds of problems.

Grandiosity and positional goods versus high-quality education

Universities have been and, to an extent, still are a source of pride and status because they traditionally have been seen to produce and certify the best and the brightest citizens, and provide the most complex, advanced, and esoteric knowledge. This implies a specific symbolic value, following from their exclusivity and level. This image still partly exists, but the university has moved from being a temple of knowledge to a factory for the production of credentials, and higher education has changed from an elite club to a mass-market phenomenon. A very large and increasing number of institutions and students cannot easily claim qualities such as cultivating and certifying a high level of intellectual competence, and few students are actually inclined to choose topics associated with this quality or are willing to work hard with intellectually demanding courses in order to improve their cognitive capacities to a significant degree (Arum and Roksa, 2011). With the heavy expansion of institutions, there is a decline in both status and possibly average quality of faculty: many institutions are struggling to find and recruit really good PhD students. The prospect of teaching beverage management, spa business, or nursing science does not attract potential top scholars. Despite this, there is still a strong, broad interest in exploiting the specific aura and reputation of universities. With the exploitation of its images comes its erosion.

The zero-sum game ingredients are strong here. The more universities, the larger the higher education sector, and the more students who graduate, the less status and market value an academic job or a degree has. Given the strong focus on reputation and rankings in this highly status-driven and conscious sector, zero-sum games do not just take place in terms of overall expansion, where added numbers lead to a drop in value for those who are already members of the club, but also within the higher education sector. Differentiation is the key factor, and most countries have rather clear, well-known distinctions and status differences. Sometimes there are bifurcations, sometimes there are three or four tiers, sometimes there is a distribution without any clear, strong divide—more like a continuum (Marginson, 2006). Expansion leads to an increased focus on such differentiation. Previously, with fewer universities and students, the dividing line between them and the rest was clear and institutions and their students within the system fairly relaxed; now status anxieties and worries are driving most higher education institutions, in particular where there are official or semi-official publicly available rankings (like those initiated by media) (see, e.g., a study of US law schools by Sauder and Espeland, 2009).

Some people may assume that rankings and status are a certain proxy for educational quality and competition, and that a good reputation is closely correlated with good teaching and the improvement of ability. But even if rankings lead to performance improvements, in particular in research, it is not necessarily clear that education quality benefits from this (Sauder and Espeland, 2009). Research and student orientation are often negatively correlated (Arum and Roksa, 2011). Research universities with a faculty good at writing specialized papers and strongly rewarded for doing so are generally ranked highest, but they are not necessarily the best at offering an excellent education. The latter may not matter so much when students are choosing institutions. 'Institutional reputation is known, teaching quality mostly is not. The acid test is that when faced by choice between a prestigious university with known indifference to undergraduate teaching, and a lesser institution offering better classroom support, nearly everyone opts for prestige' (Marginson, 2006: 3). They may or may not suffer in terms of the qualifications acquired, but their relative advantage on the labour and status markets is most certainly higher. Institutions with elite status do not need to be so sensitive to 'customers' since the provision of status does most of the trick: 'For every student dissatisfied with faculty stars they never see, a dozen potential students are waiting at the gate' (7).

As the high-status institutions retain and improve their position by keeping numbers down, 'there is an absolute limit on the number of high value institutions, and on the size of individual institutions within the prestige grouping' (Marginson, 2006: 4). The key factor is maintaining and improving status. For universities and students, 'positional markets in higher education are a matching game in which the hierarchy of students/families is synchronized with the hierarchy of universities; and the peak group in each is steeped in the habits of sustaining the other' (6).

Higher education institutions have different profiles and different strengths, of course, but the promotion of polytechnics and other continued education institutions to university status has meant that the research university is the norm and that in a uniform market, where everybody can (and should!) be ranked, newer universities tend to be far below the older ones, and are regarded as inferior copies of the latter. For non-promoted higher education institutions, not being 'a university' is often a source of great frustration, and efforts to become one is sometimes the primary objective, involving considerable resource allocation, anxiety, and conflict within the institution (Humphries and Brown, 2002). But while the idea of becoming a university may be seen as optimal, those that have made the status shift are likely to see themselves at the very bottom of the university hierarchy. The zero-sum game ingredients of higher education are strongly reinforced by the expansion of universities and the increased focus on rankings, both globally and nationally, in many countries.

Good research and good teaching clearly play a part in this process, but often not as significantly as one might assume. Of course, rankings also push institutions and people to improvements and the achievement of better visible performances, so they are far from purely destructive. But the risk of goal displacement from the rankings as a valuable support for healthy substance-enhancing initiatives, to ranking position becoming an end in itself, encourages from a societal point of view 'non-constructive' zero-sum games. Illusory arrangements easily take the upper hand. One problem here is that rankings are seldom based on really good indicators of 'substance' ('good' research and acquired qualifications), but tend to rely on easily manipulated issues, easy to tick off and count, such as those indicated earlier in the section on business schools (see also Sauder and Espeland, 2009).

Back to power

Regarding people who do not want to, or cannot, pursue extended education as problematic is the consolidated viewpoint of a knowledge-intensive society. Such views see people with a low level of education as appropriate targets for change efforts on the part of societal institutions. The problem with this discourse is not that it distorts the truth but that it creates it. That is the way power works, according to Foucault. It is productive, it produces—or, perhaps more cautiously, orders and shapes—reality, truth, the individual and institutions. In an unorganized ambiguous and open world—which may be understood and created in a great many different ways—power determines the right way to understand things. Power interacts with knowledge in ordering and regulation. Truth is created in the sense that education institutions are extended, and the education discourse guides thinking and action in ambiguous situations, as well as forms norms and templates for how people are evaluated and develop their self-images. Thus, the knowledge-intensive society becomes a socially imposed norm to which all socially well-adjusted people subordinate themselves. This involves teachers, students, and also employers. If a specific job is defined in social terms as requiring a long period of education, in reality it becomes difficult for anyone who does not comply with the norm to get access to such a job even if the person is well qualified.

There is a tendency among those who do not share education fundamentalism's predilection for school education to be regarded as a problem and in need of advice, incentives, special teaching methods, and similar techniques. One Swedish official report states that 'motivation and incentives for wanting to learn are needed. Unsatisfactory school experience and the depletion of working life may reduce self-confidence and have a passivising effect' (SOU, 1994: 164). In this context 'wanting to learn' is equated with wanting to go to school.

For an education fundamentalist, the lack of extended education, and scepticism about further studies are faults that need to be rectified. People who are negative must be converted to 'wanting to learn'. As already mentioned, it is hard to avoid the fact that there will always be people more educated than others. But education fundamentalism has pinned to its masthead that extended schooling is crucial, and those people who cannot be disciplined to accept this adjustment will be stigmatized and marginalized—people with low education cannot be employed, have no learning capacity, and cannot contribute to a knowledge-intensive society. People with a low level of education are seen as out of tune with knowledge society and close to a source of embarrassment and failure for our age—exposed to the institutional and ideological power of education fundamentalism.

Back to the early morning in and around the Central Station in Stockholm

This also provides an opportunity to return to the people I met when I got off the train at Central Station in Stockholm, briefly depicted in my Introduction to this book. I raised the question of whether people who work in travel, transport, service, and retail sectors needed to concern themselves with the knowledge-intensive society.

My response is yes, probably. They also have reason to be concerned with institutions and players whose grandiose projects involve the creation of a knowledge society—the possibilities of avoiding the power of normalization are diminishing. Grandiosity is claiming its victims.

Summary

In this chapter I have challenged the assumption that higher education is necessarily best understood as being primarily a vehicle for the improvement of knowledge and intellectual qualifications. Although I do not deny that universities in many cases considerably improve students' cognitive capacities, they sometimes appear more successful in cultivating a laid-back attitude among students and producing a favourable image of the institutions concerned.

Illusion tricks increasingly characterize the entire sector while substance— qualifications and achievements—is coming to be less valued. Large areas of higher education can be regarded as a backdrop giving a misleading impression of the knowledge society. Within this sector, illusory arrangements (branding and the manipulation of ranking positions) have become increasingly crucial. While it is of course impossible to quantify this precisely, Arum and Roksa's (2011) claim that about 40 per cent of students are not really improving intellectually gives some clue about the magnitude of the illusory element in contemporary higher education.

At the same time, as the quality of education is plummeting, we find expressions like 'world class' and 'excellence' increasingly in use.

Although learning and the development of knowledge are positive, on the whole there are also negative aspects of 'too much education' in terms of inflation, zero-sum games (longer education in order not to wind up at the bottom of the queue), and a mismatch between excessive expectations and aspirations by those who have received such education and what working life really has to offer. Many of the areas of expansion, like management, marketing, law, communication, and 'people improvement' (education, psychotherapy, social work) also promote knowledge and practice of uncertain or even dubious social value. The spread of expertise in a number of areas of life can increase dependencies on questionable authorities who promise all good things in life, but deliver mixed (or no) results.

It is important here to also point to the power aspects embedded in apparently 'well-meaning' institutions and ideologies in a comprehensive and critical review of modern higher education. The predominant education discourse is becoming a 'truth' that dominates individual self-understanding via normalization and clientization, and marginalizing and stigmatizing those interests and qualities not associated with formal education.

All this implies, of course, that we should work towards the improvement of higher education institutions rather than abandoning hopes of a more satis-factory system. This calls for realistic claims, substance in operations (intellectual qualifications), emphasis on non-positional goods (knowledge that provides positive contributions to society and life rather than better CVs), fruitful competition based on acquired knowledge and intellectual improvement, and an emphasis on core activities (rather than branding, customer satisfaction, and student services). It would be particularly import-ant and fruitful to focus on the results of such operations. Different institu-tions and programmes could be compared by means of tests and external examination of Master's thesis projects and other outcomes of learning, and institutions with poor results could either be 'named and shamed' or simply lose funding. This would encourage an emphasis on quality and increased qualifications and, in some cases, a reduction in the number of students with poor motivation and ability, and programmes that include more vocational training than (traditional) university education. All this would not, of course, remove the inherent problems of zero-sum games and the limitations on access to attractive education and jobs, but it could encourage people to engage in productive planning rather than unproductive zero-games playing. (The emphasis in this book is on the zero-sum games where one person's or institution's gain is another's disadvantage without there being a positive effect for others or for society.) In more productive competitions, rankings become less of an object for manipulation and more of an indicator of performance. There is, of course, no easy way to solve or even reduce the problems raised in this book, but there is considerable scope for improve-ment. Awareness of the basic problems is an important starting and reference point and some of the concepts and ideas offered here may be helpful.

6

Modern working life and organizations— change, dynamism, and post-bureaucracy?

Today's working life can be understood in terms of grandiose ideas, illusion tricks, and zero-sum games. These three concepts provide a rather different perspective than conventional understandings of working life phenomena suggested by signifiers such as leadership, visions, strategy, change, entrepreneurship, innovations, and human resource management.

Chapters 6–9 deal with four key themes in current organizations and working conditions. The first theme, addressed in this chapter, is ideas about major, drastic changes. People refer to the demise of bureaucracy and mass production, a transition to new forms of production and work organizations characterized by flexibility, dynamism, networks, knowledge-intensive work, flat organizations, and so on. This is worth investigating, which is what this chapter aims to do. The second theme, which is tackled in Chapter 7, is concerned with the way in which organizations try to create legitimacy in relation to the predominant norms and ideas through formal structures signalling 'the right practice', without necessarily affecting the latter to any appreciable degree—in other words, an illusion trick. The idea is that organizations are increasingly devoting their time and energy to developing shop-window arrangements—designed to satisfy various groups interested in what is going on in a given organization, but without deeper insights into its workings. The third theme, covered in Chapter 8, discusses how various occupational groups are trying to advance their positions and gain status as professionals (experts) in line with ideas about the increased importance of knowledge and expertise. They try to get a hearing for their claims for a unique and superior 'competence' that entitles them a higher status and monopoly of a given sector of the labour market. People who are not formally qualified are kept at bay. Advancing positions through professionalization is not always so simple, however, since other groups have the same ambition. This involves, for example, personnel specialists, marketers, and nurses. The fourth theme is leadership, or rather 'leadership', which is discussed in Chapter 9. It may be noted that considerable commitment and trust is invested in leadership as the key to an effective and satisfactory working life, although there is often a great deal of confusion about what it means and how such successful leadership may be conducted. Leadership is a strongly ideological area which, among other things, attracts hero worshippers. My thesis is that leadership is more a question of impressive but empty talk, and fanciful self-images rather than any distinct ideas and practices on which they are based. Views about the exercise of leadership often have a grandiose undertone that is difficult to live up to in practice.

I consider that, overall, these four themes—new organizational forms, shop-window arrangements, professionalization, and 'leadership'—provide a rich set of pictures of central ideas and trends in the working life, management, and organizational fields. Naturally, this involves trying to illustrate selected segments rather than providing a comprehensive picture.

As already indicated, this chapter focuses on the first theme—the beautiful changes in the modern organizations of our time, often described as knowledge- and network-based, post bureaucratic, dynamic, and project driven.

Rapid changes and the death of bureaucracy?

We live in a delightful dynamic age...

A rapid skimming of the media, management books, and social science publications conveys an almost unanimous impression that we are living in an age of change. Changes in the economy, working life, and society follow each other at breakneck speed. Researchers claim that 'the modern workplace continues to change at a radical and accelerated pace' (Cartwright and Holmes, 2006: 199) and that 'less and less of current organizational functioning can be called routine' (Palmer and Hardy, 2000: 230). Bureaucracy, large-scale operations, hierarchies, and planning are out of fashion. Instead, the call is for flexibility, networking, empowerment, market control, and so on. Companies and other organizations must adjust rapidly or suffer the same fate as the dinosaurs. Tom Peters, for many years the world's most famous management author consultant, claimed in 1993 that:

> ABB's T 50 programme is what makes ABB a successful exception among the doomed major companies. But it makes ABB more of a collection of small and medium-sized companies that are working together. A change of this kind is the only thing which can save the large companies of today from extinction. (cited in Tengblad, 2003: 72)

The shift to a hard-to-grasp collection of smaller companies appears to have contributed greatly to ABB's catastrophic situation in the early years of this century. Management had difficulty in getting an overview of operations and there was considerable duplication of tasks (Tengblad, 2003). Perhaps the reviewer of Peters' books has a point when he says that Peters' recipe for success is tomorrow's explanation of catastrophes (cited in Ramsay, 1996). The anti-dinosaurian thesis is defended by many others, however. Such authors consider that they can see 'a shift away from hierarchical and function-based fixed structures to more organic, network-oriented forms with team and project structures' (Müllern and Stein, 2000: 15). Miles et al. (1997), for example, argue that more organizational members are expected to develop the ability to self-organize around operational, market, and partnering tasks. This 'cellular' organization allows employees to be more entrepreneurial and identify customer needs, as well as experience psychological ownership of particular clients, products, and services. Shop floor work teams are seen as a central feature of decentralized decision-making and de-layered structures. There is reference to a strong trend away from massive, robust organizations towards flexible but more delicate structures.

This thesis was backed up by a claim of systemic dysfunctionality—that bureaucracy simply no longer works or is ceasing to be the prime coordination mechanism in a contemporary economy and society. It is now argued that a broad set of powerful economic, social, and technological changes has meant that the era of stable structures and fine-tuning of bureaucratic models is over, and the days of post-bureaucracies have arrived. As expressed by Child and McGrath (2001: 1136), vexed boundaries and top-down authority 'are maladaptive when massive change, environmental dynamism and considerable uncertainty are the norm'. It is often claimed that rapid changes mean that there is little time for reflection and critical evaluation. Things have to happen now. 'With this time concept, inventories are equated with inefficiency and reflection with sluggishness' (Müllern and Stein, 2000: 48–9). This view was cherished particularly strongly during the great days of the new economy at the end of the 1990s, but it still holds a dominant position. It is claimed, for example, that the transformation of organizations from bureaucracies and factories to networks and projects means that project groups will consist of 'actively networking, loosely-linked, disloyal individuals looking for temporary, profitable berths in the market place in a society that has turned into a cocktail party' (Dahlbom, 2000: 133).

The paradigm of the post-bureaucratic organization (PBO), which is fully in line with the 'cocktail economy', claims that the decentralized, loosely coupled, flexible, non-hierarchical, and fluid organization is, or will become, dominant. It will operate on the basis of horizontal and vertical networking, and mutual adjustment, and will be guided by visions and shared values rather than command and control. Organizations will be dysfunctional if they do not adapt to the new environment calling for these features. (Other labels for PBO are postmodernism and post-Fordism.)

It is claimed that this organizational form will replace the bureaucratic structures that were predominant in the twentieth century, characterized by the division of labour, hierarchies, rules, and the standardization of job tasks.

When addressing bureaucracy it should be considered that, in this context, the word does not imply the more everyday connotations of sluggishness, complications, and inefficiency, but instead represents a rational organization, facilitating predictability, reliability, and/or quantitative efficiency (Ritzer 2004). These more positive meanings of bureaucracy are captured by Mintzberg's (1983) concepts of machine and professional bureaucracy, referring to mass production through standards and routines leading to efficiency (such as McDonald's and airlines). Professional bureaucracy refers to organizations working mainly through standardized professional competence leading to predictable use of expert knowledge (for example, in most medical work). Well-functioning bureaucracy is achieved by, for example, clear structures, hierarchies, regulatory structures, rational procedures, and clear frameworks by those in charge of the work performed. Bureaucracy is designed to counter arbitrariness, nepotism, and poor judgement, and represents some degree of quality and rationality in organizations. However, drawbacks such as inflexibility, over-emphasis on standardized solutions, and limited creativity and monotonous and sometimes dehumanizing work are salient weaknesses.

The PBO will be achieved by horizontal and vertical networking and mutual adaptation, and is guided by visions and common values rather than by direct orders, rules, standards, and controls. It is claimed that if organizations fail to adapt to the new environment with such organizational characteristics, they will encounter major problems and find it difficult to survive.

All the usual suspects are rounded up: intensification of competition, deregulation, globalization of production, rising rates of product innovation, new forms, and the increased significance of knowledge and information technology, differentiated and rapidly changing customer preferences, the dominance of intangible services, and coping with and encouraging workforce diversity. Above all, it is maintained that bureaucracy is unable to cope with the sheer pace of change, thus generalizing observations about turbulent market environments made in earlier decades to the entire economy. The development and use of new knowledge as an increasingly important dimension in management and organization is often proposed as a reason for the collapse of bureaucracy (Davenport and Prusak, 1998). Here we can trace a double emphasis: partly on innovation-driven industries, such as consultancy, software, and pharmaceutical companies, which are regarded as increasingly crucial to the economy, and partly the intrinsic qualities of knowledge—seen as increasingly important in all kinds of areas—and calling for knowledge to be handled by groups and networks working in cooperation, rather than by means of orders and rules. Overall, this points to a knowledge economy and a knowledge-intensive society.

Flexibility is a word that has prestigious overtones in this context. Technological and market changes, in combination with the possibilities offered by information technology, are encouraging quick-footedness and the ability to adapt. The high rate of change also means that individuals need to be flexible, willing and capable of changing their employment and occupations. This involves developing new skills, making themselves employable, and working in a project format, rather than finding security in permanent, long-term employment. A more flexible labour market, and the individual attitudes that make this possible, are required. The new human being should be adaptable—willing to, and able to change places of work and occupations at frequent intervals. Careers should be 'boundary-less'.

Generally speaking, optimism about the prospect of entering the knowledge society is so strong that even circumstances that would normally be regarded as problematical are imbued with positive overtones.

> The lack of security of employment is, for example, regarded as something positive, it signals flexibility and opportunities for the new hungry generations who, in their self-realization projects have left the well-ordered charter holidays for an adventure which they have composed for themselves. (Berglund, 2002: 291)

There are, however, several sceptics and critics who regard such developments as more problematical. One of them is Sennett (1998), who shares the view that working life lacks stability and long-term qualities, and interprets this mainly in negative terms. The rapid changes and the need for employees who are prepared to adjust means that they are not able to develop a character that supports and provides a sense of stability, coherence, and direction in life. Frequent changes of employer, housing, occupation, and colleagues lead to insecure and frightened individuals, who develop a short-term and opportunistic approach. Uncertainty and anxiety predominate, and also a lack of confidence and loyalty. Life is fragmented. It is hard to find safe and lasting criteria for what is a good job, and a period of successful activity may easily be followed by dismissal if the organization is cutting back its staff, maybe to keep the stock market happy. Sennett claims that pressures to adapt and to be continuously prepared to sell your labour undermine possibilities of building up an identity and self-esteem. Even if he regards the flexibility ideal as destructive, he takes it for granted that there are strong pressures for change and flexibility, and that the modern man is a flexible individual with weak character. Fragmented personalities are common. Some authors with an awareness of history note that the concept of radical change in the current age has been with us for some time. 'Over the decades, each generation has claimed that precisely their epoch has been more subject to change and more difficult to manage than ever before' (Wikström et al., 1992: 9). One might perhaps expect that those who express such thoughts might be disinclined to make the same mistake. But no, since Wikström et al. go on to say:

> However, there is much to indicate that there is greater reason than ever to uphold this claim. Old concepts, models, tools and procedures have lost their force and we have not found any new replacements so far, and this has led to frustration, turbulence and uncertainty. We see how a previous, self-evident stability has been turned into an unavoidable mobility, and this applies at all levels in society, politics and business, and within the family and for the individual too. (ibid. 9)

One may wonder what this former, self-evident stability was based on, since previous generations have also claimed that their age was particularly turbulent.

The idea of breath-taking rapid and radical change is sometimes accompanied by accounts of risks, adjustment problems, uncertainty, and threats. But nonetheless the basic proposition is permeated by a grandiose conception of the unique character of our own age. For the most part, these accounts are positive and optimistic. Clegg et al. (1996) distinguish, for example, between an 'old' and a 'new' paradigm for organization management. The 'old' paradigm is permeated by discipline, vicious circles, an inflexible organization, administration, distorted communication, hierarchy, an assumption that members of the organization are unreliable, and so on. The 'new' paradigm is characterized, instead, by organizational learning, positive circles, flexibility, leadership, open communication, markets, and confidence in members of the organization. Here 'tacit and local knowledge of all members of the organization is the most important factor in success, and creativity creates its own prerogative' (Clegg et al., 1996: 205). Everyone in favour of the 'old paradigm': raise your hands! The grandiose features of the 'new paradigm' probably ensure a high level of enthusiasm.

People also often talk about radical changes in values. It is claimed that fundamental shifts in values involve suspicion of the exercise of power and authority and a greater emphasis on self-realization and the meaning of work—and also increased individualism (Müllern and Stein, 2000: 15). It was popular in the 1980s to refer to post-materialistic values, and those who embraced such values were termed 'inner-world people' who gave priority to empathy and personal development rather than to high pay and job promotion. Also recent studies are claimed to 'have consistently demonstrated that people rate purpose, fulfilment, autonomy, satisfaction, close working relationships and learning as more important than money' (Cartwright and Holmes, 2006: 200). If we apply need theory—for example Maslow's hierarchy of needs, which treats needs as driving forces in hierarchical terms—this involves development from lower to higher and more refined and mature motives. In other words, development is moving forwards and upwards. 'Postmaterialist' authors suggest that 'new' individuals are better than their predecessors, have been refined by the civilization process, and are more advanced in terms of motives than the bureaucracy-supporting and materialistic masses who preceded the individualists of our own time. It is considered that the education explosion and improved welfare are contributing to this process. Recessions and financial crises may lead to temporary setbacks and deviations, but do not necessarily affect the broad trend. In other words, we are on the whole supposed to be in a delightful epoch, characterized by rapid and radical change. Among other things, this is based on the idea that bureaucracy, hierarchies, and standardization are giving way to networks, flat organizations, unique solutions, entrepreneurship, and flexibility, which are the keynote for the future. The values of the labour force are supposed to comply with (or promote) all this.

... or maybe not?

In view of what is apparently a high degree of consensus on the death of bureaucracy and mass production and the idea that new values are replacing hierarchies and rules, one might perhaps regard such radical change as a foregone conclusion. Most people seem to view developments and the current situation in precisely this way. Many anecdotes are recounted in this area, but many of the arguments for new forms of organization and working-life involve the imperatives resulting from the changeability of our times, which is regarded as making bureaucracy obsolete. As a matter of interest, there is little to support this in more systematic and painstaking studies. Of course, any effort to objectively establish the truth is difficult, as Willmott (2011) points out with reference to debates in this area. 'When "evidence" is generated, selected, and interpreted in the light of particular world views, reconciliation seems no more likely than victory' (258). But there are nonetheless reasons for paying attention to what such empirical studies seem to imply.

Against the claim of people increasingly valuing qualities, such as purpose and fulfilment, over money, we can note the finding, mentioned in Chapter 4, which indicates that the number of people who think it is very important or essential 'to be very well off financially' has gone up significantly since the 1960s (Kasser, 2002). Perhaps the trend is not so consistent after all?

Since many people appear to regard the abandonment of bureaucracy in favour of more dynamic and attractive post-bureaucratic forms of organization and management as obvious, I will devote some space to studies that have investigated this phenomenon. As already mentioned, a historical flash-back indicates that our own age has no monopoly on being turbulent and subject to dramatic changes. For a long time, every decade has been imbued with a high degree of uncertainty and disruption—rapid industrialization and urbanization around the turn of the past century, two world wars in the twentieth century, the Great Depression in the 1930s, the radical years of the late 1960s, and the rise and collapse of Communism in the late 1940s and 1980s, respectively (see for example Grey, 2005; Wallander, 2003). Inventions such as the printing press, the steam engine, railways, the telephone, motor vehicles, and aircraft have all had effects arguably comparable with or even exceeding those of computers. As Wallander (2003) points out, technical changes often take time before they have any major impact. When he embarked on his career as a bank director in 1960, he was told that a society without cash transactions was in the offing as a result of the development of computer technology. But this development, which was assumed to take place within a few years, has not been implemented on a wider scale until 40 years later.

The rumour of the death of bureaucracy is not only exaggerated—according to empirical studies, it is also false.[1] There have been many changes, of course, including some cutbacks at middle-management level—the number of man-agerial posts in companies has declined—and there has been an increase in group tasks. And few people would deny the importance of IT developments. It also appears likely that there has been some expansion in knowledge-intensive occupations and companies. To some extent, they rely less on regulatory structures and standard solutions than on the problem-solving abilities of their personnel. Studies of routine manufacturing in accordance with lean production methods demonstrate a uniform picture of functional flexibility, teamwork as the most appropriate form of organization for mul-tiple functions in the new technical allocation of tasks, and assignment-oriented participation in the quality and ongoing improvement processes. So, considerable changes have occurred in industry in a post-bureaucratic direction. At least this is the case in the West where many industries function-ing with a machine bureaucracy-logic operate in China and other developing economies. But also in the West, in most other respects, bureaucracy is main-taining its grip on efforts to organize operations. Internal forms of horizontal organization and external network-type relations can and do coexist with vertical hierarchies. Most organizations draw upon a spectrum of control forms: from output, bureaucratic, professional/occupational, and customer control to charismatic and authoritative leaders and corporate cultures

---

[1] This section draws upon Alvesson and Thompson (2005).

and emotional control. To some extent this has always been true. But as environments and organizational structures have become more complex, a diversification of types of controls and coordination ensues. Different forms of control work together, rather than mutually exclude each other (Gabriel, 2005). Even in operations that call for a considerable degree of situation-adjusted and flexible organization such as fire prevention, a high degree of bureaucracy is combined with organic forms of management and coordination (Bigley and Roberts, 2001). Bureaucracy allows for a considerable variety of different organizational solutions and many changes may be regarded as changes of, and within, bureaucratic forms.[2]

Research does not give much support to the idea that organizational pyramids have been replaced to any greater extent by loose networks. Ruigrok et al. (1999) and Hill et al. (2000) found some change in the use of cost centres, flatter hierarchies, task forces, and teams rather than adherence to departments, and also increased use of IT and communication networks. But decentralization is regulated and restricted by central control of resource allocation processes and the formulation of objectives. It is interesting to note that three companies—out of a sample of ten—in the study conducted by Hill et al. that had previously been decentralized gradually became more centralized. Ruigrok et al. noted some degree of reduction in the number of organizational levels, but hierarchies are still a major factor and, if the company grows, new hierarchical structures emerge. This results in limited decentralized decision-making, and IT initiatives do not weaken the hierarchy to any great extent since the company invests in both vertical and horizontal networks. Reductions in the size of individual units and the decentring of organizations may change the form of bureaucracy, but they do not necessarily diminish its impact. Research on managers and supervisors also indicates not much radical transformation, from supervision to team coordination, but rather 'remarkable stability over time' (Hales, 2005: 501).

Alvesson and Thompson (2005) explored the nature and extent of change across three areas—work, employment, and decision practices—and found partly significant changes, but nonetheless that various forms of bureaucracy still prevailed. McSweeny (2006) found the development of an increased level of bureaucracy within the UK public sector. Even higher education is

---

[2] The beneficiaries of bureaucracy are not only top management and political elites. Unions and advocates of equal opportunities frequently favour formal rules to reduce uncertainty, provide direction, and achieve higher standards (Alvesson and Thompson, 2005). So, for example, enforcing the rights of females typically leads to an expansion of specific rules and standards, which is exactly what bureaucracy is all about (Billing, 1994). There are 'feminist cases against bureaucracy' (Ferguson, 1984), but in practice most equal opportunity initiatives take a bureaucratic form and feminist organizations also tend to adopt some bureaucratic principles, sometimes despite their initial ambitions to avoid hierarchy and formal rules (Ashcraft, 2001).

becoming increasingly characterized by the factory-like mass university, partly controlled 'by the bureaucratic accountants who reduce knowledge to something that can be measured' (Weymans, 2010: 119). As one colleague expressed it: 'Bureaucratization of the university is affecting every aspect of our activities—we are at LIU not even allowed to order books by ourselves, but this has to be done by a formal purchasing system which of course only includes a few formally selected book distributors. IT is used to formalize, control and standardize—not the mythical opposite' (personal communication). Reed (2011) also observes 'the underlying organizational resilience and historical longevity of the bureaucratic control regime' (240); at the same time as he points to changes and the presence of hybrid forms between bureaucratic and post-bureaucratic organizations.

The shift towards a service economy has been associated for some time with a post-industrial society, but it is often more reasonable to refer to an 'industrialization' of services. Ritzer's (2004) well-known thesis on the McDonaldization of society concerns the bureaucratization of services. Amongst the biggest and most rapidly growing companies of our age are the big-box retailers from Walmart to IKEA. They are all huge bureaucracies with minute standardization of their operations, but in contrast to previous bureaucracies, many only offer safe employment and career prospects to a few of their employees.

In sectors such as fast food, tourism, entertainment, media, and retail classical bureaucratic processes such as calculations, standards, routines, predictability, and quantification play a crucial role. In other words, bureaucratic forms of control are more common in some areas. Bureaucratization applies in any service sector, from call centres to hotel chains, where 'quality', standardization, and consistency in the service provided is ensured by the supervision and control of service personnel. But control via the customer has been added to bureaucratic control: including the use of evaluation forms for customers. Gabriel (2005) launches the 'glass cage' metaphor as a suggestion for replacement of Weber's classic 'iron cage' to illustrate the way in which staff are carefully kept in place. In this new glass cage, it is the customer's impression, together with the manager's and possibly also that of colleagues (the team), that monitor and control behaviour and performance.

It is sometimes claimed that globalization is promoting more flexible structures. But multinational operations also incorporate a counter-trend. Ferner (2000) observes that multinational companies have changed in the direction of a more internationally homogenized, integrated, and centralized attitude to a number to aspects in production, marketing, and personnel administration. This leads to a bureaucratization of control, for example as a result of standardized systems for rewarding senior managers and identifying employees with 'high potential'.

Much of this (over-)reported changeability is cyclical and linked to the business cycle, rather than irreversible. Different organizational ideals have taken turns at being the predominant ideal, particularly in terms of the wider attention it receives and research interest. Further, practical change processes sometimes involve greater rationality and control and sometimes references to normative and social ideals (for example, corporate culture, social relationships, and 'competence development') (Barley and Kunda, 1992).

Fashions and followers of fashion are common in organizations. Management fashion is somewhat different from consumer fashion, as there is often a genuine interest in the management world to learn, change, and improve results associated with fashion—parallel to wishes to follow the flow and appear to be on the cutting edge of things. There is an expectation and hope that the new fashion will lead to improved performance, as captured by the following definition: 'Management fashion . . . is a relatively transitory collective belief, disseminated by management fashion-setters, that a management technique leads rational management progress' (Abrahamson, 1996: 257).

But it is often difficult to achieve 'rational management progress' based on fashion, since learning and changes take time, and changes in fashion and a slow-moving reality often counteract completion of the change advocated by some other fashion. The reasons for the new fashion may no longer apply. Fashion-inspired changes often involve superficial revisions and re-labelling rather than any deeper impact, which is also seldom achieved due to the rapidity of changes. We have here a 'meta-fashion' that involves demonstration of flexibility and willingness to change, as well as specific fashions that prescribe adoption of the latest ideas and recipes for success. It is often difficult to tell which new ideas are good and which less so, resulting in soundly based new ideas, theories, and recipes lacking a stronger breakthrough and impact than those less well-supported. Sometimes it is more the case that the labels, rather than the contents themselves, the serve to represent change. The actors involved realize the disadvantage they will be at if they give the impression that they are not keeping up with the times, so they change their labels without changing the contents (Benders and Van Veen, 2001).

This does not mean that I want to deny the existence of fundamental changes in work organizations, as there are certainly changes and trends at work, and IT has made a considerable difference. The acquisition, merging, and closing of companies can create dramatic turbulence in the business cycle. Bureaucracy has often been tangibly supplemented by other forms of control, and has been ameliorated to some extent as a result of pressures opposing greater flexibility. Work teams have become more common, and hard work, profitability, and long-term relationships have lost ground to the manipulation of impressions, short-term thinking, and adaptability for some sectors of the labour force as a formula for success. But none of this says that we are not some way from abandoning bureaucracy as a fundamental organization form.

As Tengblad (2003) says, 'ideas about a dizzy rate of change, murderous competition and the emergence of a society that is dramatically different, populated by a new species of individual is not merely exaggerated, it is also misleading to a considerable extent' (178). Most companies and public sector organizations regard hierarchies and formalized procedures as essential tools that guarantee efficiency, uniform quality, and punctual deliveries (Adler, 1999).

Furthermore, fashions that inspire some movement away from bureaucracy may lead to perceived effects that trigger a countermovement. Organizations then swing between different fashionable ideals and leave space for another, perhaps opposing, fashion. Abrahamson (1996) argues that 'fashion causes organizations to centralize, lose autonomy, and become receptive to new fashions, causing them to gain autonomy, lose control, and become receptive to a new fashion that swings the pendulum back again' (274). Of course, trends are often not really so pendular, but any broad claim of a unitary trend of radical and rapid change from bureaucracy to various forms of post-bureaucracy is problematic, as trends often go in different directions and sometimes back and forth.

Why this interest in radical changes?

One may well ask: what is the reason for these often cheerful descriptions of a rapidly changing society with dynamic organizations and working life, despite their weak underpinning? In other words, how do we account for the huge discrepancy between the popular and widely shared claims of post-bureaucracy and the continued dominance of bureaucracies? A key ingredient in contemporary society is the idea of an outmoded, inefficient, and rigid bureaucracy, making it an easy target for policy-makers, management gurus, and PR-minded executives. Actors involved in, or commenting on, organizational change are eager to emphasize a more progressive, fashionable, positive-sounding vocabulary in describing management and how the organization operates.

There is a tendency to regard the world with a focus on what is considered to be changing and to ignore everything else. If the basic assumption of turbulence and change spreads, it then functions as a framework for interpretation. People think they see examples of changes, exaggerate them, and ignore other aspects. It is tempting to make the mistake of looking at history at a more general level, summarizing it in crude terms, and contrasting the relative stability that apparently characterized a past age with the imagined dynamism of the modern world.

Underlying this is the satisfaction of seeing something new. New things are fun, and ingrained, old, and unchanging aspects are boring. Changing something is regarded as development, which has a positive overtone. We are living in an age that worships novelty (Boorstin, 1961). We are looking for new and exciting experiences. Business leaders and other members of the elite class want to keep up with their times and appear to be dynamic. Many groups and organizations have a bedded interest in change hysteria: publishers, consultants, authors, journalists, companies with fashion links, and researchers who want to attain commercial success. It is clear that it is extremely profitable to launch brave new statements about dramatic changes, and about how previous principles and solutions for the economy, organizations, and working life are hopelessly out of date, and then to propagate various ideas and recipes for how these problems should be solved. It is hard to say whether the enthusiasts of change actually believe in all this, or whether they are merely cynical hucksters. Maybe they alternate between cunning plans for a sales message and being spellbound by their own persuasion—it is often easier to sell something that you actually believe in. Our age is characterized by a fusion of cynicism and naïvety.

A historical study of the way in which official committees, politicians, and others viewed future developments from their vantage point in the twentieth century showed interesting results about the function of 'the future'. The future is always invented, and typically in ways that serve certain interests. The impression is that the future overall was generally depicted as positive and full of hope, sufficiently optimistic to legitimize established routines as feasible in the long term, but also sufficiently threatening to justify established routines as essential in the short term. The future's function is to be both positive and threatening in a uniform and well-ordered manner that facilitates intervention by the political system so as to ensure that influential groups can find a common basis for their actions (Beckman, 1980b: 85–6).

Something similar also applies to our own era's contemporary and immediate future. Its function is to be interesting, exciting, fantasy-stimulating, moderately risky, and threatening for those who are slow on the uptake. But generally talk about dynamics and radical changes are presented in the abstract and it is easy to approve of such talk. An attractive future compensates for current deficiencies. Although everyday life is not always much fun—it may be predictable and trivial—this makes current developments and the (right) future that much more interesting. Potential improvements are preferable, particularly if they are successfully boosted. Hope and expectations are our friends. The idea of a knowledge society and a dynamic project organization waiting round the corner may seem particularly attractive in contrast with today's grey, bureaucracy-permeated everyday existence. The idea that our own age is particularly creative and dynamic and involves a 'paradigm shift' is clearly attractive—and this has been the case for some time. Foucault (1984) considers that this is one of 'the most destructive habits in modern thinking':

> Analysis of the present as a turning point in history, or a peak, or realization or a recurrent dawn, etc.: I think that we should be sufficiently humble to admit to ourselves that, on the one hand, the time we are living in is not exactly a unique, fundamental or breakthrough point in history where everything comes to perfection and starts again anew. On the other hand, we must also be humble enough to say—but without these serious overtones—that the time we are living in is very interesting; it needs to be analysed and broken down, and that it would be beneficial for us to ask ourselves: 'What is the nature of our own time?' (69)

It is, in fact, precisely this question that I attempt to answer in this book. We should be able to interest ourselves in our own time without necessarily portraying it as an age of fantastic, wide-ranging, and rapid changes. It is important to resist the temptation to regard our own age as much more fantastic and impressive than other times, and also consider the narcissism involved in upgrading our time and we who are living in it.[3] As Foley (2010: 9) writes: 'ages are as narcissistic as the people who belong to them: each believes itself to be unassailably superior and demands to be loved more than others. These demands are usually met. We tend to prize our own age as we prize our country—it has to be good if it produced us.'

Incidentally, one crucial aspect of our time may be said to be rather wild ideas about current rapid changes and turbulence. The fact that such highly debatable ideas about the breakneck pace of developments are widely proposed and fostered says a great deal about our current epoch, although this does prevent the prevalence of similar ideas in the past—even if they have been expressed in more moderate terms. We are living in a fantastic age, on the

---

[3] It is also important to resist the temptation to see and portray the contemporary age as particularly problematic—and therefore exceptionally interesting. Compared to most other societies and historical periods, the contemporary West includes much to be positive about. In terms of the special nature of the time, I do think that the production of grandiosity has strongly accelerated during recent decades and even though many of the phenomena pointed at in the book are evergreens, e.g., consciousness about status and interest in impressing others, contemporary society exhibits an exceptionally high degree of grandiosity, extensive use of illusions, and of social life characterized by zero-sum games, clearly exceeding those of previous times and generations. This has more to do with changes over the decades than an abrupt and radical shift. But in a reflexive spirit, I must confess that it is possible that this book also exaggerates certain characteristics of contemporary society. There is, of course, a thin line between emphasizing some aspects in order to be able to make certain key points and producing one-sided, crude, and partly misleading accounts.

threshold of something completely new, and we should be happy to experience something so magnificent.

So what? The problem of excessive infatuation with change

It may be objected that this keen interest in the rapid changeability of our age is not a major problem. Why not allow some exaggeration to give spice to life? Why shouldn't managers, other employees, students, and the general public be exposed to colourful portraits of an exciting, changing world and the need for new organizational and management principles, directed by dynamic and progressive business leaders? A great deal might be said about the relationship between entertainment value and 'more serious knowledge' (infotainment), but I will content myself with pointing to some of the negative consequences of change fanaticism. Tengblad (2003) considers that the greatest deficiency in modern working life is currently the low rating given to deeper levels of experience and occupational skills, an exaggerated faith in flexibility and suspicion of more systematic and long-term ways of working. There may also be an exaggerated desire for change that may have destructive results. Wallander (2003) points out that if a company requires an effective network of relationships, 'one should be careful not to demolish it by reorganizations. Building up a new way of working takes time. Organization consultants often appear to regard themselves as an invigorating sauna bath—the more often, the better. This is fundamentally wrong' (52).

Those who are willing to make changes are often supported by an environment that applauds such changes, possibly inspired by information about a rapidly changing world and the blessings of change:

> Such institution reorganizations signal that change is for real, and as we know only too well, the stock prices of institutions in the course of reorganization thereby often rise, as though any change is better than continuing as before. In the operation of modern markets, disruption of organizations has become profitable. While disruption may not be justifiable in terms of productivity, the short-term returns to stockholders provide a strong incentive to the powers of chaos disguised by that seemingly assuring word 're-engineering'. (Sennett, 1998: 51)

Of course, this should not be interpreted as support for conservatism, or the idea that there is often no pressure, or other good reasons for change. Change is clearly a key factor for organizations in many circumstances. But just because something is frequently important and necessary does not mean that it may not be widely exaggerated. Far too many change experiments have been initiated in relation to what can actually be achieved.

Changes that have been initiated often lead nowhere. Amundsen (2003) studied a company in which it was common to find that an organizational change had been prepared, decided, and embarked upon, but after a time it fizzled out. The result was frustration and even a 'BOHICA' mentality ('Bend over! Here it comes again.'). People become accustomed to the initiation of organizational changes but realize that this will probably not lead anywhere, so the best thing to do is to duck, carry on as normal, and avoid being drawn into the change initiative. One process of change is often abandoned when new management comes along, or there is a new phase in the business cycle or a new fashion. And then a new change attempt will start again. Managers keen on change and sceptical employees are not a good combination. It is claimed that failure to institute changes is much more common than success-ful implementation, and a common side effect is suspicion of management. In one organizational change project which we studied, the project was launched rather ambitiously, but it was not followed up and the employees reacted by regarding it as 'talk and paper for the people' or 'another example of the hypocrisy of top management' (Alvesson and Sveningsson, 2008). Ironically, one aim was to increase confidence in top management and promote 'visible leadership', but the result was almost the opposite, and this reinforced the problems the project was supposed to tackle.

Jackall (1988) considers that an emphasis on dynamic and change-oriented managers and a strong interest in new ideas means that managers on their way up like to associate themselves with and promote a given change in order to gain promotion—based on impressions of the potential results rather than what is achieved—and/or abandon the change when the fashion dies out and then concentrate on the next trend. Sticking to a change initiative over a protracted period and stubbornly pursuing it hardly seems to be a recipe for a successful career:

> A choice between securing one's own success by jumping on and off the band-wagon of the moment, or sacrificing oneself for the long-term good of the corpor-ation by diverting resources and really seeing a program through is for most managers no choice at all. Ambitious managers see self-sacrificing loyalty to a company as foolhardy. (Jackall, 1988: 143)

Watson (1994) also notes that new management ideas 'are pushed through by managers trying to make a reputation and a career, who do not stay on to see them through' (117). We have a fascinating paradox here: the strong value ascribed to new developments and change undermines chances of actually achieving any real change. Successful consultants and popular-management authors systematize this logic: they launch generally viable recipes for how change is to be handled as the only cure for current problems, and then, after a few years, claim that previous ideas have not worked, and suggest new, superior solutions. The consultancy sector partly relies on ideas and recipes becoming out of date after some time, thus permitting the launching of something new—or at least new labels and terms.

Senior executives often have limited insights into what is going on—or what is not going on. In one consultancy project which we studied, it was very unclear for those immediately concerned what changes had actually been implemented, but senior management was very pleased with the project, based on reports and convincing PowerPoint presentations by consultants and project managers. The consultancy firm received a negative rating from people in the client company with whom they were cooperating, but senior executives were satisfied (Alvesson and Sveningsson, 2011). Signalling willingness for change and change capability is more important than the actual accomplishment of changes—which calls for perseverance and an on-track focus over time. There is a good fit between a high rate of pseudo-changes and a limited number of real changes. In this sense organizational change takes place more in PowerPoint presentations and in the boardroom than outside these settings and hence may be seen as illusory arrangements (the latter could be defined as being much more visible on paper/PowerPoint than in substantive organizational practices).

One might, at this point, think that wise managements would refrain from following the fashion and projects that do not lead to any genuine changes, but it is difficult to know in advance what will be achieved, and there is a risk that people who are sceptical are perceived as conservative and slow to act. Development programmes and other initiatives that give the impression of dynamism and change orientation are good for image and grandiosity. Since other organizations are—or appear to be—heavily involved in such pro-grammes—and management books and the media tend to exaggerate the need for change and projects—people who are less enthusiastic about change projects can easily wind up in a backwater, or be afraid of doing so at any rate. In a zero-sum game for appearing to be dynamic, flexible, and favouring change, other people's ambitions and activities as regards change projects become a source of dissatisfaction, anxiety, embarrassment, and doubt, if you fail to keep up. Doing what everyone else is doing (or one thinks that they are doing) is a strong motive, reducing the risk of criticism and reducing your own anxiety. Going your own way—even if this may be sensible, upon careful reflection—in the face of other people's intensive change race can be unwise. The risks involved in dubious change must be weighed against the risk of appearing stuffy and backward. And the latter often seems to be greater than the former.

Summary

It is widely claimed that today's companies and working life are characterized by, or are well on the way to being permeated by, knowledge-intensive and flexible, non-hierarchical, network and project-based formats. Many authors say that radical changes have taken place and that sad, old paradigms and bureaucratic forms are outmoded and are on their way to the organizational graveyard. The pressure for change is strong in a dynamic economy and willingness to accept changes is crucial.

Attractive pictures of this process are widely disseminated. At the same time, however, most serious research indicates that the rate of change is not so high and that bureaucracy is still the predominant organization form. Changes are taking place in the form of decentralization and the free coupling of operations, but this does not amount to a fully fledged post-bureaucratic alternative. There are also many changes pointing to the emergence of new forms of bureaucracy. Most organizations apply a multiplicity of controls, ranging from management by results, bureaucratic, professional/occupational, and customer control to charismatic and authoritarian managers, and an organization culture and emotional control. This has always been the case to some extent. The tendency to regard modern working life as set in a radical and particularly innovative period of transition seems to be exaggerated.

Bureaucracy is a good topic to distance oneself from, and many people and organizations eager to escape the imperfections of contemporary work life and organizational practices stress their much more progressive and impressive, 'post-bureaucratic' character. Decentralization, networks, projects, flexibility, innovation, visions, and leadership trigger the right aura of grandiosity. Contemporary organizations exhibit much of this at the image level, while practices tend to be more ambiguous, or even clearly deviate from these characteristics. Given that 'progressive' organizations display or signal such grandiose qualities means that others are falling by the wayside and appear to be slow, unresponsive, or just very far from the cutting edge, and the latter lose in the zero-sum game of image, prestige, pride, and positive identity. This fuels the competition of symbolic capital in a fashion-conscious, dynamic, and change-oriented organizational world, where many are eager to display the right characteristics.

At the same time, most organizational practices and performances fail to meet this pressure and want to exhibit the right organizational structures and changes, here described as illusory arrangements. Organizations are not so easy to change, and many less beautiful features aid efficiency. Post-bureaucracy is appealing as an image and identity project in which actors draw upon particular entrepreneurial, network, and anti-hierarchy symbolism and rhetoric. This is good for self-esteem and external communication, but typically it includes more or less strong elements of illusions, as organizational performance tends to be based on more conventional and less impressive solutions. In a society and organizational life eager to sound impressive, post-bureaucracy is preached, while bureaucracy tends to be practiced. The former satisfies the need for grandiosity, the latter for the delivery of all the cheap goods and services we can get from machine bureaucracies like Walmart, IKEA, McDonald's, and airline companies.

7

Organizational structures on the beauty parade—imitations and shop-window dressing

As we have seen, an excessive interest in change—or at least the initiation of more or less well-considered projects—is closely linked to a high degree of sensitivity for what people think others are doing. As there are frequent mass media reports about the strong need for change and organizations are often engaged in various change activities, it is vital to keep up—both with the general norm and with the signalled moves of others. The risk of deviating and, in particular, falling behind is a major motive force. A key factor here is the surface—what seems to be visible from a distance and without much deeper knowledge—in an organizational and management context. This chapter focuses on the links between these aspects, in which imitations and fashions have a particularly high impact at the shop-window level (i.e., the illusion level), and where an increasing emphasis on the shop-window factor encourages imitations and fashion-following behaviour.

This chapter then takes the phenomenon of imitation seriously. But even if the desire to keep up with norms and fashions and the fear of lagging behind other organizations—in general or in one's sector—play a role, how significant is it? It may only have a moderate impact, compared with efficiency concerns, for example. And surely responsible executives, politicians, and other policy-makers are strong, independent, reasonably thoughtful, and rational actors, who generally have good reasons for their decisions and the organizational structures they are responsible for? Or is the almost caricature-like view of organizations as almost slavishly following fashions 'true'? No precise answers are possible, but research and insightful observations by respected commentators may give important material for informed reasoning.

In this chapter, I start with the phenomenon of imitation and convergence between organizations by exploring the impact of adapting new formal structures in organizations within a certain sector. There are reasons to believe that imitation of 'leaders' and following fashion are far from insignificant. Then this is related to the issue of the 'depth' of such imitation tendencies, where the window-dressing aspects are emphasized. Imitation is difficult and impractical when it comes to many operations, but certain structures are more plastic and suitable. This chapter reports a number of case studies showing some of the mechanisms and dynamics involved in homogenization tendencies and/or the display of the 'right' form of organizational structure: the cases range from diversity management in the oil industry to business concepts and formal organizational design in IT consultancy companies. All of the cases illustrate the pressures experienced to 'package' programmes and structures in specific ways.

Following John

As demonstrated in a large number of social psychology studies, the tendency to think and do as others do is a powerful factor in many situations and contexts. Thinking for yourself is often a demanding task, and deviating from what everyone else does is fraught with anxieties. Being able to refer to 'this is what everyone else is doing' is a safe move. This applies both to private individuals who are unhappy about being out of step with their environment in their assessments and views and to decision-makers at a high level in organizations. Wallander (2003), who was for many years one of Sweden's most highly respected business leaders, considers that senior executives are very much governed by a desire to be in tune with their time and not happy to diverge from what is considered to be the current style. They are keen to follow new trends and fashions in corporate management, and this means that the management ideal may shift rapidly, even if this has little to do with optimal results. Wallander considers that 'business leaders as just as fashion-conscious as teenage girls choosing jeans. They are like a herd of sheep munching at the grass. If they hear that the grass is greener on the other side of the hill, they rush away, and then all the others follow' (Wallander 2003: 115).

As I mentioned in Chapter 1, there is a strong tendency for organizations to imitate each other and regiment themselves in key respects. Some commentators denote this as isomorphism (similarity of form, image, and structure) (DiMaggio and Powell, 1983). Much of this is fashion-related, but it may also involve more long-term conformist trends, in which what are regarded as leading companies establish the norm and other companies gradually follow them. This may have a cognitive or a normative background. (In addition, there is coercive isomorphism, if the state or some other central body, for example a profession or the EU, insists on similar standards.) Cognitive isomorphism is based on uncertainty about what should be done. Uncertainty is dispersed by looking at what others seem to be doing and trying to copy them: you do not know what is the right way, and you do what everyone else is doing to avert uncertainty. Since the media and many others say that leadership means being a 'coach' these days, managers try to apply this recipe. And since other managers appear to be employing coaches—many training institutions and consultants are marketing coaching services—you do the same. In other words, the manager becomes a coach-employing coach—and appears to be keeping up with the generally accepted recipe for success.

Normative isomorphisms involve the pressure to appear to be morally well-adjusted—you achieve legitimacy by avoiding deviation. Instead, you adopt the right arrangements, structures, and language for what is regarded as desirable (e.g., appearing to be 'politically correct'). You signal environmental awareness, arrange for corporate health services, present a strategic plan, establish management groups (teams), have at least two female board members, appoint a group to handle 'knowledge management', and send employees on courses (and call this 'competence development'). In other cases, since corporate social responsibility (CSR) seems to be in tune with the times and is highlighted in books, seminars, and consultancy marketing efforts, managers develop a personal interest in having operations that may be labelled in this manner. Few want to risk being one of the few companies (over a certain size) that does not have a CSR manager and a CSR policy. Sometimes this high moral tone is denoted by forbidding employees to use hotel chains that show erotic films. Small firms are, to a certain extent, let off the hook, as they can't be expected, in the eyes of mass media, to display all the good things resourceful organizations can develop.

Isomorphism largely takes place at a superficial level, even though it can go deeper. Plans and models that attract the attention of managers can often be interpreted and applied in different ways. Hence organizations with similar formal structures and/or using certain labels to display what they are or do often turn out to be quite different in practice. For example, local dynamics, traditions, and ways of working are important and can rarely be imitated. Thus, outsiders find it hard to understand the deeper insights obtained from long-term participation that are required for adopting specific ways of operating. As a result, these organizational practices are difficult to copy. Hence, companies imitate and develop what they believe are particularly advanced structures, as described by the media, but which actually only bear a superficial resemblance. Genuine, 'in-depth' imitation is another matter, and more difficult (Rövik, 2011). Although many organizations have CSR in the form of a policy and certain activities, and hence appear to be similar, considerable variation exists at the practical level, that is, to the extent that anything at all goes on there. Sometimes, they only have the label in common, and certain buzzwords in their policy documents.

Attempts at imitation are often rather ham-fisted. Let me give an example. The setting is a Swedish regiment where an officer is explaining to her colleagues that she will be reporting on planning for the Swedish Armed Forces' operational control system. She employs a series of pictures to describe the ideas underlying this system and the process approach to be adopted, including concepts such as 'main processes', 'support processes', and 'leadership processes'. The system is to result in 'process development'.

> Why process development? Well, there is presumably a good reason since the business sector has implemented ISO 9000 certification in a great many companies and they require that their sub-contractors are certified. And this is presumably something you benefit from since this is what they do in the private sector. And we will also benefit since it simplifies our work, it will be easier to see at what level decisions should be taken and what this means. (Ydén, 2008: 182)

This clearly indicates that institutional theory is sometimes on the right track. People do things because they have noted others doing them and conclude some benefit is to be gained from the arrangements or practices in question.

The right window displays are important

As already mentioned in Chapter 1, institutional theory (Meyer and Rowan, 1977) claims that organizations are permeated by a split between legitimizing, formal structures and arrangements which primarily have a ceremonial function and work organizations characterized by productivity and efficiency. The former appear to be relevant to the latter, but the formal structures are often divorced from actual production, as they should be if the ceremonial activities are not to interfere with the productive activities.

In many cases, these ceremonial structures are an important feature of organizations. This applies, particularly, to operations with objectives that are diffuse or hard to realize. According to Perrow (1978), this is characteristic of human services organizations (HSOs) in the public sector, including health care, prisons, social work, and to some extent schools. It is assumed that the official objectives are crucial and that most activities are designed to achieve them. Countless reforms and new control and management methods are tried with the aim of improving operations and achieving better results, but they seldom succeed. Perrow considers that the attempts at improvement are ill-conceived, right from the start. The basic assumption of the key part played by objectives does not hold water. Perrow maintains that the official objectives have relatively little importance for operations, because it is hard to define and realize such goals. In addition, it is difficult to determine whether they have been achieved, as results are often difficult to measure or access. Furthermore, professionals often resist measurement efforts and other modes of monitoring their results. This reduces their degree of freedom, and they fear that it involves the risk of biased control, seldom taking complexity and quality into account.

Readily quantifiable indicators of objectives in the public sector—such as the number of hospital beds occupied, the number of pupils approved in compulsory schooling, the number of papers published at a university, and the number of alcohol tests carried out by traffic police—are dubious measures and a source of biased control. This may mean that the release of patients is delayed, doubtful or even incompetent pupils are approved, or motorists blow into balloons (breathalysers) during regular work hours when drivers are sober, rather than on a Friday or Saturday night (when the time-consuming handling of drunk drivers and expansive costs for overtime make it difficult to produce the required high numbers of testing). As a result, the fulfilment of overall objectives can easily take second place, in favour of other considerations and functions regarding what governs and motivates the various interested parties. Other factors become important instead.

Perrow (1978) distinguishes between external functions and internal motives. External functions concern non-recognized services provided for the external community that regulate the labour market and establish a sense of social order by dealing with potentially problematical elements in the population, keeping young people occupied in schools and off the street. Service organizations in the public sector also employ people, including many of those coming from a possibly over-inflated higher education system. The key functions would then be to maintain a sense of social order, keep people occupied, and reduce unemployment statistics (although, some studies indicate that many people do rather little work during a day at the workplace; Paulsen, 2010).

The internal motivation forces involve maximizing resources and making working conditions as attractive as possible for the unit concerned, preserving peace and harmony within the organization, avoiding open conflicts and scandals, and giving an impression of modernity and rationality to external audiences. The latter is achieved by adopting new ideas and organizational models and ways of working that are defined by the predominant elite groups as 'correct', and which look good in the media. Following the fashion is an important motivational force. New ideas often have mainly ceremonial importance, although they sometimes call for the investment of time and energy.

The above functions and motives do not necessarily run counter to the official objectives, and sometimes they may even help to achieve these objectives. New ideas can, of course, be an improvement. Getting enthusiastic about some new fashion can be positive, and change, in itself, can occasionally also be a good thing. As mentioned in the previous chapter, there is also often a genuine interest in the management world to learn, change, and improve results associated with fashion (Abrahamson, 1996). But often people want to jump ahead and do something that appears novel, thrilling, and impressive but interferes with genuine efforts to make improvements. There is often contradiction between goals and fashion: goal fulfilment may take second place to the desire to display something new. This is not necessarily a conscious ambition, but it may be latent in the ambiguities, both for fashion-followers and for others.

If organizational managers subordinate other considerations and take the (official) organizational objectives seriously, they will face a very difficult task. Dealing with staff with a low level of ability and interest; changing the allocation of resources without taking into account established precedents, privileges, and expectations; and redefining areas of responsibility and duties without considering how people lay claim to various roles will not meet with a positive response from all those concerned. Applying personal judgement as the best way to solve work responsibilities without considering the predominant combinations of taken-for-granted conventions, restrictive regulations, and compliance with current fashion will lead to amazement and dismay. Such a venture will meet with hostility from various groups whose self-interest, adherence to formal rituals, and desire to avoid conflicts and the risk of negative publicity will be threatened. It would also upset groups anxious about somebody deviating from what others are doing.

It is more important to establish operations that live up to socially defined standards for how things should be, with all the formal rules and structure in good order: budgets, personnel departments, management courses, formally qualified staff, diverse regulatory systems, gender equality plans and committees, etc. In other words, a conflict between an organization displaying the right surface manifestations and avoiding conflicts, on the one hand, and, on the other, one that works well in terms of actual results (which are hard to assess) may sometimes occur. It is easy to judge whether the organization's management is superficially living up to the predominant norms, but it may be difficult to determine whether the results are under par, or at any rate fail to comply with the picture presented. As a result, this may not matter so much for managers who appear to be successful.

Hence, one key aspect of organization management—not merely in HSOs but also more generally—is the arrangement of the window display: producing structures and arrangements that, in themselves, have little (positive) relevance for core operations but which give external groups that monitor activities at a distance—activists, customers, politicians, the media, public authorities, and job applicants—the impression that the organization is working smoothly. In other words, this is largely a question of illusory arrangements. The relative importance of the image varies, of course, not just depending on the type of operation, but also in terms of the theme. Organizations vary enormously in terms of salience of core operations and tangible production and my points here vary in their precise relevance for the understanding of various organizations. The production of items that can be tested clearly has a different 'substantiality' than things that cannot be so easily tested. As a result, substantial production and results often carry more weight than casual impressions and looser forms of legitimacy. And herein lies an important difference between the public and parts of the commercial world. In the private sector, market competition means that the ability to satisfy consumers sometimes reduces the importance of the ceremonial factors—the evaluation of the specific product or service is the critical point. But this is not so clear-cut as such assessments are often permeated by image-enhancing features. As pointed out in Chapter 3, people increasingly purchase the brand. An increasing number of private-sector companies are also concentrating on the symbolic sphere where the steering of expectations and a high degree of image sensitivity, etc., may mean more than the delivery of technically competent products and services. This applies, for example, to many iconic brands, to fashion and service-oriented companies, and to consultancies in many areas (Alvesson, 2004). Overall, there is an expansion of operations involving 'the corporate beauty industry'. An aesthetic and decorative surface—architecture, premises, letterhead design, elegant brochures, posters, PowerPoint presentations, company uniforms, beautiful and attractive employees, etc.—are becoming increasingly important (Hancock, 2003). This applies to both physical and verbal symbolism.

As beauty is something relative, the more aesthetically appealing competitors or colleagues become, the more ugly a company may discover itself to be (in the eyes of others or in its own). This aesthetization involves a strong zero-game between organizations. Whether the public (customers) benefits or loses is difficult to say: the organizational beauty parade may be pleasing to watch, but as resources and attention are partly taken from 'basic' practices and the services and products offered, there is a cost for the improved surface.

Let me illustrate this trend towards investment in attractive superficial structures by discussing two areas—diversity and organizational structure—where there is a clear signal value to the outside world but little, even negative, connection with 'core' operations.

Diversity and fashion: standardizing diversity management

Most people these days presumably say positive things about diversity, at least in public contexts. But, in practice, they usually prefer to work with, and spend time with, people with whom they experience affinity. They may not follow gender or ethnic lines, but may be related to age, social background, or education. Work functions more smoothly with people who share common values, meanings, and ways of thinking. Diversity management is now something that organizations are expected to handle in many countries, at least if they have major public exposure. Organizations are anxious to have and implement a diversity policy, partly to avoid problems and partly to indicate that they have systems and procedures that mean that they take gender equality and minority questions seriously—and can, as a result, 'prove' that they are good employers. But diversity aspects are also of interest in ensuring that the organization works more smoothly—treating people fairly, recruiting and promoting the most capable people, and avoiding conflicts and trouble.

An interest in diversity aspects is partly a question of a political and moral commitment to counteracting social marginalization, racism, and other injustices. It can also be regarded, however, as a meal ticket and a rapidly expanding sector in the labour market and the commercial market. As a business sector, diversity management consulting and education involves a billion dollar industry in the United States. A study by Prasad et al. (2011) provides interesting insights, and shows how important fashions are in this context. As in other major areas of societal and business activities, there are strong demands for rapid and relatively frequent innovations. This sector is characterized by companies that must continually assure clients of the current value of their services and products. One client, a personnel manager who was responsible for diversity training, justified his choice of consultant in the following manner:

> We went with XYZ because they were not into the same old ideas—you know the hippie images of the seventies. They are real professionals, and are willing to change their programs to give us something new each time. (Prasad et al., 2011: 709)

The assumption is that 'something new' means 'something better'—or at least that it looks better. Consultants also stress the importance of coming up with something new:

> that old sensitivity training stuff has no selling power any more. You've got to give it (diversity) more management appeal—link it to efficiency or performance, somehow connect it to saving money. That's the feelings of the times. (Prasad et al., 2011: 710)

Products must be standardized if the companies are to offer clients products with clear news-worthy value. Coming up with something distinct and uniform is important; it needs to be presented as clearly different from 'the old stuff'. Diversity experts monitor other companies and imitate their latest programmes. Companies develop and sell standardized products and services, for example videos, manuals, diversity audits, courses, or workshop activities. People try to link this with other fashionable themes, for example teamwork. The sales message is that diversity pays. Diversity is also sold by using harmonious and beautiful words that attract people with aesthetic values and metaphors such as 'rainbow cultures' and 'mosaic workplaces'. Against the ugly world of differentiation, exclusion, discrimination, and conflict, we find much more appealing social relations made possible through the new diversity management, with a fair amount of grandiose promises.

This profitable, harmonious and beautiful world of diversity is not so easily achieved, however. One problem is that the local relevance of diversity programmes is often limited. Leading companies in North America are often based in North Carolina and Georgia and are influenced by themes relevant for African Americans and middle-class women with jobs. In Prasad et al.'s study of Canadian oil companies, diversity issues were often associated with quite different themes, for example 'francophones'—French-speaking Canadians from Quebec. This contributed to a perception that the content of diversity programmes was often barely relevant. The main problem is, of course, that diversity is often accompanied by antagonisms, differences, and conflicts of interest, which are not so easy to handle. After participation in one such programme, a manager commented:

> It really is a feel-good exercise. You know, we can all feel good that we are this happy multi-colored family—that's going to bring in all this money for the firm. The truth is quite another matter. If people are really different, they don't get along that easily, they want to do things differently, and they get upset about how they are told to do work. (cited in Prasad et al., 2011: 718)

It was important for oil companies with a bad reputation for being conservative and backwards to give the impression that they were forward-looking and up-to-date in personnel matters. Large and well-known consultancy firms that offered the latest programmes were engaged. But their action had primarily cosmetic effects, since fashionable, standardized programmes were hardly relevant at the local level. They merely made the employees who participated in the programme sceptical. Prasad et al.'s study (2011) indicates that diversity management is mainly a question of promising rainbows and offering dreams of attractively coloured but substance-less utopias that have little to do with the darker side of identity politics and internal group conflicts.

In this context, we may also note an unavoidable but nonetheless common discrepancy between an image level and an everyday level, the key quality of an illusory arrangement. Large, well-known firms with standardized and fashionable products and services were employed in order to achieve good effects at the image level, and they were sold to client companies with fulsome promises of the extent to which diversity pays off. The effects at the everyday level almost demanded the opposite: situation-trimmed services and methods in which complexities and antagonisms were really taken seriously. Since the latter is harder to sell, costs more, and has weaker effects at the symbolic level, it usually gets lost on the way.

Packaging companies: business ideas and organization structures

Perhaps a decoupling between arrangements to make things look good, and more ambiguous, complex, and often contradictory, practices linked to ceremonial aspects, is not entirely surprising in 'soft' areas such as diversity. But this distinction also applies in what seem to be clearer, 'hard' economic, or commercial contexts, such as organizational designs and changes in relationship to the stock market and the core definition of the business (the mission or the business concept), themes that I now address.

Packaging for the stock market

The way companies are packaged and presented to customers, employees, and on the stock market is an interesting theme. Personally, I have carried out considerable research in management/IT consultancy firms and, as a result, my examples mainly involve corporate packaging designed to appeal to various groups (from Alvesson, 2000: Chapter 14).

In recent years, the IT consultancy sector has been characterized by considerable enthusiasm for mergers and takeovers, as in other areas in the business world. The experiences recounted by the business leaders I interviewed were hardly positive. (This is supported by the results of other research, for example Cartwright and Holmes, 2006; Berggren, 2002.) One manager, somewhat hardened after a number of mergers, noted with emphasis: 'Like hell did we benefit from joining up with the M-group, and like hell did we gain from pairing up with the Zeros and Digits company.' Mergers and takeovers have rather loose links with actual operations, and hence the consultants' task is not directly affected. They predicted a number of positive consequences, but apparently few of these synergies were realized in practice.

The impression is that the primary purpose of mergers and takeovers is to improve the company's stock market rating, and the scale of operations is highly important in this context. This was particularly true in the late 1990s when the new economy (also known as the IT bubble) was at its peak.

But for IT companies, especially those with stock exchange ambitions, the key factor was volumes. What type of volume or the quality of this volume was something to be kept quiet—you just kept rolling along. (company manager, cited in Alvesson, 2000: 291)

Another example of structures that were designed to impress the players in the stock market comes from a medium-sized consultancy firm with growth ambitions which modified the organization structure and established new business areas. It was considered, per se, that the change was unnecessary, maybe even negative, but financial analysts' expectations regarding transparency and insight into various fields of operations justified such a structure. Ironically, it virtually obscured what was actually going on (where the aim, in practice, was to avoid strict demarcations of operations in different areas), but it gave the impression of transparency, a businesslike approach, and a growth orientation.

At a more general level, it may be said that economic development—with periodic bursts of freed-up capital in recent decades, and short-term profit requirements—has resulted in investment decisions that have not always involved particularly wise and discerning assessments.

> Enormous pressure was put on companies to look beautiful in the eyes of the passing voyeur; institutional beauty consisted in demonstrating signs of internal change and flexibility, appearing to be a dynamic company, even if the once-stable company had worked perfectly well. Firms like Sunbeam and Enron became dysfunctional or corrupt in responding to this investor parade, but even in periods of market downturn the pressure on firms remained the same: institutional solidity became an investment negative rather than a positive. Stability seemed a sign of weakness, suggesting to the market that the firm could not innovate or find new opportunities. (Sennett, 2006: 40–1)

Nicolai et al. (2010) demonstrate how stock market analysts react positively to—and hence reinforce the effect of—the adoption of various management fashions by companies, irrespective of whether they improve efficiency. This largely involves a focus on the same information that others have, thus reducing the importance of individual, possibly richer sources of information. This is because analysts producing deviations from other people's forecasts may have disastrous consequences for their careers if they are wrong. If they are wrong in the good company of others it is not a problem. In times of uncertainty, it may be rational to do what everyone else is doing (or what you expect others to do). Therefore, fashion-oriented signals provide a clue as to how others will make their assessments, and what sort of short-term impact such assessments will have on stock exchange prices. As a result, financial analysts reward and reinforce following the fashion and the institutionalization of new management concepts. In other words, an apparently unemotional, rational stock market interacts with fashionable trends and institutionalization imbued with popular and influential management concepts, but with no tangible or proven indication of a better organization structure. Thus, share prices can give a misleadingly positive impression—such is the case at least in the short term.

The business concept

The business concept of a corporation is another theme that demonstrates the way in which factors that are irrational in substantial terms may interact with economic rationality. The business concept is supposed to provide an overall indication of what the company does and summarize its core competence and market offerings (Normann, 1977). The IT consultancy firm studied in Alvesson (2000) promised a combination of strategic and computer expertise (i.e., management). IT issues were put in a wider, business-oriented perspective and, it was claimed, involved much more than programming. Many managers and employees proudly referred to the company's business concept and considered that the company's strength was precisely a combination of management and IT skills. Strategy and management gave an attractive picture of operations, compared to being 'only' into programming. However, the extent to which people complied with the business concept was highly doubtful. This is how one subsidiary manager expressed himself when I interviewed him a few years later after he had left the company:

> This is often the way it goes with companies in this industry, it is one thing to profile yourself, but matching the profile is something else. (cited in Alvesson 2000: 292)

Another former subsidiary manager put it more crudely:

> What we live off in the consultancy world is actually resources and volume. We depend on sales and the middle level, not the brilliant analysts out front. System analysts and programmers are what counts. And that's what we lived off. We packaged and disguised that we were working in projects at Datakonsultus, but we rarely needed to take any major project risks. It was on cost-plus basis, and a packaging of volume consulting. But that's not the way they worked in England (i.e., at the British subsidiary). They believed in 'now the new view of management and IT is on the way', and we talked about this in Sweden but didn't do very much about it, but they believed in it wholeheartedly, and everything went to pot. [laughs] Volume was what it was all about! That's bulk! What we were good at was IT, that's the whole story, and that's what we earned money on too. (cited in Alvesson 2000: 292–3)

The interviewee referred to the business concept as a sales trick and a myth, and said that the business concept was rarely mentioned in discussions among senior managers.

> We didn't have that kind of competence. It was a cleverly dreamed-up and skilfully maintained myth, I might say, rather meanly. But I think it is true too.

But nonetheless I wouldn't say it was wrong because that myth held up all through the 1980s. [laughs] And that's not a bad rating at all. If people thought we were good at combining management and IT—fine. And they were happy with that, worked on their projects and made money out of programming, because that was what it was all about, really. (cited in Alvesson 2000: 293)

My impression, based on two rounds of interviews with the company's managers and others, during and some years after the phase in which the myth was fostered so strongly, was that the mixture of naïvety and cynicism was crucial. Doubts and uncertainty often evaporate in an atmosphere of enthusiasm, wishful thinking, and rationalization pressures. Naïve faith is sometimes an asset (Alvesson and Spicer, 2012). At the same time, some degree of business thinking and clear-sightedness is required if the grandiose aspects are not to be taken too seriously. Ambivalence and oscillation between naïve faith in the gilt-edged, instrumental, and pragmatic approach seem to characterize many of the participants. There is a mixture or smooth alternation, on the one hand, between a somewhat naïve view of future expectations and attempts to allow practices to be interpreted and depicted in 'myth-friendly' terms and, on the other hand, more strategic, even cynical thinking about what is involved and pragmatic behaviour, paired with sales and morale-enhancing talk that makes people happy.

But irrespective of whether senior managers optimistically believe in, or strategically, possibly cynically, sell grandiose, deceptive images, there is often a strong receptiveness among subordinates for representations that give an impression of upgrading of activities into something more remarkable and impressive. Deetz (1998) demonstrates how the overall labelling and packaging of a company's strong position influenced the members of an organization's views about who they were and what they did. When a department was relabelled from an internal support group into a consultancy organization, people's attitude towards themselves and their work changed considerably: they strongly emphasized that now they were 'consultants', and they identified themselves more closely with their unit. This change in identity occurred even though the organizational change was not particularly dramatic since the personnel were part of a corporate group with more or less the same internal customers, and they had the same jobs as in the past.

These examples illustrate the propensity to give a golden touch to the organizational framework that surrounds business and work. In other words, attempts are made to not merely support the sale of specific products and services by making questionable promises of what the customer will get for his/her money, but package the organization itself in a manner that ensures that the right symbolic or ceremonial values are achieved.

149

In a world in which corporate mergers, growth (including 'artificial' growth as a result of acquisitions), a business approach, strategy, management, and consultancies have positive overtones, it is important to develop symbols for this. Sometimes, this primarily involves the illusion level. People tend to mystify rather than clarify what they are doing, even for themselves, but maybe this is regarded as desirable. A full-blooded mystification with attractive overtones is better than a more neutral description? This appears to be a recipe for success, at least in some quarters.

One might add, at this point, that the management of mystification is seldom uncomplicated as a recipe for success. With the promotion of grandiose framings and labels, following fashions and the imitation of others, various contradictions and ambiguities often emerge. In the IT consultancy firm mentioned, some people took the business concept seriously and ran into problems. Others noted the discrepancies and felt confused, disillusioned, and cynical. Engaging in imitation and following the mass can lead to a feeling (and possibly the reality) of doing the wrong thing, with missed opportunities and suboptimal performance as a result. Building and maintaining the right surface arrangements can lead to practical problems and a waste of time and energy. All this needs to be managed—through organizational hypocrisy, myth-building, mushroom management ('keep them in the dark and fill them with shit'), and other forms of leadership and cultural management that reduce the awareness of how organizations sometimes really work in the context of strong pressures to present appealing surfaces and the contingencies of practical realities and conventions for operations. We can refer to this as stupidity management—a significant element in the smooth functioning of many contemporary organizations (Alvesson and Spicer, 2012). What's crucial here is that employees and managers are seduced by—but do not feel particularly religious about—the grandiosity, and who do not carefully scrutinize the illusion tricks backing it up.

Summary

In this chapter, I have discussed imitations and shop-window arrangements in organizations. The common factor in the management of many organizations, as well as individuals, is an attempt to associate oneself with the grandiose—and ignore the trivial aspects. Following the fashion is important. Contemporary fashions often incorporate new, more tempting aspects of grandiosity. The novelty is typically more rhetorically well supported and seductive than previously established and embraced practices and success recipes (Abrahamson, 1996; Green and Li, 2011). The mass media, education programmes, articles, and consultancy practices exert a strong pressure and encourage the advancement of positions and achieving something more attractive. The concept of the knowledge-intensive society and the idea that we are participating in the age of the great organization leap ignites our ambitions and imaginations.

Window-dressing activities are seldom obvious. They often have some links with more everyday and 'substantial' practices and effects. This applies, for example, to appealing diversity programmes and the packaging of organizations' business concepts and structures in an attractive manner, for the market and/or employees. For the most part, it is difficult to achieve strong links between grandiose representations and dominant practices—and it is often problematical if this happens. Individuals who insist on applying fine ideals or who take the organization's rhetoric and formal structures seriously tend to have deficiencies in terms of flexibility and pragmatism, and often make trouble both for themselves and for their organizations (Jackall, 1988). Grandiosity therefore needs to be handled in a pragmatic way, where promises and practices are sometimes kept apart.

In order to develop an attractive surface, organizations (i.e., their senior actors) should:

- Be fashion conscious and flexible. Be aware of what is current and modern and what others are doing (or rather say that they are doing), and be compliant.

- Combine conformism with something that appears more original in terms of visible arrangements and practices. Achieve a satisfactory mix between being basically like others but with some minor variations on an overall theme, since (hidden) conformism is more important than genuine deviation from the norm. Similarity is expressed by combining the same rhetoric and shop-window activities with something that appears to be more personal. But conformism is the dominant factor: modern organizations are trying to present themselves on a broad front as knowledge-intensive, innovative, and favouring teamwork, diversity, equality, ethics, and a quality orientation, and they regard all possible themes as strategic, etc.

- Pay great attention to surface aspects. Be aware that making things look good is crucial, that is to say avoid, disguise, or minimize factors that do not express easy access and compliance with current expectations.

- Manage organized hypocrisy. The right impression management must be combined with operative management so as to achieve special links, but also allowing for sufficient combination and/or cultivation of ambiguity so that untrustworthiness and disillusion do not take over.

- Achieve a balance between naïvety and cynicism. This applies to management that wants to encourage commitment, identification, and good morale, but also wants to avoid idealized descriptions being taken too seriously in practice. This also applies to employees, who must be able to navigate between contradictory messages without regarding themselves as hypocrites.

As with most issues there are no simple, straightforward solution to problems associated with external pressures and internal ambitions to produce an impressive surface and at the same time make operations work. So organizations attempt to balance the various ideals, sometimes successfully, sometimes creating a lot of ambiguities. In a strongly image-sensitive economy and society, paying a lot of attention to the surface, to what is fashionable and to what others are doing is common and probably good for survival and success. But, as said, there are always contradictions that can create problems. Most organizations also need to deliver products and services, and this often calls for arrangements and priorities other than those rewarded in the beauty parade.

8

A place in the sun—occupational groups' professionalization projects and other status and influence ambitions

In an age of high—even galloping—expectations of better working and living conditions, higher status, and an active role in a 'knowledge-intensive society', it is hardly surprising that many employees and occupational groups want to advance their positions. They want to have the status, attractive working conditions, and influence that they feel they deserve. There are participants in various fields—researchers, popular authors, teachers, trade unions, and representatives of various professions—who are keen to launch ideas about the importance of their specific occupation or field of knowledge, and what the general public, organizations, and clients would gain if that occupation or field of knowledge had greater influence and status. Many of these attempts to advance positions take the form of launching and reinforcing such occupations by turning them into professions. Increased professionalization is broadly viewed as a good thing, in the interest of the specific occupation concerned as well as for society as a whole. This applies particularly to occupations in the public sector, where the achievements are often hard to determine, as previously mentioned. The absence or weakness of the market as a disciplinary mechanism—showing often more interest in what is delivered (or believed to be delivered) than in formal qualification and authorization of groups—also leads to a direction of energy into professionalization projects. Scoring high on signs of being a 'profession' becomes an indicator of success. Exceptions include such occupations as engineers, managers, consultants, and advertising experts are in most countries not certified or professionalized in any strict sense—and when they are targeted for certification efforts this is attributed little significance (Alexius, 2007). (Chartered accountants are a somewhat different matter.) However, generally, there is an increasing focus on regulating which occupational groups are to be entitled to do what, by applying statutory provisions and formal requirements for education and training. As is the case with many other popular concepts, the term 'profession' is used in different ways. But the general notion is that a profession is better than a 'non-profession' and professionalization is typically viewed as a way to bring an occupation forwards and upwards in the battle for status, respect, influence, and attractive job positions. The problem is that many occupations see increased professionalization as the way to get ahead of others; success is therefore relative.

In some cases professionalization does appear to be less feasible, due, for example, to the need to be flexible about qualifications and in order to be seen as a part of top management. Here signs of professionalism are a mixed blessing and other means of position-reinforcement tactics are often used instead. The goals of status and power for the occupation are the same, but the means are different.

This chapter addresses mainly professionalization and the problem of increased competition for occupational status. It looks more deeply into two occupation—nurses and personnel specialists—in somewhat different ways. The first is about negotiations and conflicts around status and identity at a hospital unit; the second is the problem for personnel specialists to get full recognition for their ambition to be a key function in organizations in knowledge societies. The chapter discusses some basic disadvantages associated with professionalization.

On professionalization

So what is meant by a 'profession'? Sometimes the signifier refers to an 'occupation' (in contrast to 'amateurs' or people who are not members of the same profession). Sometimes it refers to all groups of employees in the 'higher' working life strata (e.g., above the blue and lower white-collar level, but below or outside managerial rank). Sometimes it refers to a limited and elite selection of occupations with particular privileges, sometimes a broader set of occupations, with many opinions about which occupations qualify for this exclusive label. As Abbott (1991) puts it:

> because the term 'profession' is more an honorific than a technical one, any apparently technical definition will be rejected by those who reject its implied judgments about their favourite professions and non-professions. (18)

There are a number of more or less accepted criteria for a 'real' or 'true' profession:

- It is based on systematic, scientifically based theory.
- There is a long and standardized formal education.

- There is a strong professional association regulating its members.
- Members have autonomy in the sense that professional knowledge rather than bureaucratic position should govern decisions and work within the professional sphere.
- A code of ethics is established by the profession.
- There is a distinct occupational culture.
- There is a client orientation.
- The occupation is socially sanctioned and authorized.
- There are criteria for certification.
- There is a monopoly of a particular labour market via restrictions of entry.
- Collective self-regulation and the professional have authority over work.

If we accept all these criteria, probably only physicians, and perhaps dentists, vets, and possibly psychologists would qualify as true professionals, since for example priests, accountants, and lawyers hardly base their work on systematic, science-based theory. Nurses, generally playing the role of support to physicians, have limited autonomy and authority at work, although in some cases that has started to shift (McMurray, 2011). In many respects, undue significance is given to official recognition, a professional association, and a formalized code of ethics. In practice, these elements may not matter very much, at least not in the business sector.

Older literature, in particular, but also more recent texts, describe professions in a way that makes one almost suspect that members of the profession's PR departments were the authors. The central role of science and knowledge, autonomy, the solving of problems vital to society, affective neutrality, and altruistic service to clients are often emphasized, producing an 'image of a largely autonomous, self-regulating and self-perpetuating institution, the altruistic members of which are filled with a desire to work for the common good in the most effective way' (Brante, 1988: 122). Contemporary views in the sociology of professions are far more sceptical of the claim that professionals have a higher form of rationality and morality than other social groups (Collins, 1990; Fores et al., 1991).

Statements made by professionals about themselves, and also to some extent researchers' (uncritical) reproductions of such statements, may be regarded as elements in their strategies for achieving, maintaining, and improving the status of their profession. In line with modern sociology of professions, what is of interest is, instead, claims about having these particular traits and what is proposed to justify a specific social position and certain privileges, including a monopoly of segments of the labour market. 'Essentialist' ideas—stressing the universal qualities of professions—have lost credibility, and there has been a greater focus on professionalization strategies and processes (i.e., efforts to gain recognition as a profession). Self-interest and efforts to achieve social exclusion—preventing other people from having access to certain jobs or tasks—is crucial for professions. This benefit for people with the formal credits is a loss of access possibilities for others. Professionalization is very much about politics and the struggle for status, power, and material rewards. It is not so much a question of the work characteristics themselves or the knowledge base of a profession (or a wan-nabe profession); rather the significant point is the ability to organize and mobilize a powerful political project to gain acceptance for claims to having special status (Collins, 1990).

An ethical code, for example, is sometimes seen as a symbolic vehicle, which supports the political interests of the profession by promoting its image as highly respectable and credible, rather than as a set of norms that actually ensures morally superior behaviour on the part of the professionals. The element of grandiosity is salient here. This is not to deny that a code of this nature cannot have some regulatory effects, reduce some opportunistic behaviour, and punish it if such cases are detected—although sanctions seem to be rare. The ideas (myths?) of technocracy, certain knowledge, altruism, rationality, and neutrality are seen as ideologies for justificatory purposes (Brante, 1988).

In this context, the 'scientification' of a given occupational area may be regarded from a status and power viewpoint, rather than because people in this occupation need it, or because their skills improve if they are subject to some particular academic discipline. The fact that questions of power, self-interest, and exclusion strategies are crucial in a professional environment does not, of course, run counter to the possibility that successful profession-alization—in one sense or another—can have positive consequences for soci-ety. It is to be hoped that academic and expert status, preferential rights of interpretation, restriction of access to the specialized labour-market sector concerned, etc., will mean a high work quality. It is difficult to prove this, however. The 'knowledge system' often has a symbolic value rather than a clear and necessary relationship with an ability to solve problems at work. It is by no means certain that qualified psychotherapists are better at dealing with problems than others, and the fact that someone has obtained the relevant formal (i.e., certified) qualification does not say much. It is not necessarily the case that all health problems are handled better by state authorized medical specialists ('real' professionals) than by homeopaths, osteopaths, acupunctur-ists, and so on. In the case of a number of social problems that also have moral implications—for example, drug abuse or criminality—alternative treatments based on collective and moral education ideas are sometimes superior to the professional treatments provided by psychologists, medical doctors, and social workers (Beckman, 1980a). However, there is considerable uncertainty in the assessment of results. While it is self-evident that members of certain certified occupational groups are better than others at certain tasks—for example, brain surgeons or commercial pilots—this does not mean that greater 'academization' and the exclusion of those without the right qualifications in all work areas necessarily benefits the general public. However, it is usually advantageous for the occupational group in question, who tend to push their own interest:

> Credentialed workers tend to redefine their jobs and to eliminate noncredentialed jobs around them. Thus the spiral of education and the rising credential requirements for jobs tend to be irreversible. (Collins, 2002: 27)

I am not investigating to what extent, and when, ambitions to acquire the status signs of a real profession or to climb the status ladder by acquiring signs of a higher level of professionalism (e.g., extended education, more operational authority, strong links with universities and research) are purely in the interest of the occupation concerned, or whether they appear to be justified from a public interest viewpoint. This is typically close to impossible to sort out. I am more interested in broad trends in which the various participants try to glorify themselves and their activities, exploit various features with a more or less sound basis, but which also have a symbolic effect, and compete with others of similar pretensions. The professional area, in this case, is a gold mine for studies of grandiosity projects and social zero-sum games.

We can see how a spectrum of occupational groups and areas try to bolster themselves in many different countries. This applies, for example, to nurses, social workers, vocational guidance consultants, teachers, military and police personnel, dental hygienists, and librarians. (I don't go into national variations here, but refer to groups that in many, if not most, countries seem to fit my thesis.) As a result, we have established new academic disciplines: nursing science, social work, vocational guidance research, military science, police studies, oral health, and library science. These disciplines provide a theoretical focus in studies for such occupations, although there is often considerable conflict between the theoretical and the practical aspects within such occupational groups. It is sometimes claimed that research and an academic approach are not particularly relevant, and that the practical aspects suffer as a result. Teachers of nursing with practical experience sometimes feel that academization has taken place 'over their heads'. Attempts to give experienced teachers research training do not always pan out—perhaps the teachers were never very interested in research, or regard it as irrelevant for their activities. Student nurses often consider that nursing science studies are not necessary, and what they need is practical know-how, not research, especially as hospitals complain about deficiencies in the students' practical knowledge. At the same time, there are also counter arguments. One nursing teacher stated that new nurses should be regarded as 'agents for changing health care. They are trained to be able to apply and understand research. They can criticize, evaluate and develop activities in the wards. And the workplaces must learn to appreciate this' (*Universitetsläraren* 19, 2003: 10–12).

It is difficult to get a clear picture of the consequences of making a profession such as nursing more academic. A lack of practical knowledge is perhaps noticed first in the case of recently trained staff, but deficiencies in this respect may well disappear as they gain practical experience, and it takes time before the impact of possible improvements in the prerequisites for nursing development make themselves felt. The tension between practical skills and academic education is also tangible in other occupations, however. In the Swedish police force, where training has been academized, i.e., turned into a more academic type of education, there are highly vocal complaints amongst the personnel that 'these new people cannot drive a car, use a pistol, or talk to people—whatever they learn these days at the National Police College'. In addition, they complain that 'the new people don't want to work outside the office, they want to become managers immediately' (chief constable, personal communication). All the police personnel I have talked to regard police work as a craft or skill, not an academic project.

A range of different outcomes of the academization of an occupation can be imagined in this context. At one extreme, there is a status boost; at the other, people snigger at what they regard as irrelevancies and a waste of resources. In terms of results, one may anticipate a wide spectrum of consequences, ranging from improved expertise to deterioration of practical skills as a result of higher status. We must also take into account the tensions that occur in the occupational groups being academized (Elzinga, 1989). For some people— perhaps a minority—this offers new opportunities for an academic career and a political advancement of positions, while others—perhaps the majority— are more interested in the practical aspects of their work and regard academization as irrelevant, or even a distraction from their real tasks. Here the status motive feels less relevant—police officers on traffic control or foot patrol may be less interested in status boosting through academic education than union management eager to lead an occupation scoring high on paper in terms of professionalism. Signs of grandiosity and the credibility of illusion are probably much more salient for the latter group, living in the world of symbolism and representations than the former, active in often messy, hands-on situations.

In this context, I merely point out possible outcomes that should be taken into account. It is important to stress that the status aspect is crucial. As a librarian I spoke to put it: 'PhD programmes and research are good because they boost the status of the occupation'. Maybe this is good for librarians, but possibly not for others, including tax payers (in countries where the state finances PhD programmes). This applies to a large number of professionalization projects that call for considerable resources.

The status problem

Representatives of occupational groups and other participants in the public debate often emphasize that lack of status is a contributing factor—poor recruitment, high personnel turnover, poor morale, poor reputation, and dubious results. They argue for higher status for the occupational group or the area concerned. The problem is that this is bound to be at the expense of someone else's position and conditions. As already mentioned, there are inevitably zero-sum games in the status context, and one might even claim that this is precisely what it is all about. The point is not that you are advancing in splendid isolation, as a completely autonomous project divorced from the rest of the world. Instead the advancement and improvement of positions is related to other occupational groups, usually primarily closely related groups, but also, at a more general level, to the aggregate of all other occupations in the labour market, which strangely is seldom taken into account. Let me illustrate some tricky aspects, taking nursing as an example.

Increased professionalism in health care—a complicated case of nursing

Registered nurses have tried to raise their status in many countries through academization, but the relative positioning is difficult to change, although in some cases the gap between doctors and nurses may have been reduced, with tensions and conflicts as a result (McMurray, 2011). However, the actual duties have not changed significantly as a result of such professionalization projects. The old and the sick still need help to wash themselves, go to the toilet, eat, and be transported. A significant part of hospital work is moderately qualified, and there is much routine work. Perhaps the increase in the number of registered nurses in relation to other personnel has meant that a higher proportion of the latter category's duties are now of a less qualified or (traditional) nursing character.

Let us look at what this may mean in an everyday context in a geriatric ward, as reported in a PhD thesis by Ulla Sebrant (2000). As a result of an ambition to increase competence, some nursing aides' posts became registered nursing posts, as in many other health service areas. The assistant nurses found this hard to accept since although their occupational group was shrinking, they felt their group was required to do just as much as before, resulting in (in some cases exacerbated) various tensions and conflicts.

> These conflicts mainly take the form of assistant nurses who repeatedly insist that the registered nurses should 'help out'. This may be due to the fact that that there are now more registered nurses, and that this is at the expense of the assistant nurse group, who are not satisfied with a situation in which registered nurses only help out when they have time. They think that they have lost out in this reallocation of staff. The registered nurses think that it is not viable to have to work with different kinds of duties... One pattern, which is often repeated, is when a registered nurse tries to be accommodating by 'taking up' a couple of patients every day, or helping out with something while doling out medicines. Another common tactic is to say you will be coming soon and then wait as long as possible. (Sebrant, 2000: 79–80)

Sebrant also notes that:

> While the registered nurses aim to work 'professionally', based on care planning and documentation, the assistant nurses want them to take on practical tasks to a greater extent... The assistant nurses want to undermine the hierarchy by asking the registered nurses to help them on their terms. This also involves the unit leader (head nurse) in a struggle, with continual negotiations about influence and identity. (Sebrant, 2000: 96)

Assistant nurses said that their workload was much heavier after some of their colleagues were replaced by registered nurses:

> Now, when the place is crawling with registered nurses, and actually the idea is that they should be helping us, nothing happens, even if we are left alone with eight patients. Some patients can manage by themselves, but sometimes there are several 'heavy' cases who need a lot of help, and there is bandaging to be done. That's really tough. (Sebrant, 2000: 98)

These accounts illustrate the everyday problems of professionalization ambitions. We can note the conflicts that can arise if many of the duties are practical, possibly less agreeable, and run counter to what the registered nurses regard as their territory and their level of competence.

Assistant nurses want more practical help and registered nurses are only interested in work in line with their competence. From the registered nurses' point of view, doing practical, 'non-registered nursing work' downgrades their status, their identity, and their self-esteem and they face the risk of less satisfactory duties, even unpleasant work. There is a considerable discrepancy between higher qualifications and the tasks that must be carried out. At the same time, there are conflicts and a lack of clarity about duties regarded as confirming identity and status, and which both groups lay claim to.

There is also a divergence of views regarding the unique knowledge base that the registered nurses emphasize as the characteristic feature of the nursing profession. Other occupational groups do not really accept this, which was clearly illustrated in the course of a conference within the department concerned:

> Information from the head nurse: 'There is a new training programme for assistant geriatric nurses on Wednesdays during the autumn'. Lisa, an assistant nurse who has read this says: 'This covers the whole lot, and it's all self-instruction'. Her colleague, Lena, agrees: 'There doesn't seem to be much new'. And Lovisa exclaims: 'I think this is a poor deal for assistant nurses, it is just nursing science'. And the head nurse (unit leader) replies indignantly: 'this is not rubbish, this is a major area—our area! We are not going to be little doctors'. She continues talking about the importance of nursing knowledge and wants the registered nurses present to say something, but they keep quiet, and silence reigns...The consultant physician looks quietly triumphant, but remains silent. (Sebrant, 2000: 202)

This example demonstrates how other occupational groups failed to share the enthusiasm for nursing science qualifications expressed by the head nurse (and many other representatives of the profession). Even in the registered nurses group, to which the head nurses belonged, there appeared to be limited faith in the importance of nursing science qualifications, at least in this department.

There are often conflicts concerning status, the allocation of attractive, identity-confirming duties, and the minimization of aspects that do not comply with an ideal occupational role. This is not a matter of a shortage of resources as much as their allocation and how divisions of labour are being controlled (and how they often escape effective control). In the hospital area, it is impossible to promote the status, formal qualifications, and ambitions of one group without affecting the relative position of others. It might be feasible to improve the position of assistant nurses by means of professionalization and training, but this would probably result in increased lack of clarity concerning status aspects and duties—and further conflicts with the registered nurses. The next stage, in accordance with standard procedure in this area, would be to improve the status of registered nurses by means of further training and professionalization, but this might encroach on the doctors' area and result in new opposition and conflicts (McMurray, 2011).

Sebrant's (2000) study illustrates the way in which the organization of duties at the ward is seen to be mainly in the hands of the registered nurses, which is not very helpful for the doctors, who complain of a lack of assistance and being continually forced to chase up the registered nurses. Productivity in complex social structures is partly a question of interaction and a smooth allocation of tasks, but this may be disrupted by changes in the status and identity of occupational groups. As a result, increasing the status of one occupational group is not a simple and unequivocally positive solution since it does not take place in a social, organizational vacuum. Status enhancement projects may solve some problems, but they also give rise to others.

Raising the status of one occupational group is always at the expense of another group. Status is, by definition, a zero-sum gain. Naturally, this does not mean to say that I regard breaking up hierarchies and reallocating status as meaningless or negative. Such actions can often be motivated, for example, by established hierarchies that are unfounded or dysfunctional. However, it is important to take into account the context and to be aware that conflicts and problems often exist with changes of status in hierarchies.

Increased levels of formal qualifications and higher scores on professionalism are often fine, but may be dysfunctional when they lead to a discrepancy between expectations of work in line with formal merits and a reality lagging behind. The emptiness of the grandiosity may be concealed, but is often exposed by close-up studies, such as the one mentioned above.

Personnel specialists—moving into the sun with the arrival of 'knowledge society'?

Of course, nurses are not unique in their pursuit of status upgrading. Personnel officers (or human resources management (HRM) specialists as they are often called nowadays) are another group that has made ambitious efforts to collectively reinforce their position.

This is an interesting occupation in many ways. Upgrading to the HRM designation is a typical example of grandiosity, changing the label in a seemingly impressive way, much more than the workplace reality faced by most personnel specialists. Few groups have adopted ideas about the knowledge economy and the crucial importance of 'competence' for current and future working life to the same extent. Personnel specialists have pursued these concepts energetically, both from a societal viewpoint and in their own interest. If competence aspects are of crucial importance for competitive capability and results, an occupational group that specializes in such matter should have greater impact, it is believed. (In some countries what is referred to as strategic HRM or talent management are also used to leverage popular status.)

As an occupational group, personnel specialists have been trying for many years to emphasize their expertise and thus reinforce their identity and improve their status in companies and other organizations. This has been achieved in a setting in which the personnel function has had, and still has, a rather subordinate status in working life. Personnel specialists often discuss their occupational identity, raising questions such as 'Who are we?' and

'What are we good at?' The problem with trying to convince others about the value of personnel activities and the contribution made is that it has failed to achieve confirmation from others, thus reinforcing the 'need' to enhance identity and status. Here the idea that we are living in a knowledge society or rapidly moving in that direction has been enthusiastically embraced (Berglund, 2002). Personnel specialists and their qualifications are regarded as having crucial importance in this context. HRM was to replace the older concept of 'personnel administration'. New and more worthy tasks were in the offing, rather than administrative routines, emergency actions for solving acute problems, and being a service unit for management at all levels. As personnel strategists, they should follow up and monitor comprehensive and long-term issues, be members of the company's top management group, etc.

These new tasks have been current for some time now and continue to be fashionable. But, in practice, personnel assignments are still dominated by routine tasks and acute emergencies that give rise to a divided and short-term work situation. The ambition of 'decentralizing' (delegating) less qualified and less attractive duties to managers has not been realized to any great extent. Managers continue to 'centralize' (delegate) such functions to their personnel departments. Personnel managers often claim that their role is changing (Berglund, 2002), and that the personnel department has developed from a primarily administrative function to playing a more active part in more wide-ranging and crucial questions. They (try to) regard themselves as consultants and partners in discussions with the CEO and top management. But much of this is wishful thinking and future developments, rather than what actually applies today. One personnel manager puts it like this:

> We are going to become a 'development department' rather than a personnel department—not product development but we must become the development function in the company and push for organizational changes—well, you name it. But we never have time to do this today because we have so many everyday transactions with all these damn papers all over the place. This is what we have to deal with every day, and then we have these acute emergencies over which we have no control. (cited in Berglund, 2002: 94–5)

Another personnel manager describes his working day in the following terms:

> I may say that I seldom manage to do what I would like to do in my role as a personnel manager. [chuckles]. It's like most of us, actually, but I would really like to work strategically, looking to the future, working with the managers more than we do. My working day often involves contacts with colleagues and staff who call me and ask things like: what happens if I am off sick or on leave. They are maybe social problems, alcohol problems, people don't feel OK, and stress and rehabilitation inquiries. There are many questions like this. And then there are a great many things that have to be reported to the authorities, you work on statistics,

reports and contacts with the social insurance offices. There's a great deal of that. (cited in Berglund, 2002: 99)

Hence, notwithstanding the 'knowledge society', many personnel specialists do not feel that they have the position and the influence that they should have as 'competence experts' in 'the knowledge society'. They consider that they are misjudged and questioned. Various strategies to rectify their situation and make their voice heard are being discussed and tested, including studying management and using business-speak so that they do not appear to be woolly headed outsiders, as well as attempting to emphasize their professionalism through standardized education and to require more research on HRM. Efforts of this kind are sometimes regarded as misguided: some people consider that specialist personnel careers are far too narrow. Wider influence calls for an education that extends beyond personnel administration, and broader experience than just personnel assignments. The professional concept is regarded as unfortunate: too narrow and theoretical rather than operationally focused, and more centred on loyalty to the profession than to the organization concerned. Many people in the personnel area see professionalization as an expression of a constricting 'guild' approach rather than as a project for qualifications and rationalization.

Lack of support for personnel specialists' ambition to be regarded as a key group in the knowledge society may be seen in light of the fact that the very concept of the knowledge society provides an idealized picture of today's working life, and perhaps of the immediate future too. Just as personnel specialists find it difficult to rid themselves of routine tasks, other departments in the organization have problems replacing unwanted tasks with more appealing forms of knowledge processes or leadership. In other words, the basic idea of why personnel specialists have suddenly become so important is debatable. While it is true that there are many, and to some extent increasing, knowledge-intensive aspects in working life, these changes are not particularly rapid or radical. And, as already mentioned, it is easy to point to other trends, for example an increasing McDonaldization of working life.

Even if employees' qualifications, abilities, and sense of commitment have become more important (in some organizations), this might mean that managers, consultants, and others work more with human resource issues, and it is not self-evident that personnel specialists will be able to concentrate on 'strategic HR tasks' and delegate all routine, operative, and sometimes conflict-oriented duties to managers. Furthermore, it is not only personnel specialists who claim that they have a key role to play in top management and strategic questions. Procurement, distribution, marketing, communications, and financing are also functions that claim that current trends are making them more important, justifying a place for them in the senior management group. A study of the marketing departments in three companies showed, for example, that these departments were dissatisfied with their role—primarily sales support—and considered that they ought to have a much more strategic function in the company (Chalmers, 2001). The cynical HRM manager may comment: 'welcome to the club'.

Grandiose ambitions of having the most attractive tasks, high status, and considerable influence and making one's mark on the organization often fall flat in an organizational world full of occupational groups with similar ambitions. In the context of this book, the interesting point is not why personnel specialists—in common with many other occupational groups that think they are entitled to a prominent position—fail to achieve their dreams, but why do they have these fantasies, ambitions, and dreams in the first place? Why not be satisfied with key administrative tasks? Why develop fantasies of occupying a strategic top position? On the whole, my answer is that today's society is driving various grandiosity-oriented institutions—spurred on by the media, education, consulting, and so on—and competition between various groups intensifies the level of claims and expectations. Regarding oneself as providing a useful service and building an identity on this basis appears to be narrow-minded, resulting in vain attempts to win a place in the sun, and often disappointment and frustration. Such feelings are shared by many other occupational groups also expecting to get a status boost.

Professionalization, expertise, and dependency

The trend in which increasing numbers of occupational groups are aiming for professionalization is often depicted in terms of rationality and improvement. Qualifications, legitimacy, greater 'competence', establishing a scientific basis for occupational expertise, and research support for practical applications all appear to be beneficial and in the public interest. It is difficult to resist the promise of 'increased professionalization'. Formal, certified knowledge, particularly associated with academic education, has considerable symbolic value and more and more people want to be associated with this. As a result, it is over-exploited, and, as indicated in Chapter 4, this is more often an illusion trick than a real qualification: a lot of education has very modest effects on learning and qualifications. But this is probably why the basic idea of a knowledge society is so popular, in parallel with a more limited interest in knowledge (in a more substantial sense associated with intellectual qualification and advanced understanding). Lofty promises are more attractive than the hard work often required to live up to the image.

In this context, we may note powerful imitation and regimentation tendencies: an increasing number of people want to have higher education, copy what is regarded as a successful 'guild' format associated with higher education, a research link, and specialization. This applies to a much greater extent to occupations associated with the public sector than those in the private sector, where competition and results play a greater part than formal aspects, and where the degree of homogeneity is less. Equality and the minimization of risk as well as equal and (thus) standardized treatment of those to be served are crucial in the public sector, for example in the medical and social services fields.

It may be relevant to point to a number of drawbacks and risks involved in professionalization. Obviously, the point here is not to study the consequences of professionalization in detail, but to demonstrate that it can often be understood in terms of grandiosity and illusion, and that this presents problems since there is a risk that the 'substance'—satisfactory work and problem-solving leading to good results—is often diminished by what often obviously appears to be 'good' at the superficial level. Rhetorical expressions like 'greater professionalization' are (far too) persuasive. One clear example is the irrelevant academization of what are largely practically oriented occupations. Variation, creativity, and adjustment to the situation may also be reduced as a result of the standardization that results from an emphasis on uniformity and a cohesive knowledge base that provides the foundations for a 'profession'. Occupational skills may be weakened when key aspects associated with professionalism are irrelevant for doing the job. As depicted in Chapter 4, there is an ongoing marginalization of other—often more important—skills as opposed to those which an increasingly unreliable higher education sector manages to uphold.

Professionalization means excluding people and locking them out. It is clearly a good thing to exclude people who have no 'real' qualifications, or the wrong qualifications, and professionalization represents some degree of quality assurance. But in many cases, a lack of formal qualifications is not the same as being unable to do a good job. The blocking of access to jobs purely on the grounds of a lack of formal qualifications may prevent the recruitment of good people and thereby weaken results.

Professionalization also sometimes involves closure and tunnel-seeing at the personal identity level. People who adopt a specific occupational identity may often find it difficult to think and act flexibly outside the parameters. As was apparent in the example of the hospital ward, a desire to maintain occupational identity among nurses may involve inhibitions as regards the duties that must be performed. Registered nurses were not happy about getting involved in patients' feeding, transportation, hygiene, and toilet requirements. This is quite reasonable, but leads to problems when job tasks and formal qualifications are at odds with each other. At a more general level, many problems cannot be handled very well on the basis of the existing professional competencies, and the professional staff may then show that they are unwilling or incapable of attempting something new, crossing occupational frontiers, or admitting that practical measures are sometimes better than professional assistance. One motivating factor may sometimes be maintaining or reinforcing one's occupational identity, but this involves a deadlock, and a client's needs are subordinated to the ambition of protecting a professional identity. Status concerns here also matters.

The locking-in of people who have wound up in a particular occupation is a special problem in the professionalization context. The fundamental idea is a long, specialized training that provides a basis for qualification and excludes others. But it also means that you are not qualified for other occupations and may find it difficult to switch to something else—apart from some simple, routine job. If you build walls to keep others out in order to monopolize a sector of the labour market, this also makes it difficult to move on yourself. This monopolization and the qualifications required are based on a prolonged period of training which is narrowly focused on the activities concerned. Starting out with something new calls for major efforts and sacrifices. In the case of demanding and, in many places, moderately successful jobs such as policing, social work, or teaching, it might be better to have greater mobility and flexibility—people who get tired of their occupation or do not fit in should do something else. But the 'professionality' ideal hinders this: a focused and standardized education tailored to a specific occupation means limited attractiveness on the labour market for other kinds of jobs.

Summary

The common factor in the examples from the health care and personnel (HRM) areas addressed in this chapter is an ambition to advance positions towards high status and attractive and qualified duties and to confirm a positive occupational identity. Avoiding less attractive and less prestigious tasks by allocating them to others is another aspect of this process. What is viewed as 'dirty work' is often an object of delegation (McMurray, 2011). This is obvious with occupations such as nurses, but also HRM people are often eager to 'delegate' unwanted tasks to managers, e.g., dealing with difficult subordinates and some routine work.

With increased interest in grandiosity, it is becoming more and more important for an increasing number of occupations and workers to avoid tasks that are not in line with the raised expectations of qualifications and high status. At the same time, it is difficult to bypass all the less glamorous, routine, boring, heavy, and dirty tasks. The more groups succeed in boosting themselves, the more difficult it becomes for them to avoid such tasks. It then becomes important for other occupations to be lagging behind. Occupations thus become involved in more or less obvious zero-sum games about high status and avoiding unsatisfying work tasks. Generally, these tasks may not be performed so well, since work morale in the context of 'non-glamorous' work may fall and other workers may also want to avoid tasks not in line with their expectations and their boosted self-image. Police officers with an academic degree may not want to take care of drunken people who have urinated on themselves in the street or perform routine alcohol testing of car drivers in large quantities, for example. Sick people in hospitals may get less help with their body functions if most of the staff believe strongly in a knowledge society and status upgrading and feel it is not their job to help patients get to the toilet, etc.

Various discourses—presented and fostered by occupational associations, researchers, writers of popular books, and others—support occupational position-advancement projects and, based on such arguments and the perspective of the various occupational groups, higher status and greater influence are considered to be a good idea and in the best interests of the organization and society as a whole. What is good for individuals and their occupational group is also deemed to be good for their employers and society as a whole. So we are often told.

We can also see a discrepancy between beautiful ideals and everyday practice in various attempts by occupational groups to improve their position by means of professionalization. Many occupations are in the process of being academized and professionalized. The prospect of higher status, better working conditions, and benefits for society is presented. Naturally, all professionalization projects probably have more or less serious ambitions to achieve something positive, not just for the occupational group concerned but also for others, and qualifications are often part of this. At the same time, this wealth of professional enhancement aspects also involves many illusion tricks that tend to signal an attractive image rather than saying anything about the occupational group's qualities and ability to achieve good results. In many cases, academization, ethical guidelines, and qualifications may be regarded as window dressing. Such arrangements are becoming increasingly important for more and more occupations. It is a question of making things look good from the outside, with the help of pseudo-structures and labelling, and disassociating them from what people actually do.

We may note increasingly intense competition among occupational groups as professionalization projects become more popular. Attempts by one group (guild) to achieve status, influence, and a monopoly in a certain type of work collide with similar projects and aims held by other groups. Various groups must latch on to status-enhancing efforts if they are not to be left behind, and so professionalization becomes a zero-sum game. If one group appears more professional, others will look less so. More and more resources will be spent on position-improving by more and more occupations, but the net (or average) effect for the occupations involved will be zero.

The extent to which employers and clients win or lose no doubt varies considerably. Of course, sometimes professionalization may mean improvements of qualifications and lead to better performances. Sometimes increased status markers make occupational skills less relevant for work. Struggle for status can also be costly and lead to waste of resources. Probably, the interests of clients and society as a whole suffer as a result of a 'guild' approach, non-discriminatory, heavy emphasis on formal qualifications, and seemingly impressive but vocationally irrelevant education, reduced mobility, and lack of competition. But, as Perrow (1978) notes, the official objectives in much of the public sector—which is where enthusiasm and support for professionalization is most widespread—are not what primarily governs activities.

The other side of the higher status coin is that it is also a *status-reducing project*—for some other group. Sometimes this is quite tangible; for example, if registered nurses improve their status, this clearly affects doctors and assistant nurses, although the effects on others may be more diffuse in other cases. It may certainly appear to be desirable to raise the status of a number of groups—ranging from teachers to assistant nurses, from policemen to cleaners, and skilled craftsmen and factory workers. Of course, the existing status hierarchies are not the result of some natural law. But, as the example of the registered and assistant nurses shows, cooperation between various occupational groups is often a delicate matter. And the social limits of status enhancement can hardly be avoided. Not everyone can have high status and great influence. Zero-sum games apply in this area. Competition for a place in the sun increases when an increasing number of occupational groups conduct grandiosity projects—and are exposed to them.

Success is achieved at the expense of someone else.

9

Leadership—a driving force or empty talk?

However, if, as we have seen, more education, training, and professionalization is not always the ideal way to improve society and its institutions, maybe leadership can do the trick and achieve fine results? And maybe this is the answer to the frustrations experienced by many groups and individuals? Perhaps good leadership can lead to a better working life and results that will satisfy shareholders and tax payers? This is what is claimed, on a broad front today—perhaps somewhat too widely.

Leadership can be seen as a way of boosting the status and position of managers. Going from mere managers to becoming leaders parallels the efforts many occupations undergo to become more professional. 'Leadershipization' and professionalization can therefore be seen as parallel phenomena, triggering and reinforcing each other. The status boosting of groups of employees makes managers extra eager to add a new impressive quality to what they do.

Recent decades have witnessed an enormous expansion of interest in 'leadership'. Contemporary discussion and books about managerial leadership certainly cover a broad terrain, and there are no limits to what leadership is supposed to accomplish in terms of improving the feelings, thinking, values, ethics, change-mindedness, and the satisfaction and performance of followers (subordinates). The leader has become one of the dominant heroes of our time—even a mythical figure. When faced with major crises or even mediocre performances, cries for superior leadership are heard. All kinds of institutions, from firms to schools and universities to churches, are supposed to benefit greatly from more and better leadership. Whatever the problem, leadership has become the solution, and it is a standard recipe for success. Much of this interest in leadership revolves around change and development, and the ability of leaders to get people involved in and committed to opportunities beyond their everyday realities. Employees may be bored, tired, or alienated at work, but effective leadership is expected to address such problems. Followers are thought to be inspired and influenced by leaders, thus overcoming uncertainty, narrow mindedness, and low motivation. Through the good leadership, the lazy become energetic, the opportunistic are turned into committed organizational members, and those with weak morality will be guided by ethics, or so a lot of the leadership industry promises. Of course there are also more sober and nuanced thoughts in the field as well, but not many, unfortunately.

Most leadership academics and practitioners claim that leadership is, like health, a good thing: 'leadership is vital for healthy organizations' (Western, 2008: 5). It is crucial for the functioning of institutions such as firms, schools, hospitals, welfare agencies, and the police. We are told that 'a leader is responsible for direction, protection, orientation, managing conflict and shaping norms' (Heifetz and Laurie, 1994: 127). This may sound unproblematic and self-evident, but it puts the leader in the role of the big star while everybody else comes through as followers who are directed, protected, helped in terms of avoiding conflict and beholden to the norms shaped by the leader. This view has its problems: perhaps the idea of leaders exerting leadership over followers is overrated?

This chapter discusses the current great popularity of, and faith in leadership, and shows the excesses of dominating views of leadership. It reports some studies encouraging caution about too much enthusiasm. In practice it is not easy to live up to the leadership ideals propagated by the leadership industry.

The leadership craze

In organizations, leaders and leadership are often viewed as key drivers. We normally expect managers to perform leadership activities, although most people realize that there may be informal or shifting forms of leadership. Nowadays, we often evaluate how managers perform as leaders. To be a manager is not so good, but to be a leader is almost always regarded as much better. Leaders are often portrayed as strong, directive, and persuasive, with the ability to get others to follow visions and missions in a voluntary and non-coercive manner, thereby initiating change and motivating subordinates (Barker, 2001). Leaders initiate and communicate ideas and values in a convincing manner, partly by applying their charismatic abilities. The growing literature and research on leadership presents many seemingly impressive and morally uplifting examples of the deeds of the leaders. There is often a heroic lustre in many of these portraits of the charismatic and visionary leader. Successful organizational outcomes, turnarounds, mergers, and acquisitions are routinely attributed to the extraordinary traits, heroic abilities, and skills of the leader.

There is generally a strong ideological undertone (and often overtone) in this context, not only in business or pop-management leadership writings ('management pornography'), but also in academic leadership theory: leaders and leadership are to be celebrated. As Spoelstra and ten Bos (2011: 182) remark: 'leadership scholars generally produce all sorts of beautiful images of leadership'. People easily become enchanted with leadership stories, models, and vocabularies, and fail to think critically.

Leadership with a capital 'L' usually refers to leaders who rely heavily on their personal abilities and often, although not exclusively, conduct their leadership from a position of authority, applying mainly overt although non-coercive strategic and visionary means in order to influence people's feelings and thinking quite directly. Such leadership is strongly related to change and development, and usually referred to as charismatic or transform-ational leadership. Increasingly, people in management are supposed to act as leaders in facilitating change, and indeed the capacity to act in this way is often what is deemed to separate leadership from management (Barker, 1997). Zaleznik (1977) illustrates such a view of the influence of leaders as 'altering moods, evoking images and expectations, and establishing specific desires and objectives... The net result of this influence is to change the way people think about what is desirable, possible and necessary' (71). This cer-tainly sounds appealing and definitions like this mean that people love to associate themselves with the label of 'leadership'—and many academics probably feel that this is more rewarding than being interested in managerial tasks, supervision, or something similar—which are increasingly seen as un-remarkable, perhaps even trivial.

For a couple of decades, the most popular direction, also in academia, has been so-called transformational leadership (TFL). This claims to be capable of transforming followers from instrumental wage-earners into devoted organ-izational citizens. As enthusiasts claim,

> Leaders transform followers. That is, followers are changed from being self-centred individuals to being committed members of a group. (Sashkin, 2004: 175)

This is different from transactional leadership—which is about instrumental aspects of work and negotiations with subordinates, and about rewards and conditions for their contributions. TFL is broadly viewed as superior. It is often seen as being about how leadership accomplishes something really extraordinary. TFL advocates assume that the so-called leader has significant influence on followers' self-confidence, enthusiasm, identification with the group/organization, and voluntary compliance. The leader represents agency, while it is implied that follower agency and social conditions do not matter much. The literature, not only pop-management (business press) but also academic work (cited in this chapter), is full of strong claims about the grandiose accomplishments of TFL people:

> After crafting an image of what the leaders want the organization to achieve, they charismatically communicate their vision to their followers . . . Moreover, transformational leaders connect followers' self-concepts to the organization's mission and vision through idealized influence, inspirational motivation, intellectual stimulation and individualized consideration. (Hartnell and Walumbwa, 2011: 232)

'Wow!' is perhaps the appropriate response when reading about the miracles referred to in the above quotations from Sashkin and Hartnell and Walumbwa. Here we have larger than life characters who are able to accomplish all this. If you like hero mythology this sounds good, but any consideration of the realities of the business world may invoke the feeling that it is perhaps too good. Extensive, in-depth research on the creation of and changing culture indicates that this is difficult to achieve (Alvesson and Sveningsson, 2008; Martin et al., 1985), but TFL authors seldom consider the organizational literature, preferring instead to focus on the dyadic relationship between leaders and followers, thus leaving organizational reality out of the picture, and having little appreciation of the complexities of organizations (Jackall, 1988; Watson, 1994), including the inclination of 'followers' to be active and to resist leadership initiatives and acts (Collinson, 2006; Lundholm, 2011). Organizational changes are supposed to be accomplished mainly by positive means, through influencing rather than coercion. Leadership often refers to voluntary compliance, where people believe in and accept the leader's ideas and messages. Cost-cutting and enforced changes are not a salient part of the picture. Instead, the emphasis is often on new and superior values, adaptation to a changed world in terms of cognitions and mental maps, gathering around an attractive vision, and improved morale and increased commitment. When behaviour, standards, and performance controls are in focus, it is more common to talk about management than leadership, even though no clear distinction between can be made.

Prominent CEOs, entrepreneurs, and key political figures in the mass media are often used to illuminate the importance and nature of such heroic leadership. These people are seldom studied in much depth, so media representations are frequently the dominant factor, and these are often guided by the need to sell a good story and not complicate things too much. These sell-a-good-story motives also dominate many of the popular management books, which are entertaining and easy to read. They often seem persuasive, but may say little about the complications and messiness of what actually has occurred in the cases that have inspired such good stories and are said to be accurately portrayed (Hansen, 1996).

Post-heroic leadership

In contrast to various dominant, heroic approaches to leadership, such as transformational leadership, a relatively recent trend in the literature suggests that leadership might involve more mundane and everyday activities, or little 'l' opportunities. Leadership here is seen as related more to collaborative action, distributed among organizational actors. One idea in this context is to emphasize the relational and process aspects of leadership, and that most people in an organization are involved in the exercise of leadership. This approach to leadership is sometimes framed as post-heroic and seen as a more progressive, participatory, and shared view of leadership (Huey, 1994). By decoupling leadership from heroic connotations, the post-heroic approach is said to encourage more humanistic and democratic workplace relationships. Leadership is, here, linked to ordinary and sometimes perhaps even trivial acts, but may nevertheless be significant for the commitment and engagement of employees. Managers informally walking around and talking to their subordinates are, for example, presumed to have a positive influence on people and the work climate. In many senses, it may be argued that leaders largely spend their time doing what other people in the organization do: they talk, listen, joke around, and chat. But when they do more or less the same thing as other people, it is assumed that this has a different and much more powerful impact. However, it cannot be taken for granted that the small talk of managers is of a higher quality or greater significance than the small talk of peers. Perhaps most subordinates are not impressed by or bothered that much about a chat with their manager. The latter may have an agenda and be good at communication during small talk, but so might others and even a skilled small talker may not be that influential in his or her chats with subordinates.

By framing leadership as a matter of listening and chatting, managers may express signs of social competence, progressiveness, and humanism. This might be seen as the opposite to the grandiose heroism of the dominant views of leadership. Perhaps this is a good example of anti-grandiosity? There are elements of this, but much of the post-heroic talk includes its own small-scale grandiosity.

The post-heroic approach to leadership thus suggests that the seemingly trivial things managers do can also be labelled leadership and are (potentially) of great significance. The message is that leaders matter, that leadership is important, and that meaning, motivation, a sense of direction, and, most important, the confirmation of identity are outcomes of rather mundane activities, but are nonetheless labelled leadership. The very idea that ordinary people respond strongly to, and are dependent on, a person performing 'leadership' is thus reinforced. Rather than acknowledging that everybody can listen, small talk, interact, and be open for discussion, and that all these ordinary acts may not mean that much, the idea is that 'leaders' are extraordinarily vital here, that it is their listening and informal interactions that have a very special meaning and matter significantly for employees. The claims then comply with the following formula: mundane acts conducted by a manager = leadership and lead to all sorts of positive effects on followers (Alvesson and Sveningsson, 2003c). There is an idea that managerial doings function like magic, in contrast with situations when other people are small talking, listening, paying attention, etc. In the leadership framework, the seemingly trivial becomes grandiose in nature and effect. When 'leaders' do more or less what all people do, then it becomes very special and remarkable, at least in the eyes of parts of the leadership industry—and in the eyes of many managers themselves.

Leadership as moral peak performance

It is very common to describe leadership in positive ways. Most versions of heroic and post-heroic leadership emphasize the centrality of the moral virtues of the leader. Leaders are good people, leadership stands on a sound moral ground, and real leadership accomplishes positive results. This is a credo in most leadership talk, both in pop-management and academic literature and in the claims made by many managers themselves. Moral issues are not always clearly espoused in this context, but the undertone is one of positive features scoring high on morality. In many specifications of transformational leadership, we find elements such as the leader having genuine concern for others, being busy empowering and developing potential and having integrity, and being trustworthy, honest, and open (Alvesson, 2011). All this indicates a person who is also morally superior to an average person, who presumably scores much lower in these respects.

Efforts to boost the moral qualities of leadership are common. One example of this is 'Superleadership'. This involves leading followers to lead themselves by means of 'empowerment' and the development of 'self-leadership' skills. The Superleader is a fine person who 'focuses primarily on the empowering roles of helping, encouraging and supporting followers in the development of personal responsibility, individual initiative, self-confidence, self-goal setting, self-problem solving, opportunity thinking, self-leadership, and psychological ownership of their tasks and duties' (Houghton et al., 2003: 133). The Superleader does this by means of a range of orientations and behaviour, all of which echo positive moral ideals such as encouragement of learning from mistakes, avoiding punishment, listening more, talking less, creating independence and interdependence, and avoiding dependence.

Bass and Steidlmeier (1999) also make a case for there being truly good leaders. There are some concerns that charisma may not always be so good, leading to questions of whether transformational leadership is necessarily a blessing (the so-called Hitler problem). These authors confidently claim that authentic transformational leadership is always on the side of the good, it 'must rest on a moral foundation of legitimate values' (184). If not, what may for some be seen as 'leadership' does not deserve this fine label. A similar trick is to define people like Hitler as tyrants, not leaders. One basic difficulty is that this equation between effective leadership and a high moral level displays a naïve view of contemporary working life and business (Alvesson, 2011). Being flexible, adapting pragmatically to the situation, following the market, and doing what your boss and your customers ask can be significant rules for coping with life in many companies. Insistence on integrity, honesty, concern, etc., may earn some respect, but are also likely to be seen as inflexible and negative for corporate profit and, not least, for the ethical person's career (Jackall, 1988). In particular, in the current economy of persuasion, with an emphasis on grandiose claims, illusion acts and arrangements, the prospects for people who insist on integrity, and a high level of morality appear to be risky—for their peace at work and career, and for the organization. A strong moral compass may well be a source of frustration for superiors and customers, and hence a career liability.

Leadership in practice I: not so much of it

Irrespective of exaggerated claims in the literature and by managers in organizations, as well as by large sections of the general public, it is important to ask the question: what does leadership look like in practice? As most studies of leadership take the form of questionnaires or interviews with one party in a manager–subordinate relationship, they typically give a superficial, biased, and unreliable picture of something that is very difficult to grasp and vulnerable to expectations, ideologies, personal convictions, and sympathies or antipathies. Much of the research readily available reproduces cultural scripts or folk theories and outcomes of wishful thinking (i.e., that all good things go hand in hand). It is, for example, common to find that informants believe that good leaders who are appreciated by their followers lead to good organizational results, and studies based on such views may say more about the predominant leadership ideology than leadership practice. Given an ideological bias and superficial methods, much leadership research and—even more so—popular writing on the subject are unreliable, and we do not know as much as might be assumed, despite vast amounts of research and writing about leadership (Alvesson, 2012).

However, like other close-up studies, my own research group's work tries to combine repeated interviews with the manager and subordinates and/or observations and also learn about the organizational context. We also try to avoid strong ideological assumptions about leaders leading followers (e.g., Alvesson and Sveningsson, 2003a, 2012; Lundholm, 2011; Sveningsson and Larsson, 2006). It appears that managers frequently claim to conduct their leadership with capital 'L': working with visions, values, the overall picture, strategic issues, etc. However, it has been found that they are less capable of exercising their espoused leadership ideas in practice. A study of middle and senior managers showed, for example, that while they said they were working with strategic issues, developing cultures, working with visions and values and other seemingly important and impressive things, administrative, operative, and technical issues actually dominated their work (Alvesson and Sveningsson, 2003a, 2003b). Discrepancies between what they espoused and what they practised were common. Many managers are reasonably good at talking leadership in line with pop-management recipes, supported by management education and/or business press, but less so in 'walking the talk'. This is, of course, a good example of grandiosity: impressive representation, questionable substance (i.e., practice and accomplishment), falling short of promises.

An illustrative example is one senior manager, who talked about how work had changed from being operational to strategic. When asked to further explain his leadership as strategic, he ended up talking about a rather directive way of governing:

> There are many different ways of working. I think that as a manager here one has to implement significantly more directive ways of handling of people, that is, that you say to people that you must concentrate on this development for a month. I want you to learn about this. I think that you have to have a much more directive way of handling of people in these operations.

While managers can often regurgitate some textbook and pop-management views of leadership, any deeper sense of the meaning integrated in their practices is less common than one might expect. Carroll and Levy (2008) point to the uncertainty and ambivalence managers express about the meaning of leadership. In their study of managers, leadership was viewed as appealing and desirable, but people were often uncertain of what it means. Their participants realized that while management is not so exciting, it is more robust and easy to grasp and do. The studied managers were 'eager to acquire the leadership mantle but unable to make sense of it in isolation from their partially unwanted management one' (Carroll and Levy, 2008: 93).

Managerial practice is mainly about participating in meetings and performing administrative and operative tasks. Often pressing administrative and technical duties allow little space and time for leadership, apart from event-driven, reactive forms (Holmberg and Tyrstrup, 2010). For most managers, operative questions take the upper hand, and time, energy, and leadership ability with a capital 'L' are rare.

When I was talking to a woman, who had formerly been manager of a communications firm, and who appreciated a lecture I had given—in which I claimed that leadership is not so common—she said that she had had a guilt complex because she had not had time to exercise leadership—she thought this was something that other managers did in the course of their work. As many people like to present an idealized picture of what they are doing—this is also broadly communicated by the business press as well as in education and in talks—clear insights of what people outside one's own domain are doing may often be lacking.

Managers in many companies are caught between two forces: talking about leadership and celebrating their work with visions, values and strategies, and practical constraints and administrative demands, which often take precedence over more transformative or heroic leadership behaviours. As suggested by Sveningsson and Larsson (2006), managers' claims of leadership may occasionally be so inconsistent with actual practice that the idea of being a leader could be regarded as a fantasy product. It refers more to dreams and imagination than with subordinates' and observers' beliefs about what the leader-wannabe manager is doing and accomplishing.

It is clear that heroic conceptions like transformational leadership play roles other than informing leadership practice, for example offering material for identity constructions and legitimation. Such concepts give managerial tasks a glorified aura. They fit nicely into contemporary ideals of grandiosity: portraying the current reality as extraordinary, impressive, and hopeful and disregarding the messiness and imperfections of social practice.

Leadership in practice II: shit happens

In addition to the mentioned difficulties for people trying to exercise leadership—shortage of time, the messiness and event-driven nature of organizations and work, and managers' inability to translate general ideals into specific practice—there is the problem of actually influencing subordinates. While many people may, to a degree, be receptive to leadership efforts, they are often not particularly focused on the manager and not particularly inclined to let themselves be influenced in the very radical ways suggested by, for example, transformational leadership theory. Even if there is some interest in followership (Bligh, 2011), much leadership thinking and leadership writing ignores or marginalizes the subordinate aspect. The views of subordinates are regarded as a function of (effective) leadership—in other words, what the leader does determines the followers' feelings and behaviour. The 'followers' are often considerably more independent, unruly, and variable than this, at least in modern non-authoritarian countries and organizations. They deserve to be taken seriously, including as a 'threat'—or possibly as a corrective—to the impact of the leader's ideas. Many subordinates prefer autonomy and rely on peers for support and help, and are not so interested in managers who hold meetings or tell them how to think and act (Blom and Alvesson, 2011). One may ask how many people in contemporary Western workplaces do really see themselves as followers, to be led by a leader? It is one thing to accept being subordinate to a manager, which may be seen as reasonable or unavoidable, but it is another issue to be prepared to follow a leader transforming one's basic orientations to work and to adapt one's values, meanings, and mindset accordingly. Of course, this happens, but by no means in all cases.

An example illustrating my point is the following event in an industrial company. A young worker was asked to report to the marketing manager who tried to persuade him to say 'business' instead of 'product' when referring to the rock drills produced by the company (from Alvesson and Björkman, 1992). It was part of a corporate effort to make the firm more 'market-oriented', to make people in production recognize that there are customers buying the 'business'/product, and to create a common orientation across the different areas of the company. This attempt to adopt the term 'business' encountered sustained resistance from some employees. According to the shopfloor worker:

Roland [the factory manager] has also been brainwashed with that term. I am convinced that the expression originates from the marketing manager. I have nothing whatever to do with the 'business' rock drill. It is the marketing side which has to do with the business. *There* it is a matter of business, but not *here*. I am not interested in getting closer to the market. I have enough to do as it is. [The marketing manager] tried to impress upon me that it is a matter of businesses, not the product. He tried to find out what kind of person I am. I thought it was a damned thing to do. His job is to deal with the market. He should not come down here and mess with me, that's my own boss's job. Roland also thought it was a bit unpleasant. [He was also there.] You wonder what kind of people they have up there. (cited in Alvesson and Björkman, 1992: 147)

This worker's strong negative reaction can partly be accounted for by reference to his work situation—it is the physical product that he operates on, not a financial transaction. The term 'business' simply does not appear meaningful and relevant. The effort to impose this kind of meaning on his work experience backfired heavily and the result was the opposite of what the marketing manager wanted to accomplish. Instead of a common understanding and greater appreciation of customer and market considerations, the outcomes were the underscoring of differences in a world view, negative perceptions, and distance between marketing and production people. This example illustrates that leadership in the sense of managing meaning and understanding is often difficult in practice.

In an observation of manager–subordinate interactions in a bank, it was clear that subordinates were often not so inclined to accept their managers' ideas and suggestions (Lundholm, 2011), partly because they had good reason not to do so. They frequently argued back, and the interactions ended with the manager partially retreating, as a consequence of the objections or general reluctance of the subordinates. In verbal interactions, it was sometimes not obvious who was supposed to be the leader and who was supposed to follow. Some ingredients of ceremonial or ritual confirmation of the manager's position as an authority ('sham hierarchy') were visible, but not much leadership in line with the leadership literature could be seen.

A case study of a cultural change project in a high tech firm indicated great problems for managers in dealing with values and meanings. Top managers had no real success in inspiring middle level managers to take on initiatives and the latter treated instructions to work with values in workshops with subordinates as 'tick-off-activities' (done, now over to something else) rather than as something that triggered efforts to work with values, understandings, and practices ambitiously, thoughtfully, and on an ongoing basis (Alvesson and Sveningsson, 2008). Visible leadership was preached, but it was difficult to see examples of it. As is not uncommon, persuasive words were in circulation and people broadly were sympathetic to the ideals and values presented, but found them vague and with uncertain relevance for their own practices.

When discussing issues around leadership it is important to recognize that the vast majority of managers are also subordinates and must adapt themselves to their own manager, and overall demands made by the organization and the market. A narrow understanding of managers as leaders inspiring followers neglects the broader organizational context and the many constraints making the great majority of managers—being middle- or low-level managers—more like sergeants than generals. Balancing demands from both above and below is an important and difficult task for many (Wenglén, 2005). And then there's the question: 'Who is actually leading whom?' It may be the case that the leader leads and the others follow. Perhaps there may be a strong manager (or an informal leader) and weak, uncertain, or inexperienced co-workers, particularly in the case of a crisis. Managers and informal leaders have more say than others—almost by definition. But everyone in the workplace is participating and exerting an influence. This often involves a complicated interaction, and it's by no means certain that the manager is the supreme Influencer via Leadership. One study found that managers saw their subordinates (co-workers) as the most significant source of feedback and the relationship as perhaps not so strongly leader-driven, indicating that the influencing process may be almost the opposite of what most leadership researcher and management writers assume (Kairos Futures/Chef, 2006). (If leaders are central and they lead their followers, one may perhaps assume that the manager's superior would be more significant for feedback—a key influencing mechanism—than the subordinates. Whether they really are subordinates in anything but a highly formal sense is also worth considering, even though the managerial prerogative typically produces at least some degree of subordination.)

This is, of course, not to deny the existence of leadership in one form or another, but clear-cut forms do not appear to be particularly common—outside the management literature and in self-descriptions of managers which may include a fair amount of self-serving bias. In our extensive research we find very few, if any, leaders who transform people, guiding them through visions and values and generally performing extraordinary, or even mundane, acts with a specific magic, and who have a considerable impact on followers (Blom and Alvesson, 2011; Lundholm, 2011).

Leadership fuelling fantasies of grandiosity and identity-boosting

Finally, it is important to draw attention to how the leadership discourse tends to paint contemporary society and its organizations in bright colours. There are certainly some leadership theories that are dry and lifeless. Traditional distinctions such as initiating structure and consideration (or tasks versus a relation orientation) are hardly intended to cheer people up, but the dominant approaches in recent decades have much more rhetorically impressive features. Leadership is typically portrayed as totally decoupled from issues of supervision, such as telling people what to do and making sure they have done it to a satisfactory degree, reminding, enforcing, appealing, pointing out formal rules to be followed, reports to be filled in, and other boring or frustrating tasks that must be carried out. These parts of superior–subordinate relationships and organizational reality have little or no place in contemporary leadership texts. Working life, as most people probably know it, does not appear particularly relevant in popular leadership talk and texts. What comes across here is a vibrant, enchanting reality. The leader is inspiring and develops people, a good role model, never nagging or constraining them or getting involved in disputes about subordinates' demands for pay rises, their efforts to avoid boring or stressful tasks, turning up late at work, or taking an afternoon nap in the office.

Leadership discourse provides an ideologically appealing view of contemporary organizations. Whether it distorts reality can be debated, 'reality' is very seldom there to be simply inspected or measured, but leadership discourses generally offer a much improved version of the real world and how it should be handled. The common factor in the work of popular leadership authors appears to be: Why not become enthused by the escapism provided by an abundance of vocabularies and leadership stories rather than being caught up in the imperfections of organizational constraints and demands and managers busy trying to make the organizational machinery work?

We have argued that the reason for the popularity of such authors is that they inform identity-boosting efforts rather than managerial practices and perform a broadly legitimizing function. Various constraints—including the pressure to carry out administration tasks—and inabilities seem to make it difficult for managers to be guided by leadership theories such as transformational leadership, and apply them in practice. Contemporary organizations appear to offer more fertile soil for flexibility, adaptation, and moral comprise than insistence on authenticity and integrity. The strong faith of leadership researchers in the latter as a success factor is rather peculiar, unless one regards leadership as an ideology and as part of a zeitgeist eager to beef up our social reality with terms, prospects, representations, and fantasies that flavour the (hyper-)reality we experience with pleasurable and comforting overtones.

Leadership: illusion acts and zero-sum games

Leadership in a more ambitious sense—the type that transforms followers—is a difficult project whose primary expression is probably leadership training programmes, management best-sellers, and interviews in which people talk (too freely) about what they are doing and display a selective and idealized view of themselves and their doings. Naturally, managers are often of some importance, and sometimes they even have considerable impact, through leadership or in other ways. However, leadership as a central practice and key ingredient in what takes place in working life seems to be overestimated. Ideologically oriented accounts of leadership and a tendency to attribute responsibility for positive or negative outcomes to particular individuals are a contributory factor in this context (Meindl, 1995). Sometimes, woolly headed references to coaching, visions, etc., can be a pretext for not implementing supervision, in the sense of making sure that the important work is carried out—a function that is not fully in line with beautiful ideas about leadership, making people grow through coaching or 'Superleadership'. In many cases, myths about modern management in the form of leadership constitute a splendid illusion trick.

But what does all this have to do with my third central theme in this book—the zero-sum game? Does leadership fit in here? No doubt, it is possible to imagine a seamless leadership in which all parties can benefit—managers, employees, and customers/clients—and sometimes this happens. However, there is also a zero-sum aspect in all this talk about leadership and strong tendencies for leadership to increasingly colonize working life. This is because the greater the focus on leadership and the more there is of it, the greater the emphasis on 'non-leaders' as followers and subordinates rather than autonomous employees capable of operating independently. With the celebration of leadership and leaders, professionals become decreasingly self-sufficient and increasingly subordinated. If the leader has a decisive impact on ideas, thinking, and values, there is less scope for others to have any influence. If modern leadership advances the position of managers, those who do not hold such a position must fall into line to some extent and reduce the independence of their thoughts and actions. If leadership is to take on more and more important tasks and functions—everything from responsibility for achieving results and ensuring that everything is done in the right way (in formal terms) to making sure that people do not work too hard (and burn themselves out), that they apply gender equality, act ethically, are environmentally aware, develop their 'competence', are included in a vision, are 'growing' as individuals, and can talk about their problems, to name a few—all indicates that other people's responsibility for this is limited. Maybe individuals persuaded by leadership ideas refrain from influencing other people in a positive direction since this is a task for leadership? If chatting with the manager is leadership and therefore much more important for subordinates than chatting with colleagues, the value of colleagues' chat is reduced.

The emphasis on the ideological position of leadership entails a weakening of everyone who cannot claim to exercise leadership or be a leader. In this sense, the increasingly grandiose claims of leadership also involve zero-sum games. I do not wish to overemphasize this aspect—leadership can also play its part in the development and qualification of people, and plus-sum games do often occur. But, in an age when leadership is celebrated and those associated with the grandiose label are upgraded, there are grounds for reminding ourselves that authority, status, and influence for one group cannot be strengthened without reducing opportunities for others in these respects.

Some incapacitation of 'non-leaders' is implicit in an idealized picture of leadership. And this emphasis on the exceptional significance of leadership also implies that pay and other privileges for leaders—often connected with persons holding managerial positions—should be much greater than that for other people. This distinction between significant leaders and insignificant others is not always explicit, but it is, of course, an implicit factor in a focus on leaders and leadership. This (over)emphasis on the importance of leadership legitimates and is the driving force behind significant and increasing differences between key leaders and others.

Summary

A major and expanding leadership industry gives a somewhat beautified picture of relations and practices referred to as leadership. When leadership is referred to, words and terms with positive overtones dominate. This applies to almost all the best-selling leadership books, depicting a streamlined, harmonious world in which everything fits together. Transformational, authentic, Superleadership, and other impressive forms of leadership are espoused, creating considerable enthusiasm among managers and other leader-wannabes. But this is much more visible in educational seminars, interviews, questionnaire responses, and ceremonial speeches than in specific managerial practice. Here the complexities of organizational life, time constraints, obnoxious and not so leader-focused subordinates—often seeing themselves as professionals and/or skilled workers rather than followers—and the inability of most managers to translate grandiose notions of leadership into practice lead to a reality that falls short of delivering what the leadership industry promises and what leader-wannabes hope for and perhaps expect to do. All this turns much leadership discourse into an example of illusion tricks rather than something that mirrors or guides managerial practice. The leadership ideal is espoused rather than enacted.

In this chapter, as in Chapters 6–8, I have discussed certain aspects of current working life and organizational circumstances, based on my three fundamental viewpoints: grandiosity, illusion tricks, and zero-sum games. This is, of course, a vast area. I have chosen to concentrate on four broad but nonetheless manageable themes:

- Claims for rapid and pleasing shifts from bureaucracy and mass production to more organic, network-based, knowledge-oriented organizational structures.

- Institutional processes that generate coordination of structures and shop-window arrangements that present a positive external image.

- Professional claims aiming to advance the interests of occupational groups that want to achieve higher status and influence.

- Claims to conduct leadership with a capital 'L', with the aim of establishing involvement and common values in a harmonious world.

My idea is that these four themes encapsulate typical attempts to create a grandiose and idealized organizational and working life environment and, in particular, the problems involved in such projects. The dynamic world which has been depicted calls for greater 'competence', professionalization, strategic orientation, and leadership, but does not always live up to such fine ideals.

A large number of commercial and other entities are in the process of producing rhetorically attractive ideal identities. Managers and other representatives in various fields of operations learn that they are—or should be—'strategists' (cf. Knights and Morgan, 1991) and 'leaders'. This involves convincing others—and maybe yourself—that what you are doing is important and fine. As far as possible, everything that is everyday and trivial is to be converted into something that is more impressive. In a world permeated by grandiosity in which leadership, corporate development, competence issues, strategies, coaching, corporate culture, visions, entrepreneurship, innovations, etc., are stressed, realism is not necessarily the best solution. Instead, there are a multitude of illusion tricks—a whole world of activities, arrangements, and labels that look good, but have little bearing on the core operations. Managers try to give the impression, via small talk with employees and other mundane acts, that they are leading them and therefore significantly influencing their thoughts, values, feelings, and actions.

Without denying the importance, possibilities, or existence of leadership in a substantial sense—clear actions indicating an overall direction that people comply with—leadership is more typically found in the media, courses, and management talk than in practical applications. Although managers are leaders in ceremonial contexts, such as chairing meetings and giving speeches, deeper studies indicate that they are more often administrators, managers, or, in particular, meeting participants. But references to leadership permeate modern working life and organizations. And this is a key label for various fragile managerial identity projects.

Everyone aims for a place in the sun, and a generous soul may feel that they no doubt deserve it. Ideas about the marvellous knowledge society, mass-professionalization, and being a leader open up this prospect. But it is difficult to see how what is promised and what is demanded can be delivered. The idea that people are generally highly qualified in a knowledge society is at odds with the significance and centrality of leadership. The space for grandiosity is limited and when too many occupations, groups, and functions claim it, they tend to undermine each other's success. Occupations aspire to become professionals while managers are eager to see and present themselves as leaders. When one group moves symbolically closer to grandiosity the others tend to respond. If individuals in an ordinary occupation claim to be professionals, being merely a manager does not sound so impressive. The seductive idea of being a 'leader' is here the solution. Credible grandiosity is not without its limits in organizations and working life, as there are tensions between leaders calling for followers and professionals demanding autonomy. If everyone is struggling for the place where the sun is shining, many people will find that they have wound up in someone else's shadow.

10

The triumph of imagology—a paradise for tricksters?

Having addressed the three broad subject matters in Chapters 2–9—consumption, higher education, and working life/organizations—it is now time to connect these themes, to formulate additional ideas, insights, and results based on synthesis as well as summaries and conclusions. This will be done here and in the final chapter.

Below I address further the significance of expectations and desire. The title of Kovel's (1981) by now somewhat dated book, *The Age of Desire*, is probably much more appropriate today than 30 years ago. Recession and financial crises in some countries can temporarily attenuate the rampage of desire for some groups—with reduction in the material standard of living, concerns other than desire may require attention—but this does not disturb the overall picture of the dominant inclinations in post-affluent society.

I start the chapter by addressing post-affluence and, in particular, how expectations of the good consumption and working life are gradually raised so that reality, when salient, may be a source of frustration and disappointment more often than delivering what it should. People in ads are always happier and more beautiful than the consumers trying to imitate them. The institution recruiting students seldom undersells the quality of its teaching, or the employment that may follow for graduates. The job title increasingly promises something better than the actual job tasks. Having pointed at the misfortunes of reality—or 'shit happens'—I then make some specific links between education, work, and consumption, before moving quickly over to how statistics often support competitions in showing the right numbers to make things appear to be good, sometimes at the expense of the quality of the phenomena the numbers are supposed to say something about. I also address how the understanding of grandiosity and illusion tricks can be further developed through the use of Kundera's concept imagology. Here, in particular, I draw upon Kundera's claim that people occupied by imagology constitute a broad, diverse, but rapidly expanding set of occupations leading the road to grandiosity.

Untrammelled expectations

We are living in an age of continuously raised expectations—for higher consumption, improved material welfare, better opportunities for higher education and well-paid, qualified, and high status jobs, and greater happiness. We also expect producers, employers, experts, and the state to fulfil these expectations. We are permeated by very strong encouragement of our desires, which are continually spurred on by various entities making exaggerated promises about what is positive and desirable:

> This craving has hence become a goal in itself in recent decades. There is an insatiable desire to lay claim, and anyone who is not driven by this force is depicted as someone who has lost faith in the possibility that life can be better, someone who has given up. (Östberg and Kaijser, 2010: 30)

This escalation of expectations is particularly noticeable in key areas. Grandiose features are often the symbolic response to substantial inability. When you cannot deliver, there is a greater emphasis on pseudo-structures and other illusion tricks. This applies, for example, to higher education and modern working life, which acquire a golden shimmer when the radiance of the knowledge society is reflected by higher education institutions, occupational groups, and workplaces. This also applies to consumption, some of which involves items that are not essential but which put a gilt edge on life and have become an increasingly dominant feature of (post-)affluent societies.

The institutions that incite grandiosity fan the flames on a large scale. 'Be something great!', the higher education institutions promise. 'I am a leader, not a manager' is the cry in the organizational world. 'Don't sell comfortable shoes to women. Promise beautiful feet!' is what the marketers propose. These untrammelled expectations often have an ambiguous, or even contradictory, relationship with a world that is far from perfect. It is true that this picture is imbued with representations and virtual images—the prevalence of illusion tricks (e.g., pseudo-actions, pseudo-events, pseudo-structures) makes 'reality' rather ambiguous, and not always particularly important. Boorstin and the postmodernists like Baudrillard (1983) have a point when they claim that reality has lost ground to hyper-reality, i.e., simulations and illusions. But, of course, reality has not yet lost this battle (that is to say aspects of reality that do not involve engineered representations and that are not geared to giving the right impression).

Concrete circumstances ('reality') often have a corrective effect when they do not correspond to what the promoters of expectations and grandiose representations promise. This gives rise to problems, both for those who have swallowed the prospects presented and for those who must answer for exaggerated expectations. Let me give an example. This concerns a personnel manager who recruited a number of young graduates and subsequently pointed to a violent collusion between high expectations and a working life that by no means lived up to such aspirations:

> 'People who have recently graduated have such high expectations and demands. They expect to be working with strategies and to be general manager before they are 30. "Where is my career plan? I want to have a personal coach", they say.'

Her voice quivered with irritation and indignation, and she continued:

> 'They have preconceived ideas about how things should be, how a company should function. And they complain about how bad things are in a workplace compared with how they should be. . . . People are sometimes unwilling to perform routine duties such as copying or even putting things in an Excel file. They want to concentrate on PowerPoint presentations and work with top management groups.'

Accounts like this are sometimes explained away by saying that the older generation does not understand young people but, in the case in point, the personnel manager was only in her early thirties. Without wishing to over-generalize, I think it says quite a lot about expectations and pretensions.

These expectations are no doubt partly derived from the media, but higher education also has a major share of the blame for this situation. Universities and other higher education institutions too often convey seductive pictures of what students may expect when they complete their studies, including intellectual stimulating, creative, and high status jobs. (I am relying here on my own subject, business administration, which is the major topic of study at many universities, and in many ways typifies higher education today.) Higher education institutions must attract students, ensure they stick to their programmes, and make them as satisfied as possible. This is defined as 'quality'. The students, of course, are particularly satisfied with a presentation of the more exciting, high status, and influential aspects of working life. This means an emphasis on senior management and strategic and consultancy operations, getting the students to identify with such activities and believe that this is what they will be dealing with when they complete their fine education. This attractive picture has some of the features of a confidence trick, but it also means that the programme appears to be successful in the outside world. Then, of course, a personnel manager, such as the person cited above, may ask what you are actually studying in the higher education world; however, working life provides no tangible, broad, and systematic feedback and correction. And naturally the picture is hardly uniform—there is considerable heterogeneity in individual careers, particularly in the long run. Gradually, for some individuals the experiences of the imperfect reality may become weaker: some probably gradually find qualified jobs; others probably adjust and develop a more realistic view with moderate expectations.

Fanning exaggerated expectations is a common formula for success in education, marketing, the mass media, politics, and public relations. Expectations have a life of their own, despite often weak foundations in reality. In the above example, the people hired by the personnel manager directed their frustrations at the company in question and its shortcomings, rather than at higher education and the media. The young graduates thought the company was at fault: 'Why doesn't it function better?' was apparently a common reaction. This is how untrammelled expectations can continue without being unduly affected by an inadequate world. It's real life that's at fault; it lags far behind in terms of grandiosity.

One key question is: Why is reality often unsuccessful in making expectations more realistic? Why do people like the upset ex-students become so perplexed by the imperfections of the company that employed them? Advocating, in all seriousness, the ideal that half the population should have higher education and regarding this as justified in modern working life (without any real counter-arguments) illustrates the untrammelled dissemination of expectations and the centrality of grandiosity. A mass culture and the expansion of mass-media representation have weakened the distinction between appearances and (other aspects of) reality, partly because representations and illusion tricks are key elements of contemporary reality.[1] And the mass media help to create a world in which the boundaries between illusion and reality are obliterated. The screen media are, of course, crucial in this context, but science also contributes to the revival of infantile tendencies and primitive fantasies as a result of an endless series of technological wonders, miraculous medicines, genetic manipulations, electronic devices, etc. Lasch (1984) cites Chasseguet-Smirgel, a psychoanalyst who considers that one of the key factors underlying the current change in mental disturbances in a narcissistic direction is scientific advances that may be regarded as confirm-

---

[1] Some would argue that contemporary society is pluralistic and fragmented and the one-dimensional mass culture is gone. Of course, there are enormous social variations as well as homogenous forces creating effects. I am content here to mention that the latter certainly are in operation: just imagine Hollywood, CNN, global fashions in consumption and management, McDonald's, IKEA, Starbucks, domination of a few global management consultancy and accounting firms, Facebook, much talk about knowledge, innovation and education, etc. For a strong case in favour of the standardization theses, see Ritzer (2007).

ation of a possible reunification between the ego and the ideal ego, that is to say the re-establishment of infantile fantasies about omnipotence. According to Lasch, 'Contemporary culture conveys the impression that everything is possible. Like modern art, modern communications, and the production of consumer goods, it has "cleared the air of objects", thus allowing fantasies to flourish unchecked by a sense of the intractability of the material world around us' (1984: 193).

As I have tried to indicate, the education sector, in particular, and many areas of working life are committed to communicating ideas in which an increasing proportion of individuals and institutional arrangements live up to grandiose fantasies about success. Knowledge and education are liberated from the need for specific insights, abilities, and deeper forms of understanding. Work is increasingly a question of applying idealized pictures of what you do and are able to achieve—manipulation of symbols rather than concrete production. This results in a situation in which reality is rather ambiguous and unstable, but also raises question marks about our ability to assess reality and our own position in the world. In a world permeated by fluid realities, infiltrated by pseudo-events, it is hardly surprising that reality also appears to be an uncertain factor. In this situation, it is often difficult for the individual to make sensible choices. In particular, there is a strong tendency to be continually uncertain and never really satisfied with what you have achieved. A feeling of missed opportunities—a better career, more rapid promotion, a more attractive employer, and a better and higher standard of consumption— is exacerbated. There are undoubtedly choices—perhaps too many—but people have the impression that they cannot live up to them in a satisfactory manner. This frustration originates in continually being on the lookout for opportunities, and feeling that other people may be more successful than you are. The keynotes of this are opportunism, a search for promising employment, willingness to change jobs, and a focus on image and CVs (Sennett, 1998). You have a feeling of inadequacy in working life, and this shows up in consumption as well as in many other areas: 'one never has enough and what one has is never good enough' (Gabriel, 2005: 24).

Some links—education, work, and consumption

In previous chapters, I have discussed three main areas for this study under separate headings—with the exception of the serious and increasing gap between education and working life—the over-education problem. In this section, I will also look at some links. These are partly a matter of the general change of social regulation in which traditional forms of control are partly being replaced by frameworks and techniques for consumer regulation that are also used in other spheres, involving 'the substitution of "seduction" for "repression", advertising for authority, and the endless creation of needs ("fashion") for norm imposition' (du Gay, 2000: 70). Contemporary forms of control of the consumer thus become paradigmatic, to some extent, for the exercise of social control in a broader sense. Employees and students also become socialized into responding through a consumer-appealing logic, although this is, of course, mixed with other regulatory practices associated with the specific social field. Education drives expectations and demands for a better working life, that is to say a working life that complies with the 'knowledge economy' label, and where people primarily use their brains in creative jobs in which they can develop. Consequently major areas of working life find it difficult to live up to these requirements for a knowledge-intensive working life, in a substantial sense. Knowledge companies are certainly important, and an increasingly significant factor in the economy, but this only applies to certain aspects of working life. References to a knowledge economy, the professionalization of occupations, and leadership ideas about visions, etc., are making the rounds without having any significant bearing on what actually happens in most workplaces, in daily work or core activities (to the extent that there really are material aspects of any great importance).

At the same time, ideas about what goes on in organizations—particularly in the private sector—that are cultivated in the media, management books, and public appearances by consultants and business leaders also present an idealized picture of working life and its requirements. This is lapped up in education, and achieves a good interaction between these two spheres—at the very least the symbolic and rhetorical level. On a more practical level, there is more friction and divergence between practice and grandiose images, as illustrated by the example of the frustrated personnel manager cited earlier in this chapter.

Generally speaking, an increasingly protracted formal education is an important factor when competing for jobs. Thus, the admission ticket for a given job is becoming more expensive as more years of schooling are required; however, this does not guarantee that the actual job or employment conditions are any better. Although a formal education often ends up being ignored in the job context, the expansion of education and exaggerated expectations of a knowledge-intensive working life are shown to go hand in hand.

Consumption ideas and the hedonism encouraged and reinforced also have a considerable impact in the education world. Intellectual effort is losing ground to a customer orientation in which students are expected to tick the 'very satisfied' box in the questionnaires that are supposed to measure quality. Learning ideals are subordinated to the goal of student satisfaction. The key requirement is to do something meaningful, have fun, and only make a modest effort. Demanding subjects, such as the natural sciences and some languages, are losing students, while less demanding areas (such as business, media and communication, and perhaps social science as a whole) are highly popular.

Consumption, at the right level, is also a crucial aspect of establishing beneficial networks that the more prominent universities can facilitate, and since the actual studies and intellectual learning represents a declining proportion of the student's time, the 'social capital' is becoming an increasingly important aspect. 'Economic, social, cultural and even physical capital may influence whether students gain access to the most desirable networks when in college. Having the "right" clothes, body, hygiene practices, hair style, accent, cell phone and musical taste can matter' (Stevens et al., 2008: 133).

Consumption and working life are, of course, closely linked in several respects, and perhaps these links are becoming increasingly important. Clothes and other forms of consumption are defined as expressions of identity and clues to the individual's 'inner life'. Hence success in working life is becoming more and more a question of impression management, including mastery of consumption's symbolism. We can see here a long-term trend from a situation in which clothing and other consumption were formerly an expression of social position and social conventions, to being regarded as personality attributes (Sennett, 1977), and hence as clues to characteristics and potential.

A growing proportion of jobs are more about 'aesthetic and emotional work' (Thompson et al., 2001) than about occupational skills and technical and intellectual qualifications. It is important to be properly dressed for such work, look good, and behave in a pleasant manner. Sometimes, it should not be noticeable that work is involved—the staff should give the impression that they think this is fun or that customers are friends. The customer must feel in a good mood. This applies, for example, to large areas of the service sector— 'pink labour'—in which agreeable interactions with customers are a crucial feature. Entertainment centres, hotels, restaurants, airline flights, and shopping are examples of areas in which the appearance, clothing, and style of the staff are of decisive importance. No great occupational knowledge is required for the most part. (However, this does not mean that the job does not provide considerable scope for quick thinking, social skills, a practical approach, etc. When I claim that many occupations do not call for higher education-type knowledge, I am not implying that such jobs do not require certain skills.)

The third theme, somewhat different from the two discussed earlier, involves how consumption can compensate for a person who is stuck in a frustrating job. Consumption as therapy is a well-known phenomenon. 'It was tough reaching the age of 30, and therefore I spoilt myself with a new hair style/fur coat/larger car' can be an alternative to going to a psychologist or getting involved in some active project (or quite simply accepting minor frustrations). The escalation of expectations and aspirations in a working world that often fails to provide a delightful existence and confirmation to the right extent can spur on the 'need' to handle narcissistic problems via consumption and restore damaged self-esteem.

In particular, this third theme—but also the other two—can be illustrated by the following story. A person with an administrative job in a global management consultancy firm noted the following in a study I conducted with business firms:

> Something that is extremely good about this organization is that on the few occasions that I have bought something at NK [an upmarket department store], it just takes five minutes before I meet someone else who works here. This has happened every time. And this has a lot to do with how you perceive yourself. And I think this conception of yourself is absolutely essential because otherwise people couldn't really do the job they do. But at the same time, I think that many people working here are sufficiently flexible so that they can tone themselves down in their contacts with clients. But I see them here in the office, and I think there's an enormous difference between how they are when they are here. Some people actually sit in some cubby hole [when they are with a client] and do their programming, and they are not allowed to move around, and should be seen and noticed as little as possible. They are not allowed to push themselves on the clients. But when they get back to the office, they get quite a different reception. Then it's a case of 'Now the consultant is back!'

People who write about management consultancy and refer to it publicly often stress that the key aspects are advice to senior management on crucial matters and organizational changes. In reality, things are not always so attractive. Some employees, particularly the younger ones, say they feel like 'corporate slaves' (Kärreman and Alvesson, 2009). Much of the job might involve working with operative questions—qualified but routine tasks of a technical nature in rather low-profile circumstances. But this is seldom stated. People who stress their consultant status with clients may find that they get nowhere. They sometimes encounter suspicion of outsiders coming in as experts, and also irritation about their high pay. Work results are often ambiguous. In other words, it is sometimes difficult to get confirmation (Alvesson, 2004). A well-known company name and the accompanying status and identity support, combined with high pay and consumption opportunities, can compensate for this frustration. Perhaps the management consultant's identity finds its clearest expression in the consultancy atmosphere in the office, references to the work and successful career when talking to friends, distributing business cards (on which the employees are entitled to be called managers after a couple of years), rather than in the job itself. Hence the consultant makes his or her clearest impression of being a 'consultant' mainly as a company representative, rather than at the operative level.

More generally, consumption can work like a compensatory mechanism for imperfections and frustrations at work. Through the outcome—rather than the content—of work, one can develop, maintain, and repair a sense of success and satisfaction and exhibit signs of professional standing. The notion of consumer freedom becomes highly attractive in the light of all the constraints at work—particularly strict for those very eager to maximize this consumer 'freedom'. The latter is often bought by accepting considerable lack of freedom in work and career (long work weeks, strong subordination to bosses and clients important for one's career, etc.).

The beauty of statistics ideal

Needless to say, statistics can be used for all purposes and some of it has been mobilized in this book for my own sceptical project. Often quantitative material that is publicly communicated is used to produce favourable impressions. High and increasing numbers indicate success. The key role played by readily communicated statistics is a major problem. Numbers often conceal quality issues, something seldom explained or analysed in mass media or political contexts. Statistics should look good, and should preferably be used to support impressive journalistic statements.

Here is an example. According the Swedish National Agency for Higher Education, 'the proportion of students from working-class homes has increased from 17 per cent to 23 per cent of all new students over the past 10 years. In terms of numbers this means a virtual doubling of the number of students with a working-class background' (DN, Debate, 1 June 2004). 'Biased social recruitment has declined radically', it is proclaimed triumphantly.

This sounds good—and that was the whole point. The problem is that working-class children often wind up in programmes that do not comply with the traditional picture of a university education, and their future careers—as pre-school teachers, recreation instructors, or nurses—are low paid, with low status and little influence. In teaching education, nowadays a part of the university system, 'a growing proportion of the students come from backgrounds with no study tradition, and the extent to which the upper social layer is deserting teacher-training programmes is astounding', according to Lindblad, a professor of education (interviewed in *Skolvärlden*, 9 November 2005). Standards of knowledge and intellectual ability among student teachers are deteriorating. In this context, the term higher education proletariat, mentioned in Chapter 4, is illuminative.

The proportion of the population with higher education in Sweden and other countries is often compared. Statistics that indicate lower figures for the home country are normally regarded as a sign that things are not good. It is seldom feasible to complicate the discussion by pointing out that the 'higher education' label says nothing about the standard of learning and knowledge, and that only a small proportion of those registered as having completed full-time higher education have actually done so—most of them study on a part-time basis. In other words, more or less appealing statistics for the volume and expansion of higher education live a life of their own, disconnected from the education and qualifications that can be achieved. In an it-should-look-good world, what counts are those things that can be easily packaged and presented to a world that seldom provides any special insight into the questions involved. Ironically, this is legitimized by a reference to the 'knowledge society'.

A few years ago, I was invited to lecture at a Canadian university. During my stay, I saw in a newspaper that a leading politician in the education field was dissatisfied that only 20 per cent of the Canadian population had a university education, while the corresponding figure in the United States was 28 per cent. Maybe we are not sufficiently ambitious, this politician said, but he also hoped that Canada would surpass the United States within 10 years (*The Globe and Mail*, 25 March 2004). A few hours later, I was listening to my hosts, who were teachers of management. They were complaining how bad many of their students were and considered that the whole idea of education was doubtful as far as the majority of students were concerned. Only 10 per cent or so would ever get a managerial position that corresponded to the contents of their education, they thought. One teacher also talked about relatives and acquaintances working for Air Canada who were doing jobs totally unrelated to their degrees, for example a stewardess with a degree in law. Her brother had a degree in history, but was actually lifting baggage on and off the conveyor belt at the airport.

Certainly, 20 per cent does not look so good if your neighbour achieves 28 per cent, but if we leave the magical world of illusion tricks and focus instead on the limited amount of learning achieved and the inadequacies of working life, then perhaps the figure of 28 per cent is bad news, particularly in view of the stiff criticism of higher education voiced in the United States and the rapid increase in the number of students awarded a formal university degree. Naturally, one may claim that education and knowledge have a value in themselves and may enhance life outside the world of work. Higher education should not be simply adapted to the requirements and opportunities offered in working life. But it is not self-evident that it is a good idea to increase the number of students who study for several years if they subsequently only get unqualified, routine jobs.

Economic growth is another crucial area for statistical enhancement. Falling behind other countries in terms of GDP or growth rate is a source of anxiety and criticism—it is regarded as a clear sign of failure, and even crisis. If every effort is made to achieve rapid growth and you fail or under-perform, this is clearly not a success story. On the other hand, this kind of Olympic Games thinking is slightly absurd in this context. There is no doubt that most countries in the world need economic growth, and that there are some reasons why rich countries should also have this aim to some extent, but must they come in first or give priority to this goal? Since it is hard to understand that further dramatic increases in consumption offer any great dividends in the form of satisfaction associated with material objects, and even more difficult to see how this might increase human happiness, success in the growth Olympics appears to be an expression of mindless priorities rather than the winner being the world's leading nation. This is particularly relevant in view of the enormous environmental problems that growth creates.

The problem with figures for economic growth or the number of university graduates is that they do not say much about the values with which they are habitually associated: greater satisfaction in terms of material welfare or greater knowledge. But, as I have tried to show in this book, there are no such self-evident correlations of this nature—quantitative expansion is not necessarily accompanied by qualitative enhancement, but may even result in emasculated education with lower value in the labour market, or poor consumption decisions (the destruction of value as a result of the premature discarding of products, and failure to use them due to lack of time), not to mention greater 'consumer stress'. What we can see here is a quantitative increase and a qualitative decay. But quality does not count in the education and growth Olympics—the logic of simplicity is what matters here. The decisive factor is 'how many' and 'how much'.

The prevalence of grandiosity mechanisms

As suggested in Chapter 1, our era is characterized by an enormous accumulation of institutions and mechanisms that encourage grandiosity. It might even be claimed that our existence is being colonized by these to an ever-increasing extent. A strange mixture of fantasy and desire seems to typify our age. This trend is spurred on by politicians, mass media, schools, higher education, and other forms of training and education, consultants, therapists, and similar experts in 'human improvement', marketers, lifestyle experts, career coaches, and occupational groups with professional aspirations—all selling a vision of a potentially more appealing life, if only we buy their products or employ their services. An ever-increasing range of opportunities is offered by education, therapy, travel, clothes, housing, and all kinds of products. Underlying this are technological developments, but above all the difficulties faced by companies in selling their products—and this means that consumption propaganda, in a broad sense, has become one of the main features of economic operations. Since the 1950s, the crucial problem has not been production, but rather the need or desire to purchase the particular product or service that the company in question is selling. Other institutions—politics and education, for example—have imitated and been drawn into this powerful logic. Politicians and educators increasingly seem to be marketers. Ambitious promises and the cultivation and exploitation of people's narcissistic fantasies about a grandiose future—via education, careers, and/or consumption—have taken over. In addition, we have the expansion of higher education, accompanied by an army of graduates, many of whom are forced to create a demand for their services by inventing more or less off-beat needs.

Kundera (1992) suggests the term *imagology* to summarize a whole range of related phenomena: advertising agencies, statesmen's communication consultants, product and fashion designers, hairdressers, and people in show business who dictate the norms for beauty and guidelines for external appearance. All these people have 'look-good' jobs. We can point to the compositional change in the economy and labour force from brown, blue, and white collar to pink and gold collar labour. The former worked with farming, industry and craft, and bureaucracy, respectively, while the latter are in routine, respectively, more well-paid jobs within what broadly can be seen as the beauty business(es).

We may, however, extend this concept somewhat, as Kundera does when expanding his arguments, and regard imagologists as the entire range of people who are involved in pseudo-events and the production and communication of ideal images and illusion tricks. Many participants in the public debate—pop-management authors, journalists, some consultants, many academics, some business leaders, marketers, politicians, and many representatives of occupational groups—can be classified as imagologists. And actually, one might say that a high proportion of elitist and high-status activities are of an imagologist nature. People orchestrate illusion tricks and communicate grandiose ideas in this context.[2] An imagologist may be identified if he or she

---

[2] Many top managers and consultants engaging in strategy work can also be seen as imagologists. At one university, top management was heavily engaged in work with renewing the overall research strategy. An inquiry of the 40 faculty members that had received the largest research grants during recent years revealed that none of them knew or cared about the university's strategy.

contributes the most 'bullshit' in a cliché competition. More than 40 years ago, Boorstin noted that this type of activity was widespread and was regarded as highly respectable in the United States, which was a pioneer in this area.

> The making of the illusions which flood our experience has become the business of America, some of its most honest, most necessary and most respectable business. I am thinking not only of advertising, public relations and political rhetoric, but of all the activities which purport to inform, comfort, improve, educate and elevate us: the work of our best journalists, our most enterprising book publishers, our most energetic manufacturers and merchandisers, our most successful entertainers, our best guides to world travel, and our most influential leaders in foreign relations. Our every effort to satisfy our extravagant expectations simply makes them more extravagant and makes our illusions more attractive. The story of the making of our illusions—'the news behind the news'—has become the most appealing news of the world. (Boorstin, 1961: 5)

Heroes undoubtedly exist, and artistic, humanitarian, and scientific performances do, too. Progress is also being made in the political and economic spheres. Here we can find examples of genuine greatness—in contrast with what I denote as grandiosity where the achievement or the quality is weak and does not match the representation. But such examples of genuine greatness are rare. For the most part we must stick to the adage: 'No knight is a hero for his page', which is to say that almost no idealized image stands up fully to closer inspection. These days, we could rewrite this as: 'Who can achieve grandiosity without pseudo-events and spin doctors?' Since major achievements are rare and often of a long-term nature, evaluation is complex, and they must give way in the face of grandiose projects, supported by Potemkin scenery, pseudo-events, and statistical cosmetic surgery so as to attain the desired effect.

In some sense, we may say that imagology has taken over and that we have all adopted this logic to some extent. There is undoubtedly a surplus of imagologists. Arguably the imagology business is one of the largest business areas—and certainly the most rapidly expanding. But most of us, even those who are not primarily or obviously imagologists, perform this function on a part-time basis—more or less consciously and voluntarily. Not all see themselves as heavily engaged in personal branding, but putting a lot of energy into the aesthetics and format of PowerPoint presentations, business cards, dress, homepages, CV boosting, Facebook activities, etc., is quite common; that is, for many the display of the right image is important. It is difficult to resist the tendency to load aspirations and activities with grandiose features and adapt to illusion tricks unless you want to wind up in some hopeless backwater. If other people are trying to give themselves and their institution a golden shimmer, you may well appear to be dry-as-dust.

In 1976, Herbert Simon was awarded the Nobel Prize in economics for his studies of decision-making in organizations. Simon's principal work, which was published in 1945, was entitled *Administrative Behaviour*. Thirty years later, a book with this title would have hardly reached the market and, if it had, its influence would have been minimal. The title simply does not sound sufficiently attractive and grandiose. In the 1980s, I participated in a seminar which was largely on the same theme. The presenter, a serious and acknowledged academic, had written a book entitled *Strategic Decision Making*. Like Simon's book, this was aimed at an academic group in which precise definitions and restrained rhetoric were to be expected. In other words, this was not a question of management pornography where the author tends to 'lay it on thick'. When asked whether the term 'strategic' had some special meaning, the presenter honestly replied 'no', it just meant that major decisions were involved. The title was simply a means of attracting interest. And we cannot exclude the possibility that a book entitled *Big Decision Making* would have had fewer readers. I suspect that a contemporary author would have been reluctant to admit that 'strategic' did not have any meaning in relation to the contents of the book, and perhaps he or she would not even have understood the question. Of course, something that is important is something strategic. My impression is that this term is used habitually nowadays to refer to something important. 'Strategic importance' is a common expression, but people might just as well say 'important-important'. But that would not sound so good, although in a world weighed down by substance, this should be a strong selling point, making the subject even more important. Hence the emphasis on 'strategic'.[3]

This is something that Herbert Simon did not have to worry about very much. He could happily use the modest *Administrative Behaviour* title for his book, but it nonetheless attracted attention and gave him a Nobel Prize. Even though the term 'administration' had a less negative meaning in 1945 than today, it hardly qualified as grandiosity. This makes me feel a little nostalgic.

Part-time imagology pops up all the time. The somewhat unscrupulous labelling of everything as 'scientific' (for example, nursing science, fashion science, sports science, leisure science, and military science) has already been mentioned. In the course of an air flight I recently heard the cabin personnel informing passengers about the airline's 'service concept', which simply involved information about what could be purchased. No real concept was presented, but OK, 'service concept' doesn't sound too bad. Sometimes we are part-time imagologists against our better judgement. Fairclough (1993), a

---

[3] One often reads that hotels are 'strategically located', typically suggesting that they are nearby to tourist attractions.

British language researcher, found himself unwillingly faced with a temporary imagologist situation. When reading through his own application for a university promotion, he noted that his account reporting fairly neutral information only constituted part of the text, which was permeated by implications of a more grandiose nature in which meaningless but beautiful wordings appeared constantly, for example references to his 'influential leadership'. He did not believe much of this and some of the claims he made were contrary to his principles but, in retrospect, he noted how the spirit of the age and the norms for selling oneself had drawn him in. This orientation makes it more difficult for performing credibly compared to people fully buying into leadership and other glamorous ideas and claims.

In Chapter 4, with some assistance from Naomi Klein, I referred to an advertising executive, back in the 1920s, who warned his employees against visiting the factories that made the products that were to be given a rosy hue in advertisements.

Insights about the real circumstances would complicate matters and run counter to the right mentality. Managing the escalating decoupling between substantiality and the production of illusion tricks is easier if the latter are believed in. It becomes more difficult to work with illusion tricks if you have deep knowledge of what representations are supposed to refer to. The smooth, non-critical participation in illusion tricks and grandiose images plays an important part in the success of people who want to make a career in dominant institutions. Knowledge leads to doubt, scepticism, and hesitation. In the example above, Fairclough was frustrated and ashamed of the way he expressed himself—as a critical language scholar—and he was far too familiar with the contexts involved to smoothly sell himself as a person worthy of promotion through reference to his 'leadership'. The knowledge society, the new economy, higher education for all, the diversity of rainbow cultures, leadership as the key to corporate salvation, brand as value-builders, greater professionalization—they all sound attractive and delightful, and a mastery of standard rhetoric would appear to be a useful accomplishment for elite groups in society. A high degree of buy-in is a key resource here.

But the use of high-sounding phrases brings on the cynics—or else the inability of a muddled everyday world to deliver what the imagologists promise. I do not actually believe that most people are particularly cynical or selfish, even though the imagology business focuses on shameless promotion of the self-interest of the organization, occupational group, or political party concerned. Integrity is hardly a virtue held high in regard among imagologists. But division of labour and the emphasis on nice-sounding messages means some protection from contact with reality, facilitating adaption to work with grandiosity and illusion tricks without too much moral friction. Ignorance is sometimes bliss and works as lubrication for the enthusiastic carrying-out of pseudo-reality activities. Some lack of knowledge about working life in a 'knowledge society' probably facilitates enthusiastic propagation of this concept (more about this in the next chapter).

A cosmetic statistical presentation would appear to be less convincing if the person who cites it has doubts about what the numbers are actually saying. The Canadian education politician who pushed for higher percentages of a youth cohort in higher education might risk stumbling over his text if he listened to and reflected on the picture presented by the university teachers I spoke to—students with little interest or ability, labour market prospects with no resemblance to the contents of the education programme, and students responding to the question 'Why have you studied this subject?' with answers such as 'To earn as much money as possible' or 'I don't know'.

A journalist who wrote a series of articles on problems in higher education reported the following impression after an interview with a minister of education in a European country:

> [I] felt that he appeared to be relatively out of touch and extremely unwilling to discuss any problems whatsoever as regards the existence of problems in the country's higher education. Rather scary. (Personal communication)

Knowing too much of what really goes on then may make it difficult to express positive messages. Ignorance may in this sense increase credibility. The will to not know may be a strong contemporary motive, facilitating many individuals' careers (and ease of mind). Maybe this captures a picture of an imagologist in our age, and something of a successful formula for other imagologists, when a lack of deeper knowledge is quite simply an asset.

Summary

In this chapter, I have underscored the overall triumph of imagology and further illustrated the role of making things more and more remarkable and impressive. I have also pulled together some of the themes addressed in the previous chapters on consumption, higher education and working life, and organizations, and shown how they influence and reinforce each other. Expanded higher education drives notions of the knowledge society and the latter provides a rationale for the expansion. Zero-sum games, meaning that those with higher credentials tend to do better than others, add credibility. Consumerist orientations and modes used to regulate consumers function to some extent as a general paradigm for controlling people and making institutions like universities and workplaces function. Seductive language and images, the raising of expectations, and the appeal to ideals as providing immediate satisfaction and happiness without too much effort and sacrifice are basic ingredients of contemporary culture, permeating not only the consumption sphere but in many ways other sectors of society.

Escalating expectations are contingent on making promises and appeals to desire, with an emphasis on seduction that characterizes companies, professions, schools, and other institutions. In this sense we are witnessing the triumph of imagologists, a variety of occupations trading in grandiosity and illusion tricks. Apart from full-time professionals, many people become part-time imagologists. Delivery of the goods by means of representations, for example, in CVs, titles, certifications, and improved statistics, do something to make people feel satisfied and give the impression of positive developments. But, as emphasized, the illusion element is often very strong, giving rise to various problems. Even if reality—in itself seldom concrete and open to a variety of impressions and interpretations—tends to produce all kinds of problems for the more appealing world of illusions, the latter's persistence and 'reality-penetrating' capacity often protect people from too much painful contact with the more brutal aspects of reality. In the final chapter, I will investigate these factors more systematically.

11

The costs of grandiosity

A critical reader might well ask at this point: What is the real problem? Why is this author so worried about what most people may see as positive things in life: increased consumption, more education, promises about a working life with stronger ingredients of milk and honey? The sceptical reader may want to challenge this text and pose the following critical questions:

- Why not just accept what people want? Isn't it natural that people want more—and more? Of course, people are looking for more things and want to increase their consumption. And if they want to pay the earth for things with certain brand names, maybe they will be more satisfied with that?

- So what if there is a lot of higher education, even if all the graduates do not get jobs? It's good to keep people occupied and out of the way in a cheap and agreeable manner. And don't the students always learn something in all these courses? They don't perhaps become smarter, but education is better than unemployment.

- Why not permit new and finer titles and labels? Why not make elites and others happy through using knowledge vocabulary to describe society, economy, and the population? And if all these university colleges, polytechnics, and other higher education institutions want to call themselves universities, why not be generous? The division between universities and university colleges only favours those snobs who work or study at the former places. And the liberal awarding of titles like 'marketing director' and 'professor' might give the people concerned a nice title on their business cards and make them happier, perhaps more motivated, and make their spouses proud.

- Who cares about 'real' equality of opportunity for women and minorities if there are fine equal opportunity policies and programmes? If we have a sufficient number of women who are promoted to fill their quotas on the board and in higher education, we will have sufficient equality to comply with the statistics, and then everyone can be happy. Equality enthusiasts will be pleased by the policy formulations and statistics, and those with other views might be happy to note that nothing much is happening in substantial terms. So we don't need to concern ourselves with this. Why disturb the picture, as has been done in this book?

If an increasing proportion of individuals and activities involve imagology, could this contribute to a more amusing and attractive world? Perhaps this is not as 'real' as older versions of reality, in the sense of being part of everyday life, but there are other advantages. The world filled with grandiosity and illusion tricks is aesthetically appealing and much more attractive than a boring reality. It is much more interesting to listen to managers that call themselves leaders and who say that they are dealing with visions, strategies, coaching, and other impressive things, than hearing that they spend their time in meetings discussing technical issues and are engaged in making the bureaucratic system work. Who would not prefer to listen to accounts of leadership that enable people to grow, rather than task management assignments that involve ensuring that personnel also perform boring but useful tasks? Why not listen to the typically fantastically fine values in the CEO's PowerPoint presentation rather than be forced to think about the values that actually rule in the company? Such values are probably ambiguous, hard to define, and rarely edifying—in contrast with an aesthetically, pedagogic, and encouraging PowerPoint version. 'Customer orientation', 'sustainable development', 'emphasis on human resources', and 'technological excellence' all sound good, very good in fact. Normal people would prefer to consign gender equality to a question of stopping middle-aged men from voting in other middle-aged men on company boards rather than being confronted with their own gender-stereotyped choice of occupation and family life. And who would not prefer to have a cold beer served by a beverage manager with a Master's degree rather than by someone with no special training? Reality is often messy and not much fun, while pseudo-events and other illusion tricks radiate elegance and a sense of security and clarity. Maybe it is not so important that they are superficial and misleading.

> The pseudo-events which flood our consciousness are neither true nor false in the old familiar senses. The very same advances which have made them possible have also made the images—however planned, contrived, or distorted—more vivid, more attractive, more impressive, and more persuasive than reality itself. (Boorstin, 1961: 36)

Hence, the value of pseudo-events and pseudo-structures (i.e., the level of the illusion) cannot be denied. Reality has encountered stiff opposition from imagology, which clearly has strong assistance in the development of hyper-reality, especially as a result of a bombardment of digital images from various local and international sources that undermine an anchoring in time, place, and social contexts, and modify a sense of a stable ego (Kincheloe and McLaren, 2000: 284). However, I don't fully accept Kundera's and Baudrillard's (and to some extent also Boorstin's) theses that imagology and hyper-reality have disposed of reality. Postmodernism has made its point, and social constructionism offers good insights, but perhaps they should not be pursued too far—they easily lend themselves to theoretical legitimation of grandiosity and illusion tricks. Slogans such as 'everything is a construction' and 'there is no relationship between a representation and "reality"' (should there be such a thing) leaves the space open for imagologists. As Jackall (1988) notes, the principles of postmodernists and PR experts are much the same. The strengths of imagology—but not its omnipotence—must be recognized and, to the extent that the market is right, its position is well deserved. In other respects, it may be said to fit in with a market society perfectly since it provides simple, unambiguous, comfortable, aesthetic, cheap, and well-packaged 'solutions'.

In the preceding chapters, I have stubbornly stuck to a somewhat old-fashioned concept of reality as a possible contrast to the grandiose ideas and illusion tricks contributed by pseudo-events and imagologists.[1] So far, no victory in the battle between reality and pseudo-reality has been declared in many areas, and a grey reality is still giving as good as it gets, with the stubbornness of an inebriate, and this is particularly clear in an era of financial crises, recession, and a potential environmental disaster. In a 'knowledge society', at least in the United States, there are still three chaps heating frozen meat at McDonalds and similar workplaces for every IT expert (Sweet and Meiksins, 2008). In this sense, I have asserted a killjoy's perspective, and possibly made life a little bitter for some—to the extent that my message is accepted and taken seriously.

---

[1] I use different terms that have considerable overlap: illusion, imagologists, pseudo-reality, window-dressing, representations. They point at different nuances and evoke somewhat different associations, but on the whole refer to those aspects of social life that are more or less systematically targeted for creating a positive, one-sided view of phenomena, in the service of status enhancement, reassurance, and identity boosting. For those not able to associate themselves with such beautiful, self-serving representation, elements of worry, envy, and inferiority may be more salient experiences. All this is part of zero-sum games. Of the above-mentioned overlapping concepts, illusion points more to the overall effect of arrangements being there or used for influencing impressions and experiences, functioning as a surrogate for practices, or 'substance' and backing up grandiosity. Window-dressing refers to something similar but points at specific activities and arrangements more directly intended to have an effect on the impressions of primarily external audiences. Imagologists indicate a (wide) group of occupations making reality more aesthetic. Pseudo-reality indicates the world of mass media and/or communicative forms claiming to mirror or at least refer to a reality out there, while representations is a wider and more neutral concept also incorporating the less problematic aspects of efforts to describe or indicate phenomena.

Four major problems associated with the triumph of emptiness

In addition to the fundamental problem of a sense of reality, persistently interfering with the formal structures and verbal representations displaying illusions and leading to ambiguities and frictions, one could point to four specific problems caused by the growth of grandiosity and its support in the form of a wealth of illusion phenomena, that is to say pseudo-events, pseudo-structures, language boosting, and so on. The first problem is that real costs are involved (in the form of qualitative losses), the second is a depletion of trust and confidence (a valuable asset for any well-functioning society or institution), the third is reinforcement of the narcissism (that is supposed to be satisfied by grandiosity), and the fourth is the production of what may be termed 'functional stupidity'.

Increased quantity leads to decreased quality

In the areas discussed in this book, there is a tendency that greater quantity sooner or later means deterioration in quality. It might be rather defeatist and mechanical to claim that this is an automatic effect, and I would not like to propose that it is a universal law. But nonetheless, growth often occurs at the expense of quality. This has already been discussed in connection with higher education, so I will turn to other areas instead. This tendency is particularly clear in the consumption field where material welfare has doubled over the past 30–40 years, but not even the most fanatical consumption enthusiast would consider that there has been any proportional, tangible increase in satisfaction and well-being. In fact it appears to rather be the case that such factors are constant or have even declined somewhat (Pugno, 2009).[2] As demonstrated in Chapter 4, greater consumption volumes are often accompanied by less urgent desires, more socially positional products, a poorer basis for consumption decisions, less maintenance, stress/lack of time in connection with utilization, greater materialism, and a focus on the regulation of identity and self-esteem in terms of consumption.

In working life too, greater quantity in the ways addressed here may lead to deterioration in quality. As we have seen in Chapter 7, as organizations imitate superficial structures that signal success, they become more like

---

[2] Of course, one should be very careful in taking any indication of such an ambiguous phenomenon as 'happiness' (or subjective well-being or satisfaction) too seriously. Nevertheless, we should (sceptically) consider these studies as giving some input for consideration since issues around economic growth and consumption are far too important to be neglected. Adopting radical constructionist views is likely to lead to political marginalization rather than contributing to important discussions in society.

window-dressing and less effective for operations. Imitations often mean weak support and commitment at the local level, and tend to be pale copies of the original. Consequently, insistence on the adoption of some recipe for success often does not work in terms of improved practices or 'substantive' results. Too many change projects are staged—this gives an impression of dynamism and strong leadership, but these projects often make little progress and have no positive outcome.

As a result of the 'professionalization' of an increasing number of occupational areas, science, education, and monopolization of work areas are cited to promote the status, identity, and privileges of the occupational group concerned, rather than the advantages for clients. Academization is no doubt appropriate in some occupational groups with a clear academic core (for example, physicians) for whom a long education is essential and where it is important to achieve homogeneity and minimize risk. But the value of academization is more doubtful in the case of other groups trying to imitate such professional status and authority—at both the substantial and symbolic level. The more occupational groups that follow the same recipe for success, e.g., are academized, the weaker the overtones of the academic world, in terms of both qualitative internal mobilization and the impression made on outsiders. The number of talented and interested candidates for university jobs in the population is limited and the quality of university teachers is probably declining as a result of greater amounts of teachers. With the mass university and accompanied increased bureaucracy some of the charm and attractiveness of a university career is possibly also lost, further reducing the number of talented people willing to start and continue a research and teaching career in academia.

A limited group of professionals with high status can be afforded a high degree of autonomy. With the experience of being an exclusive elite, often a feeling of extra duty and commitment follows. However, with mass professionalization involving many occupations claiming and, to one degree or another, being certified, the traditional privileges of 'real' professions such as a high degree of autonomy and status become eroded. More and more fine-grained regulations and constraints follow, fuelling and fuelled by an experience of being a wage earner or white collar worker that does not stand out in terms of importance and contributions. The average professional of today is subordinated to bureaucracy and managerialism. This is partly an effect of quantitative expansion, partly of an increasingly weak or questionable base for claims of professionalism for many of the occupations concerned.

Leadership as a distinct source of influence is being weakened by the extension of 'leadership' to cover 'everything', including handling emotions, aesthetic aspects, fun at work, 'visions', and other poorly defined aspects, to become a speciality in which 'leaders' should exercise their authority. Leadership tends to have vague yet comprehensive meanings, but to the extent this concept is taken seriously (as it often is), there are marked asymmetries between 'the leader' and 'followers', in which exaggerated expectations are attributed to the former. The launching of leadership as the answer to all kinds of problems in all possible areas—from universities to churches and from companies to trade unions—involves a dilution in terms of ideas and practice. As I have demonstrated in Chapter 9, this often winds up in empty talk and vain hopes, a pale attempt to copy the leadership referred to in the mass media or presented in management courses (Alvesson and Sveningsson, 2003a).

A roughly similar logic applies to high-status branded goods. The whole point is their distinction value—the greater the quantitative dissemination, the less qualitative value they have. It is implicit in the concept of the social limits to growth that expansion does not lead to a corresponding improvement in general satisfaction.

The more we have of something, the greater the tendency for a qualitative deterioration per unit. The price of retention or augmentation of a position is rising. This price may involve longer education, a higher degree of professionalization (more links to science, higher barriers against other occupations, more of a guild approach, more ceremonies surrounding ethical guidelines, etc.), or a higher price for consumer goods that are socially attractive. If the individual is neither prepared nor able to pay this higher price, there are no opportunities for an attractive job with influence and status, a cottage with a lake view, or a mobile telephone that will make friends and acquaintances jealous.

One might, in this context, launch the concept of an inevitable leakage. Efforts and sacrifices only achieve a modest outcome, due to the wastage that occurs as a result of the deterioration in quality associated with increased volumes. This is hardly surprising in the positional goods area, where the attempts of others to enhance their position counteract the effects of one's own efforts. But also time constraints easily means that quality is lost as part of the 'quantity problem'. That is to say, limited time means poor choice and imitation means that with the expansion of copying efforts the model's original qualities are lost in transition, and positive elements of the imitation tend to be marginalized when copying is multiplied, leading to copies of copies rather than originality being a common framework and a driver for new arrangements.[3]

[3] A similar problem is indicated by Ritzer (2007) referring to how the rationalizing processes in the world based on mass production and use of standards led to a loss of distinctiveness, uniqueness, quality, and richness. He sees globalization as the increased domination of social forms 'centrally conceived, controlled, and comparatively devoid of distinctive content' (36), ranging from restaurant chains like Burger King, coffee houses such as Starbucks, to luxury goods such as Gucci bags.

Erosion of trust

Another problem is the responses to grandiosity and illusion tricks when they are perceived as inconsistent with 'substantive matters', that is, practices and accomplishments. In contrast with my discussion in the previous section, I now address the way in which symbolism and trust are undermined by the imagologists' progress, rather than the decline of quantitative benefits. There is, of course, also a qualitative aspect in this, but the focus is not on how bad or good it is, but rather on the faith given to an institution.

Illusion tricks are about trying to maintain or enhance legitimacy and/or grandiosity, but frequent use of these tricks leads to an uncertain or even negative outcome. Naturally, this covers a wide range—where it-must-look-good practices may result in anything from greatly impressing the environment, an acceptable degree of legitimacy, to an embarrassing belly flop. I have stressed the probability (or risk or opportunity, depending how you look at it) of (a) illusion tricks that not only exist in parallel with a certain practice, but also lead to a deterioration in such practices, and (b) institutions that might deserve a better fate but deplete their confidence capital. This may lead to a reduction of faith, not only following from bad practice and performance, but from the perceived discrepancy between this and the promise indicated by grandiosity claims and illusion tricks. Even a reasonably good practice falls short of promises of 'excellence' or 'world class'.

There are many examples of the way in which investments in a better image result in a loss of quality of substance. Resources put into the impressive surface mean fewer resources for practices other than window-dressing. The backing of knowledge society claims through expansion of mass education, accompanied by weaker and less interested students and loss of status of universities in many countries, leads to palliatives in the form of professorship titles for a high proportion of the teaching staff (at least in the UK and many other countries). The value of the title and trust in the carrier as a credible knowledge authority tends to be weakened or lost. Over the past couple of decades, the Swedish armed forces, like in many other countries, have been cutting back resources and the number of trained national service personnel, but have not reduced the higher ranking levels. There are close to a thousand lieutenant colonels but the so-called 'emergency defense force' can, in the best case, mobilize only one real battalion (SDS, 27 September 2004). In other words, the armed forces are well equipped with titles, but not with combat personnel. They also made an effort to equipping themselves further on the image front by trying to change their 'all communications' logo (at a cost of millions of Swedish kronor—and at the price of making a number of employees even more frustrated, partly because they liked the old logo, partly because they thought this was a misuse of resources; SDS, 14 November

2005). Here we find an institution weak on substance but seemingly compensating through rather lofty efforts to boost the level of the illusion, leading to lowered trust among those being informed about the development.

A somewhat different example is the accreditations and honours awarded to institutions assessed to meet certain quality criteria. In principle, the quality criteria should imply that a recipient has certain characteristics. This is the prototype for 'non-grandiosity' where the representation reflects the subject matter it is supposed to communicate something about. But in many cases this alignment is difficult to accomplish and the representation becomes decoupled from what it is supposed to say something about. Bell et al. (2002) report that the UK award Investor in People became an objective in itself for organizations to strive for, rather than a confirmation of the high-quality HR practices that the award was supposed to encourage and honour. In many organizations oriented to exhibit arrangements and practices that could be ticked off in assessments, the chase for the badge became the ultimate goal and good HR practices became subordinated to manipulations to match the criteria. This has led to less than optimal processes, including problems concentrating on doing good work also in ways that were not anticipated to be part of the tick-off-the-boxes procedure for assessment. For some personnel, this meant a distrust in the award and a feeling of embarrassment for having received it.

Cynicism may also result from observing how institutions of which one is not a member boost their image. In the *Guardian* supplement on 'Superbrands' (3 March 2012), one will find Warwick Business School listed alongside Coca-Cola, FedEx, and Pampers as 'one of the strongest consumer and business brands in the country':

> Warwick business school is the UK's top provider of finance and business research and education, and has the ambition and capability to become Europe's leading university-based business school. Its mission is to publish leading-edge research that has real impact; to produce world-class business leaders; and to provide a lifelong return on investment for students, alumni and partners

This may sound impressive, but it also triggers responses like this one from a leading UK academic: 'No wonder there is a problem retaining staff!'

This is a response from a researcher whose institute is being turned into a 'centre of excellence':

> I work with my colleague effectively and produce research work everyday with or without this center. I think that the center concept just another form of new structure that 'they' usually bring in and keep changing all the time. I assume that there must be new sets of evaluations and regulations that we need to do. I doubt about it. I don't think we will gain anything more than a new bunch of paper work and reports. (Personal communication)

Let me broaden this discussion somewhat by raising another example of re-labelling. In the private sector, the increased emphasis on persuading people to buy everything that is produced, involving a disassociation from 'needs' or (lasting) satisfaction, has been accompanied by references to 'value creation'. And, certainly, making your neighbour jealous may have some value. But in this case the loss of substance is disguised by the rhetoric. One might also regard value-creating activities as a question of value destruction, in the form of a source of frustration, or a new fashion as a definition of what is no longer fashionable, etc. One might at least claim that the jargon in this area trivializes the concept of value in this area.

The certification of individuals on more or less dubious grounds is an increasingly widespread trend. For example, in a recent email I received, I noted that the sender was not only a professor and dean of a higher education institution, but is also a Certified Chartered Marketer and Chartered Business Consultant. The question is whether this person is better as a marketer than as a consultant (as he is not only 'chartered' but also 'certified chartered' in the former capacity) and whether he requires higher remuneration in the marketer capacity.

Certification is popular. In Sweden, charity collectors on the street can receive certification after a two-day course, and many people can acquire the label of certified coach, after they have paid a fee and participated in some kind of brief training program. Gradually, the idea of certification moves from a possible indicator of some acquired and guaranteed quality to a pure illusion trick—saying nothing about any underlying competence.

I have previously mentioned the promotion of a number of polytechnics and other higher education institutions to university status, the scientification of all kinds of areas, and the establishment of university courses in areas such as surfing, Robin Hood, Harry Potter, fashion science, and beverage management.

The overall trend involves a kind of symbolic pollution (Alvesson and Berg, 1992), potentially weakening faith and commitment to society and its institutions. In some cases distrust may not be bad: established institutions often need to be critically scrutinized and perhaps be treated less respectfully, but on the whole the criticality and scepticism that can be triggered by symbolic pollution are problematic. The attractive features can be perceived as simple trickery and bluffs—at least to the extent that the outside world sees through them. If and when this happens, there is an undermining of the capital of trust built up by the institutions concerned. Pseudo-reality backfires and there is a risk that reality becomes seen as besmirched rather than beautified. The grandiose—like simple confidence tricks—falls flat and become vulgar and a lie—many people guess that there is something nasty hiding behind the attractive scenery. Higher education, universities, and various titles appear to be desirable because they are associated with various qualities. Traditionally, universities have established their reputations on the basis of studies at a high intellectual level and with a high research content. In countries where the title of (full) 'professor' is applied to a superior position, rather than to all teachers, this gives a picture of highly qualified, experienced researchers. But this is now often old hat, with the exception of a few elite universities. The downward pressure on quality is a powerful factor. A 'race to the bottom' is a typical sign of grandiosity—although image and the quality it is expected to refer to are disconnected, the disconnect is concealed.

The symbolic capital associated with university status is still considered worth fighting for, however, even—and maybe especially—by higher education institutions not characterized by a high proportion of competent researchers and teaching at an advanced level. In the event of success in this respect, if such efforts weaken this symbolic capital and undermine the university concept, this is not primarily a problem for the institution concerned. Even if the fine club of which you become a member loses status as a result of your membership, this is nonetheless a status boost for yourself.

A 'good' society is based on confidence. But when actors increasingly exploit symbolic resources they are not only destroying the positive qualities of the object of exploitation, they are also contributing to the creation of a suspicious and cynical society. This is perhaps one of the most serious consequences of the massive enhancement of grandiosity, illusion tricks, and the qualitative undermining of societal institutions.

All this is not to say that it was 'better before'. My point here is not to make a strict comparison. At earlier times institutions like the church, the university, the military, and the government may often have been addressed with uncritical and naïve respect, leading to strong subordination and excessive status differences. My ambition is only to indicate that the heavy expansion and exploitation of grandiosity and illusion as routes to success lead to not just sound scepticism and resistance, but to a loss of trust, cynicism, and opportunism.

While pointing this out, I am not saying that this is the only or major response. The trends and current social situation described in this book take many forms and lead to a variety of experiences and psychological effects. The undermining of trust is one possible consequence. It can exist parallel to, or in sequence with, other responses, such as people being seduced into cultural dopes naïvely celebrating a beautiful world. Or, as we will turn to now, reinforcement of narcissism.

Narcissism

This book has been primarily concerned with economic, social, and cultural factors, but much of its content may be regarded and understood at a psychological level, and the narcissism concept is important is this context. This may be seen in the psychological basis for the popularity of grandiosity, while narcissism is a result and an extension of grandiosity. This has been touched on in previous chapters, but I will now remind readers of its relevance.

In psychology there is a differentiation between healthy and pathological narcissism. This must be seen as a continuum rather than as discrete forms. What is of major interest here is neither healthy emphasis on the self or the positive interplay between individuals and conforming performances, relations, and affiliations nor people suffering from psychic disorder. It is rather the socially reinforced problematic or shaky forms of narcissism associated with contemporary culture that is of interest. The key aspect of narcissism then concerns unstable and vulnerable selves and a culturally oriented exaggeration of subjectivity, accompanied by the need for confirmation of idealized self-images. The sense of self is inflated, it is overheated, and objects are overinvested in terms of a personal meaning, involving either positive conformation or doubt, uncertainty, a feeling of insufficiency—in relation to all available signs of grandiosity. A fragile identity is accompanied by general frailty: a risk that imperfections and problems lead to increased anxiety, relationship problems, overconsumption of pharmaceuticals, health issues, burnout tendencies, and so on.

This is linked with an explosion of ideas, dreams, and fantasies. This tendency embodies a potential for liberation and change, although I am not emphasizing this aspect in my book. The person concerned is not locked into established conventions in terms of traditions, gender, social class, and family, but inspirations come from various sources. Ziehe and Stubenrauch (1982) refer to cultural 'free-setting'. The opportunities are, for example, that identity is no longer regarded as something which the individual more or less takes over and which last throughout his/her life. 'Identity can be tested, changed, be stylized and resumed' (30). People, especially young people, are forced into this 'identity process', that is to say, working with their own identity project with only limited assistance from established traditions (support/obligation), to develop a specific identity. This cultural liberation produces a strange double tendency. People become, to a continuous extent, liberated from social and cultural factors. Gender, for example, is not given and solely constraining, but something we can play around with and 'un-do' (Butler, 2004; Deutsch, 2007). At the same time, cultural free-setting involves great strains and difficulties for people exposed to a multitude of identity-proposing and undermining regulatory efforts and mechanisms

(Knights and Willmott, 1989), leading to the identity process becoming a struggle, riddled with anxiety (Alvesson, 2010). This means that individualism has 'crossed over to cultural narcissism' (Twenge and Foster, 2010: 100).

Our desires, dreams and fantasies are exposed to an unprecedented diversity, as a result of the bombardment of images provided by advertising, the media, and the 'consciousness industry'. This increasing scope for personal expectations, dreams, etc., in relation to realistic and practical constraints increases intrapsychic conflicts (Frimodt, 1986: 83).

The latter means that individuals often have considerable difficulty in developing a strong and stable identity. Ziehe and Stubenrauch (1982) refer to a remarkable 'superheating' of subjectivity. This may be the result of an excessive discrepancy between expectations, demand, etc., and what reality offers for the great majority.

> This gap between the realities of life and culturally produced expectations, between everyday life and the explosion of expectations in our minds and hearts, may be a vital motive for needs and fantasies of change. But it may also be expressed in the form of depression, suffering and somatic illness. Both aspects demonstrate the ambivalence in the cultural liberation process. (33)

Many of the phenomena discussed in this book may be understood as mechanisms that both create and try to fill in this gap. This is double-edged in that the problem and the solution reinforce each other. The grandiosity projects described in this book are closely related to narcissism. This relationship is dialectical: grandiosity projects encourage narcissism but can also be seen as providing a response to the reinforced need for confirmation. A knowledge society, the professionalization of occupational groups, claims for a place in the sun, higher education for almost everyone, the upgrading of titles on a large scale, the inflation of education grades, shop-window arrangements designed to confirm an attractive self-image can all be associated with narcissistic fantasies, bringing individuals some way from healthy to not to so healthy, occasionally also pathological forms of narcissism. A key issue is that such fantasies are relatively loosely linked with actions, achievements, knowledge, and other aspects that can establish individual and collective self-images in a substantial and robust manner. Grandiose projects contribute to a fragile and hollow confirmation of identity. Completion of a demanding education and achieving high grades or promotion as a result of protracted efforts may build character and stabilize identity, but performing such feats without any substance in the form of learning, achievement, or demonstration of ability has no such durable effect. Pseudo-events and other aspects associated with grandiose ideas lead to a kind of 'pseudo-confirmation'. There is a great danger that the fundamental problem is merely exacerbated: having a university degree, being a member of a 'profession', gaining a title that gives an outsider a false impression, or buying high-status goods involves an uncertain fluctuation between envisaging oneself as fantastic and a depressed sense of emptiness coupled with the realization of the hollowness of all this. The result is a strong desire for confirmation. Increasingly, much of what appears to provide confirmation is too hollow to work properly: the response is often an ironic grin when you receive an academic degree in spa management or Robin Hood studies or a misleading vice-president or professorial title where qualification and job authority fall short of most people's beliefs about what the title represents. Self-doubt about what you know and can do does not help either.

In this sense, the narcissism-confirming (grandiose and illusory) projects and institutions discussed in this book are incapable of solving the problems that create a demand for them in the first place. In particular, this involves illusion tricks which form a vicious circle—narcissism interacts with institutions and mechanisms that encourage grandiosity, and they reinforce each other the whole time. The psychological consequences of this are far from trivial—too much uncertainty about what one does and the institutions supposedly providing backing, for example a solid education, plus a fragile identity run counter to a sense of well-being. It leads to increased vulnerability and to all kinds of mental problems. Not surprisingly, most indicators point at later generations becoming more and more narcissistic, both in terms of psychic problems and in terms of the normal psychology and its vulnerabilities (Kasser, 2002; Lasch, 1978; 1984; Twenge et al., 2008; Twenge and Foster, 2010).

Functional stupidity

A fourth possible cost of the grandiose society and its economy of persuasion is the cultivation of a particular form of stupidity—what Andre Spicer and I call 'functional stupidity' (Alvesson and Spicer, 2012). We define functional stupidity as a socially supported lack of reflexivity, substantive reasoning, and justification. It entails a refusal to use intellectual resources outside a narrow and 'safe' terrain of adaptation to and exploitation of a given social situation. It has nothing to do with low intelligence—people can be intelligent (be good at IQ tests) and be functionally stupid. Functional stupidity can provide a sense of certainty, which allows social life and organizations to function smoothly. This can save the social order and its members from the disorder and friction that comes with doubt and reflection. This mainly means that you follow the flow, avoid too much scepticism and resistance, and let yourself be persuaded by all the beautiful representations on offer. You repress the doubts and unpleasant feelings of 'What the hell is going on here?' Functional stupidity means that you refrain from critical thinking, reflection, and the posing of broader questions about values, ideals, and representations of reality.

One can see functional stupidity as an important 'resource base' for contemporary social life, particularly in a work and organizational context. Contemporary economic life and society, with its emphasis on persuasion, images, and seduction, fuels specific forms of functional stupidity. These forms of stupidity and narcissism go together: the need for confirmation and positivity softens the brain in some respects. Messages are accepted, not because they can stand scrutiny, but because they create an appealing, beautiful grandiose world, making its inhabitants feel good and boosting their self-identity. Positive appearances are then accepted and one refrains from exploring what is beneath the surface.

There are, of course, important general barriers to broader thinking, such as lack of knowledge, information, time, or cognitive capacity. There are different routes to and sources of functional stupidity, including totalitarian regimes, group thinking, highly routinized work, and charismatic leadership, all discouraging free thinking and careful reflection. However, an economy of persuasion is, in the context of this book and of contemporary (Western) society, the most significant factor. Here we find a reluctance to use cognitive capacity in a broader, deeper, and sharper way outside the predefined paths set out by institutions, ideologies, and identity templates that emphasize grandiosity.

Functional stupidity then is not purely or even mainly about cognition. It also relates to affective issues such as motivation and emotion. The *motivational* aspect of functional stupidity involves an unwillingness to use one's cognitive capacities, apart from in narrow, instrumental ways. A lack of intellectual curiosity, close-mindedness, and an orientation to comply with dominant social logic without much interest in adopting an alternative viewpoint are all important factors in this context. This means a fixed self-identity as an 'organization man', a brand enthusiast, a committed consumer eager to create the good life and expecting happiness through material goods, and a believer in your abilities as guaranteed by your CV or your standing as a 'professional'. This fixed self-view overlaps with the inclination to see the grandiosity and its backup of illusory arrangements as positive and worth taking seriously in a world where you should not be too fussy about the accuracy and truthfulness of things. Be positive and don't spoil the fun are cultural guidelines supporting the suppression of doubt and a naïve faith in the things that can add some glamour, status, and self-esteem.

Related to this are the *emotional* aspects of functional stupidity. Anxiety and personal insecurity may reinforce functional stupidity. Embracing grandiosity and its backup is emotionally motivated: the offerings of a positive sense of self and confirmation of an idealized version of self, one's profession, organization, and contemporary (knowledge) society hinder critical scrutiny. Of course, this overlaps with the boosting of narcissism.

In this sense, there is an interaction, indeed a strong overlap between inability and unwillingness to shut off the use of reason for critical thinking, reflection, and questioning. Impeding these faculties is, of course, not just a matter of individual capacity and motivation. Societal, organizational, and occupational contexts are central, as are regimes offering consumption as an easy solution to all problems. These contexts are not in themselves anti-reflective but can, in principle, cultivate or discourage thoughtfulness, critical reasoning, and dialogue. This book draws attention to those dominant social institutions that tend to reduce these qualities.

Functional stupidity contributes to maintaining and strengthening institutions. It may also motivate people, help them develop their careers, and subordinate them to socially acceptable forms of work and consumption. At a more general level, functional stupidity helps people to be adaptive and socially smooth. Such positive outcomes can further reinforce functional stupidity. There is a positive conditioning in accepting and enacting grandiosity, bypassing the messiness and imperfections of reality, and instead concentrating on hyper-reality—pseudo-actions and events, signs and window-dressing. If you accept grandiosity, more of its fruits will probably benefit you—in careers and in social life circling much around consumption and brand fascination. But functional stupidity can also give rise to negative consequences, such as the trapping of individuals and organizations into problematic patterns of thinking. This can lead to individual disappointment, economic failures, and social problems. Such negative outcomes may prompt individual and collective reflexivity, which can effectively undermine functional stupidity and make people less impressed and seduced, and more inclined to resist.

Some doubt may also emerge from the wealth of criticism that stigmatizes branding, advertising, commercialism, fashions, and luxury goods (e.g., Klein, 2000). Also the realization that much of the identity-confirming symbolism associated with the inflation of grades and titles and the promotion of occupations and organizational activities to professionalism, excellence, etc., are quite hollow may trigger doubt. This kind of suspicion can spur insights that can undermine the attractiveness, status, and self-confidence of image-producing institutions. Even if grandiosity is seductive, it easily backfires.

As emphasized throughout this book, we live in an economy of persuasion, circling around promotion, desire, and expectations. This creates a particular consciousness—a mentality bearing imprints of the combination of the id and the ad (as Foley, 2010, puts it) more than careful reasoning and assessment. In post-affluent societies, far from all people can confidently claim that they are clearly contributing to social well-being by producing something that improves the lives of people, leads to a better society, or something similarly meaningful and uplifting. A large part of all work fuels the desire for positional goods, meaning that the 'creation of value' for (some) customers entails the 'destruction of value' for others. The noise and often intelligence-insulting messages of a massive communication of grandiose images lead to uncertainties and a lurking sense of inferiority that contributes to the reproduction of an insatiable need for identity confirmation, and a responsiveness to persuasive tactics promising meaning, and fuelling the confirmation of identity.

The massive investments in seduction and enchantment are the key to the switching off of too much doubt and scepticism. Functional stupidity is needed—switching off independent thinking and critical questioning makes it easier to be seduced by visions, brand value talk, and the notion that workers belong to the same extended family as their CEO (even though senior executives may earn perhaps ten or even a hundred times as much as low-level employees and may be enthusiastic downsizers and outsourcers). The point here is not that work with visions, branding, and other techniques of persuasion are necessarily stupid, or that it is necessarily unwise to accept them (or pretend that one does). Rather, I am saying it may be easier to create a strong belief and clear enthusiasm for the messages if critical, reflective thinking, and thoughtful communication are severely constrained.

Refraining from thinking through what one is doing and reflecting on its purpose then becomes a real resource for adapting to 'institutionalized myths'. Elements of 'stupidity management' (Alvesson and Spicer, 2012) in the economy of persuasion then involve encouragement *not* to think about what really works, but instead normalizing imitation, fashion-following, and conformism, as well as celebrating grandiosity as a general virtue. This entails a general receptivity to institutionalized processes, and the specific support of institutional work processes, including discouragement of questions such as 'What is the point of this?' and referring to the safe quasi-reason 'everybody else is doing this' as a justification. Then one can comfortably relax, be seduced, associate oneself with the illusions, and have faith in a world producing the pink and gold of hyper-reality we so often prefer to a grey and multicoloured reality.

A COMMENT ABOUT COSTS

These four problematic features are intimately connected with contemporary social dynamics involving grandiosity, illusory arrangements, and zero-sum games. The latter tend to produce qualitative losses, erosion of legitimacy, narcissism, and functional stupidity. These outcomes are somewhat different and, in the case of the erosion of legitimacy (and its appendix, cynicism), this is almost the opposite response to functional stupidity (that is, faith and naïvety). It is, of course, hardly surprising that there is a variety of triggered responses. There is frequently strong uncertainty or ambivalence: most people probably realize that increased consumption in rich countries may be a mixed blessing, that an improved title (i.e., a finer title without changes in job content or conditions), a university degree achieved as a result of modest efforts, and attribution of a mysterious 'brand value' to a specific object involves a fake element, but they may still stick to and take the improved symbolism seriously. Fleming and Spicer (2003) refer to cynical consciousness. Ambivalence or swinging between naïvety (functional stupidity) and cynicism may be a trademark of our time. People may swing between overall contexts and situations, and also over time. It is probably common that a period of seduction and naïvety is replaced by experiences of distrust and cynicism after some time in working life, in education, or during the life cycle of a new fashion.

Of course, I am not claiming that the four problematic features discussed here are the only, or even the main characteristics of our time, institutions, and lives. Needless to say, there are other key elements in social life and development than those associated with grandiosity and positional goods: reduction in prejudices, acceptance of sexual diversity, equal opportunities, scientific progress, better healthcare, increased freedom and opportunity, and broad access to knowledge and freedom of expression (within the boundaries of political correctness and other things that sound fine). Some of these work in other directions than grandiosity. The costs portrayed here are the effects of grandiosity, but there are a variety of balancing and opposing forces. The latter mean that quantitative expansion leading to qualitative losses, erosion of legitimacy, increase of narcissism, and cultivation of functional stupidity are far from absolute and that the social patterns observed are quite complex and diverse. Most people are not cultural dopes—at least not all the time. Also brand-oriented consumers are often insightful (Bertilsson, 2009). Despite this somewhat optimistic note, there are reasons to take a rather sceptical view seriously.

Despite everything: a place in the sun?

But maybe there are other solutions. Possibly, this book has expressed a gloomy picture, in which apparent improvement projects hardly deliver the goodies promised. I have, among other things, claimed that grandiose ideas of attaining a position of superiority are seldom realized. It is difficult to achieve a place in the sun by means of various illusion tricks. The obstacles are the inadequacy of our world and similar ambitions on the part of other individuals, occupational groups, and organizations. The social boundaries of growth lead to a zero-sum game.

But let me move towards completing this book by citing a happy ending about trainee teachers. The teaching profession in many countries has certainly experienced a decline in terms of status in 'knowledge society', and teacher training in many countries is characterized by weak students and a low level of requirements, probably reflecting and contributing to the establishment of a broader education of a less than impressive nature. But one result of this not particularly demanding education is that people appear to be able to acquire a place in the sun. This is not in a metaphorical sense, since the number of attractive positions in society is limited and the teaching profession is further from achieving such positions than ever, but in more literal terms.

At any rate, Ylva, a teacher trainee in Sweden, says 'with a laugh' that 'I think we have too much spare time. We study two or three days a week, and then we go and sun bathe' (SDS, 14 April 2004). Maybe this is not so bad—at least if the weather is good. Perhaps we should be less ambitious in our concern about education and working life and radically modify our ideas about freedom. Possibly there is something wrong about Ylva's (and my) attitude that teacher trainees have too much time off. Maybe we should accept a school world, and to some extent a working life, dominated by an easy-going approach.

We may recall Keynes's calculation that if we had devoted the productivity increases of the previous half-century or so to shorter working hours rather than consumption, a full working week would be only 15 hours. Perhaps certain students in higher education are on the way to realizing this option. But this is achieved by moving quite far away from what is broadly dressed up in pretentious and self-satisfied terms such as knowledge, learning, competence development, a knowledge-intensive society, professionalization, and so on, although this may be tricky since teacher training and other forms of education encourage slack and hedonistic attitudes and at the same time broad groups are emphasizing growth and consumption as the key to happiness and identity.

In an international economy exposed to competition, growth also calls for a great deal of hard work. No doubt, it is tempting to keep people in a good mood and establish legitimacy by means of suggestions of grandiose undertones and overtones that support narcissism, while pretending there are no negative consequences. But one alternative is to accept hedonism in a more relaxed and less consumption-orientated, grandiose, and illusionistic manner. The following anecdote may give food for thought:

A fisherman in South America was taking care of the catch of the day in his little boat as a North American tourist was passing by.

'What lovely fish you have there. Do you catch a lot every day?'

'Well, I take a trip, and then I get this much, maybe.'

'What do you do the rest of the time?'

'I play a bit with my children, play cards with my friends, take a siesta in my hammock, drink a glass or two and discuss things with people in the bar.'

'But why do you waste time like that. You could be making three or four trips a day, and with the money you make you could buy another boat, employ someone and make even more money.'

'Well, and then what?'

'With smart investments and hard work you could build up a little fishing fleet within 10–15 years, make real dough and then sell the whole caboodle, retire and do what you like.'

'You mean that I could take a fishing trip every day, play with my grandchildren, play cards with my friends, take a siesta, take a drink or two and meet people over a glass of wine in the bar?'

The vulgoeconomy—a sketch

As mentioned in Chapter 4, Burenstam Linder (1969) said several decades ago that we had perhaps entered the 'vulgarization phase of growth', or were well on the way. I latched onto this idea and, in view of the fact that material welfare in most post-affluent countries is now roughly twice what it was when this book was written, I consider that today's economy may be described as a vulgoeconomy. This concept points a little malevolently away from the more rational aspects of a modern economy—which certainly has its advantages, in particular in a historical perspective, inconceivable innovative achievements, efficiency, and flexibility. The highly impressive characteristics of such developments are frequently and strongly cited by predominant groups and are so familiar that I largely ignore them in this book. But the fact that technological and economic developments in the twentieth century have been accompanied by fantastic progress does not mean, of course, that the growth ideal will continue to be equally desirable or sensible as it was, say, a century ago or in poor countries of today.

In a vulgoeconomy most material needs and desirable aspirations have already been satisfied, and economic development is more a question of escalating and maintaining a high level of demand for goods and services as a result of major investments in consumer influence. Such goods and services then form part of a social zero-sum game. In other words, the challenge in a vulgoeconomy is to create demand—production is rarely the bottleneck, and persuasion is a key feature. Strong persuasive pressures lead to a tendency to over-bidding. Grandiose projects are promised and grandiosity becomes a crucial feature of what is packaged and sold. But this logic of attractive promises and the intensive communication of ideal images is not only confined to commercial institutions. The vulgoeconomy, with its accompanying persuasion logic, is becoming a paradigm that influences society and culture over a broad spectrum.

An increasing number of institutions are drawn into this logic, or encourage it. They 'have a strong interest in getting people to believe that purchasing the right car, the right soft drink, the right watch or the right education will radically improve their chances of being happy, even if this is at the cost of mortgaging their lives' (Csikszentmihalyi, 1999: 826).

Competition to gain attention and an audience for messages is increasing. In a crowded marketplace name recognition is crucial. This applies not only to organizations that must persuade potential customers about the excellence of their products—other organizations also appear to be attracted by this logic. This is no doubt a question of legitimacy to some extent, but it also involves narcissism at the organizational level—we also want to be seen! Illusion tricks with powerful, simple, and attractive messages contribute to visibility (and subsequently disguise things that they do not want to be too visible). In addition, the visibility of others generates invisibility for the organization concerned. There is a zero-sum game for attention and it is not much fun if you wind up in a backwater.

The cockroach-elimination logic mentioned in Chapter 3 has spread in this context from 'mere' consumers and has been intensified. People are becoming increasingly immune to 'ordinary' messages—you must work harder and harder to achieve an impact in societal arenas in which competition for attention and showing yourself is becoming increasingly intensive, and the scope for each new persuasion attempt is more limited. An increasing number of current organizations, political bodies, special-interest groups, etc., are into symbolic pollution, strongly engaged in branding.

The surplus of physical objects and bombardment by sales promotion and demand-stimulation messages is not merely a positive aspect, in that something good is implicitly promulgated—there is also a negative side. The presentation of some good objects implies that older objects are less satisfactory in comparison. (Occasionally this may involve some totally new object but, for the most part, there is competition between what is for sale and what people already have—and which they may not wish to replace if they do not have some 'assistance' or pressure to urge them on.)

The rather pretentious (maybe even grandiose) term 'value creation' is often applied to consumption in modern business jargon—this simply means that customers get something they are pleased with. In the modern fashion-oriented economy 'value destruction' is also an important feature. The production of dissatisfaction is a key feature, even if it is often implicit. This is obviously clearest in the case of fashion goods, an emphasis on which implies that everything that is not the latest loses value. But at a more general level, this means that an economy of affluence tends to encourage dissatisfaction with what you already have.

In this economy, goods and services that provide individual satisfaction (freedom from hunger or the experiences of life in the raw) independent of others' consumption levels have come to play a diminishing role in comparison with items that have a clearer place in zero-sum games. In other words, the positionality factor has increased. Since the goods and services, etc., covered by the zero-sum game are dynamic and constantly changing, they have a destabilizing impact on the individual's position and satisfaction. It is hardly feasible to adopt a relaxed attitude to consumption (or education qualifications, a professional title, or even your organization's compliance and visibility). Retention of status quo—for example, maintaining an average position as regards social success and demonstrating good taste—also calls for continuous efforts to keep pace with economic growth and the level of expectations. Contentment means that you fall behind and at risk of being classed as a failure.

The increasing sociality of consumption and satisfaction, and the increasingly strong emphasis on consumption as a key factor in activity in life means that identity questions tend to become more tangible and problematic.

Individuals are moulded into consumers in the vulgoeconomy. To some extent, this logic makes itself felt in education and working life. Other sources of identity—activity, relationships, knowledge, material work results, and morality—are losing ground. Economic institutions account for a higher proportion of the socialization process. The influence of consumption often focuses on making identity less certain, and on boosting and providing misleading impressions. The intertwinement of undermining and confirmation of a sense of self is crucial in the consumption-triggering process. In the vulgoeconomy there is an interweaving of individual identity with consumption activities. This is particularly explicit in the case of high-status brands. In a branded world of products in which companies invest enormous resources to animate objects, there is simultaneously a tendency to objectify souls.

Summary

There is broad political agreement, in many Western and other countries, about the importance of the expansion of higher education, our existence in a knowledge society in which expertise and qualifications are central features; professionalization, statistical equality, and diversity are to be promoted;

good leadership leads to a good working life; and efficient organizations, economic growth, and improved material standards are the key guiding rules. 'Grandiosity for everyone' could be the political slogan of our time.

In my opinion much of this talk has limited substance and contains a considerable amount of simple trickery and self-deception. No doubt many individuals see through this more or less, but even if they are partially aware, most institutions and individual actions are permeated by the logic of grandiosity. It is tempting to abstain from or marginalize critical reflection and buy into various notions of grandiosity and all the representations, formal structures, and activities boosting this.

Much of this agreement is at the it-should-look-good level. Grandiose ideas about competence development, professionalization, a knowledge economy, equality of opportunity, ethics, leadership, and material welfare are based to a large extent on illusion tricks in the form of pseudo-arrangements and other imagological tricks. Many groups think that this is to their advantage, but the advantages are often illusory—apart from for the imagologists. On the other hand, this may be a question of avoiding losses. It is important that things don't look too bad or that one educates oneself less, professionalizes oneself to a lesser degree, or mobilizes less symbolism about equality of opportunity, ethics, strategies, or leadership than other people. It is best not to wind up in the wake of others as regards the inflation of grades and titles.

With the stubbornness of a drunken man, I repeat: This is primarily a question of values of a positional nature, where the social limits to growth mean that the exchange depends on the way you manage in relation to others. Attractive projects that aim to shine over others often unfortunately wind up with no sign of improvement in the searchlight, and in many cases the spotlight blinds bystanders. And even if you stretch up and stand on your toes, you do not see any better if everyone else is doing the same.

Underlying the grandiose society's illusion tricks is the triumph of emptiness.

Bibliography

Periodicals

Dagens Nyheter (Sweden)
Sydsvenska Dagbladet Snällposten (Sweden)
The Globe and Mail (Toronto)

Publications

Abbott, A. (1991). 'The Future of Professions', in S. Bacharach (ed.), *Research of the Sociology of Organizations*. Greenwich, CT: JAI Press.

Åberg, R. (2002). 'Överutbildning—ett arbetsmarknadspolitiskt problem?', in K. Abrahamsson et al. (eds), *Utbildning. Kompetens och arbete*. Lund: Studentlitteratur.

—— (2003). 'Unemployment Persistency, Over-education and the Employment Chances of the Less Educated'. *European Sociological Review* 19 (2): 199–216.

Abrahamson, E. (1996). 'Management Fashion'. *Academy of Management Review* 21: 254–85.

Adler, P. (1999). 'Building Better Bureaucracies'. *Academy of Management Executive* 13, 4: 36–47.

—— (2002). 'Critical in the Name of What or Whom'. *Organization*, 9: 387–395.

Alexius, S. (2007). *Regelmotståndarna* [Opponents to rules]. Stockholm: EFI.

Alvesson, M. (1995). *Management of Knowledge-Intensive Companies*. Berlin/New York: de Gruyter.

—— (2000). *Ledning av kunskapsföretag*, 3rd edn. Stockholm: Norstedts.

—— (2004). *Knowledge Work and Knowledge-Intensive Firms*. Oxford: Oxford University Press.

—— (2010). 'Self-Doubters, Strugglers, Story-tellers, Surfers and Others: Images of Self-identity in Organization Studies'. *Human Relations* 63(2): 193–217.

—— (2011). 'The Leader as Saint', in M. Alvesson and A. Spicer (eds), *Metaphors We Lead By: Understanding Leadership in the Real World*. London: Routledge.

—— (2012). 'Studying Leadership—Taking Meaning, Relationality and Ideology Seriously', paper. Lund University.

—— and Berg, P. O. (1992). *Corporate Culture and Organizational Symbolism*. Berlin/New York: de Gruyter.

—— and Björkman, I. (1992). *Organisationsidentitet och organisationsbyggande*. Lund: Studentlitteratur.

—— and Köping, A.-S. (1993). *Med känslan som ledstjärna. En studie av reklamarbete och reklambyråer*. Lund: Studentlitteratur.

—— and Spicer, A. (2012). 'A Stupidity Based Theory of the Organization'. *Journal of Management Studies* 49(7): 1194–1220.

—— and Sveningsson, S. (2003a). 'The Good Visions, the Bad Micro-management and the Ugly Ambiguity: Contradictions of (non-)Leadership in a Knowledge-Intensive Company'. *Organization Studies* 24(6): 961–88.

—— —— (2003b). 'The Great Disappearance Act: Difficulties in Doing Leadership'. *Leadership Quarterly* 14(3): 359–81.

—— —— (2003c). 'Managers Doing Leadership: The Extraordinarization of the Mundane'. *Human Relations* 56(12): 1435–59.

—— —— (2008). *Changing Organizational Culture: Cultural Change Work in Progress*. London: Routledge.

—— —— (2012). 'Un- and Repacking Leadership: Context, Relations, Constructions and Politics, in M. Uhl-Bien and S. Ospina (eds), *Advancing Relational Leadership Theory: A Conversation among Perspectives*. Greenwich: Information Age Publishing.

—— and Thompson, P. (2005). 'Post-bureaucracy?', in S. Ackroyd et al. (eds), *Oxford Handbook of Work and Organization Studies*. Oxford: Oxford University Press.

Amundsen, O. (2003). 'Fortellinger om organisationsendringer', PhD dissertation. Trondheim: Norges teknisk-naturvitenskapelige Universitet.

Arum, R. and Roksa, J. (2011). *Academically Adrift: Limited Learning on College Campuses*. Chicago: University of Chicago Press.

Arvidsson, A. (2006). *Brands: Meaning and Value in Media Culture*. London: Routledge.

Ashcraft, K. (2001). 'Organized Dissonance: Feminist Bureaucracy as Hybrid Form'. *Academy of Management Journal*, 44(6): 1301–22.

Asplund, J. (1989). *Rivaler och syndabockar*. Göteborg: Korpen.

Barker, R. (1997). 'How can we train leaders if we don't know what leadership is?' *Human Relations* 50(4): 343–62.

—— (2001). 'The Nature of Leadership'. *Human Relations* 54: 469–93.

Barley, S. and Kunda, G. (1992). 'Design and Devotion Surges of Rational and Normative Ideologies of Control, in Managerial Discourse'. *Administrative Science Quarterly* 37(3): 363–99.

Barnett, R. (2004). 'The Purposes of Higher Education and Changing Face of Academia'. *London Review of Education* 2(1): 61–73.

Bass, B. M. and Steidlmeier, P. (1999). 'Ethics, Character, and Authentic Transformational Leadership Behavior'. *Leadership Quarterly* 10: 181–217.

Batteau, A. (2001). 'Negations and Ambiguities in the Cultures of Organizations'. *American Anthropologist* 102(4): 726–40.

Baudrillard, J. (1983). *Simulations*. New York: Semiotext(e).

Bauman, Z. (1988). 'Is There a Postmodern Sociology?'. *Theory, Culture and Society* 5: 217–37.

—— (2001). 'Consuming Life'. *Journal of Consumer Culture* 1(1): 9–29.

Beckman, S. (1980a). *Kärlek på tjänstetid*. Stockholm: Arbetslivscentrum.

—— (1980b). *Långt borta och nära. 1900-talets politiska framtider i ekonomisk-historisk belysning*. Stockholm: Liber.

Belk, R. (1988). 'Possessions and the Extended Self'. *Journal of Consumer Research* 16: 1–38.

Bibliography

Bell, E., Taylor, S., and Thorpe, R. (2002). 'Organizational Differentiation through Badging: Investors in People and the Value of the Sign'. *Journal of Management Studies* 39(2): 1071–85.

Benders, J. and van Veen, K. (2001). 'What's in a Fashion? Interpretive Viability and Management Fashions'. *Organization* 8(1): 33–53.

Berggren, C. (2002). 'Från fusion till fission. Om storeföretag, fusioner och innovationer', in G. Ahrne and R. Swedberg (eds), *Ekonomin i samhället*. Lund: Studentlitteratur.

Berglund, J. (2002). *De otillräckliga*. Stockholm: EFI (PhD dissertation).

Bertilsson, J. (2009). *The Way Brands Work*. Lund Studies in Economics and Management 114. Lund: Lund Business Press.

Bigley, G. and Roberts, K. (2001). 'The Incident Command System: High-Reliability Organizing for Complex and Volatile Task Environments'. *Academy of Management Journal* 44(6): 1281–99.

Billing, Y. D. (1994). 'Gender and Bureaucracies: A Critique of Ferguson's "The Feminist Case against Bureaucracy" '. *Gender, Work and Organization* 1(4): 179–94.

Bligh, M. (2011). 'Followership and Follower-Centric Approaches', in A. Bryman et al. (eds), *Handbook of Leadership Studies*. London: Sage.

Blom, M. and Alvesson, M. (2011). *Leadership on Demand*. Lund: WP.

Boorstin, D. (1961). *The Image: A Guide to Pseudo-Events in America*. New York: Atheneum.

Bourdieu, P. (1984). *Distinction*. Cambridge, MA: Harvard University Press.

Brante, T. (1988). 'Sociological Approaches to the Professions'. *Acta Sociologica* 31: 119–42.

Braverman, H. (1974). *Labour and Monopoly Capital: The Degradation of Work in the Twentieth Century*. New York: Monthly Review Press.

Brunsson, N. (2003). 'Organized Hypocrisy', in B. Czarniawska and G. Sevon (eds), *Northern Lights*. Malmö: Liber.

Bryman, A. (1999). 'The Disneyization of Society'. *Sociological Review* 47: 25–47.

Burenstam-Linder, S. (1969). *The Harried Welfare Class*. New York: Columbia University Press.

Butler, J. (2004). *Undoing Gender*. New York: Routledge.

Carroll, B. and Levy, L. (2008). 'Defaulting to Management: Leadership Defined by What It Is Not'. *Organization* 15(1): 75–96.

Carter, P. and Jackson, N. (1987). 'Management Myth and Metatheory—From Scarcity to Postscarcity.' *International Studies of Management Organization* 17(3): 64–89.

Cartwright, S. and Holmes, N. (2006). 'The Meaning of Work: The Challenge of Regaining Employee Engagement and Reducing Cynicism'. *Human Resource Management Review* 16: 199–207.

Chalmers, L. (2001). *Marketing Masculinities*. Westport, CT: Greenwood Press.

Chevalier, A. and Lindley, J. (2009). 'Overeducation and the Skills of UK Graduates'. *Journal of the Royal Statistic Society* 172(Part 2): 307–37.

Child, J. and McGrath, R. (2001). 'Organizations Unfettered: Organizational Form in an Information-Intensive Economy'. *Academy of Management Journal* 44(6): 1135–48.

Clegg, S. (1989). *Frameworks of Power*. London: Sage.

—— et al. (1996). 'Management Knowledge for the Future: Innovation, Embryos and New Paradigms', in S. Clegg and G Palmer (eds), *The Politics of Management Knowledge*. London: Sage.

Collins, R. (1990). 'Changing Conceptions in the Sociology of Professions: Formation of Professions', in R. Torstendahl and M. Burrage (eds), *The Formation of Professions*. London: Sage.

—— (2002). 'Credential Inflation and the Future of Universities', in S. Brint (ed.), *The Future of the City of Intellect*. Stanford: Stanford University Press.

Collinson, D. (2006). 'Rethinking Followership: A Post-structural Analysis of Follower Identities'. *Leadership Quarterly* 17: 179–89.

Csikszentmihalyi, M. (1999). 'If We Are So Rich, Why Aren't We Happy?' *American Psychologist* 54(10): 821–7.

Dahlbom, B. (2000). 'Nätverkande. Om organisering och ledning i e-samhället', in K. Ydén (ed.), *IT, organiserande och ledarskap*. Stockholm: Försvarshögskolan.

Davenport, T. and Prusak, L. (1998). *Working Knowledge*. Cambridge, MA: Harvard Business Press.

Deetz, S. (1998). 'Discursive Formations, Strategized Subordination, and Self-surveillance', in A. McKinley and K. Starkey (eds), *Foucault, Management and Organization Theory*. London: Sage.

Deutsch, F. (2007). 'Undoing Gender'. *Gender and Society* 21(1): 106–27.

DiMaggio, P. J. and Powell, W. W. (1991) Introduction, in P. J. DiMaggio and W. W. Powell (eds), *The New Institutionalism In Organizational Analysis*. Chicago: University of Chicago Press.

du Gay, P. (2000). 'Markets and Meanings: Re-imagining Organizational Life', in M. Schultz et al. (eds), *The Expressive Organization*. Oxford: Oxford University Press.

—— and Salaman, G. (1992). 'The Cul(ture) of the Consumer'. *Journal of Management Studies* 29(5): 615–33.

Easterlin, R. (2001). 'Income and Happiness: Toward a Unified Theory'. *Economic Journal* 111: 465–84.

Elzinga, A. (1989). 'Kunskapsanalys och klassanalys—med fokus på omvårdnadsforskning', in S. Selander (ed.), *Kampen om yrkesutövning, status och kunskap*. Lund: Studentlitteratur.

Fairclough, N. (1993). 'Critical Discourse Analysis and the Marketization of Public Discourse'. *Discourse and Society* 4(2): 133–69.

FAO. (2011). *Global Food Losses and Food Waste*. Rome: FAO.

Featherstone, M. (1991). *Consumer Culture and Postmodernism*. London: Sage.

Ferguson, K. E. (1984). *The Feminist Case against Bureaucracy*. Philadelphia: Temple University Press.

Ferner, A. (2000). 'The Underpinnings of 'Bureaucratic Control' Systems: HRM in European Multinationals'. *Journal of Management Studies* 37(4): 521–40.

Ferraro, F., Pfeffer, J., and Sutton, R. (2005). 'Economics Language and Assumptions: How Theories Can Become Self-fulfilling'. *Academy of Management Review* 30: 8–23.

Fleming, P. and Spicer, A. (2003). 'Working at a Cynical Distance: Implications for Power, Subjectivity and Resistance'. *Organization* 10: 157–79.

Florida, R. (2001). *The Rise of the Creative Class: And How It's Transforming Work, Leisure, Community and Everyday Life*. Basic Books: New York.

Foley, M. (2010). *The Age of Absurdity*. London: Simon and Schuster.

Fores, M., Glover, I., and Lawrence. P. (1991) 'Professionalism and Rationality: A Study in Misapprehension'. *Sociology* 25, 79–100.

Fosstenlokken, S., Lövegren, B., and Revang, Ö. (2003). 'Knowledge Development through Client Interaction: A Comparative Study'. *Organization Studies* 24: 859–79.

Foucault, M. (1976). *The History of Sexuality*. New York: Pantheon.

—— (1977). *Discipline and Punish*. Harmondsworth: Penguin.

—— (1980). *Power/Knowledge*. New York: Pantheon.

—— (1982). 'The Subject and Power'. *Critical Inquiry* 8: 777–95.

—— (1984). 'The Ethic of Care for the Self as a Practice of Freedom: An Interview with Michel Foucault', in J. Bernauer and D. Rasmussion (eds), *The Final Foucault*. Cambridge, MA: MIT Press.

Frank, R. (1985). 'The Demand for Unobservable and Other Nonpositional Goods'. *American Economic Review* 75(1): 101–16.

—— , Gulovich, T., and Regan, T. (1993). 'Does Studying Economics Inhibit Cooperation?' *Journal of Economic Perspectives* 7: 159–71.

Fromm, E. (1955) *The Sane Society*. London: Routledge and Kegan Paul.

—— (1976). *To Have or to Be?* London: Abacus.

Gabriel, Y. (2005). 'Class Cages and Glass Palaces: Images of Organizations in Image-conscious Times'. *Organization* 12(1): 9–27.

—— and Lang, T. (1995). *The Unmanagable Consumer*. London: Sage.

—— —— (2006). *The Unmanagable Consumer*, 2nd edn. London: Sage.

Galbraith, J. K. (1958). *The Affluent Society*. Harmondsworth: Penguin.

Giddens, A. (1991). *Modernity and Self-Identity*. Cambridge: Polity Press.

Grafton, A. (2011). 'Our Universities: Why Are They Failing?' *New York Review of Books*, 58(18) (24 November).

Green, S. and Li, Y. (2011). 'Bringing Rhetoric Back in: The Reintegration of Rhetoric and Institutional Theory since Alvesson 1993'. *Journal of Management Studies* 48: 1662–97.

Grey, C. (2005). *A Very Short, Fairly Interesting and Reasonably Cheap Book about Studying Organizations*. London: Sage.

Habermas, J. (1972). *Knowledge and Human Interests*. London: Heinemann.

Hales, C. (2005). 'Rooted in Supervision, Branching into Management; Continuity and Change in the Role of First-Line Managers'. *Journal of Management Studies* 42(3): 471–506.

Hancock, P. (2003). 'Uncovering the Semiotic in Organizational Aesthetics'. *Organization* 12: 29–50.

Handal, G. (2003). 'My Classroom Is My Castle'. *Forskerforum* 167: 18.

Hansen, E. J. (2002) *Uddannelsesystemerne i sociologisk perspektiv*. Köpenhamn: Hans Reitzels forlag.

Hartnell, C. and Walumbwa, F. (2011). 'Transformational Leadership and Organizational Culture', in N. Ashkanasy et al. (eds), *The Handbook of Organizational Culture and Climate*, 2nd edn. Thousend Oakes, CA: Sage pp 225–48.

Heath, D. and Heath, C. (2008). 'A Dirty Shame'. *Fast Company* (126): 60–1.

Heifetz, R. and Laurie, D. (1997). 'The Work of Leadership'. *Harvard Business Review* (January–February): 124–34.

Hill, S., Martin, R., and Harris, M. (2000). 'Decentralization, Integration and the Post-bureaucratic Organization: The Case of R & D'. *Journal of Management Studies* 37(4): 563–85.

Hirsch, F. (1976). *Social Limits to Growth*. Cambridge, MA: Harvard University Press.

Holmberg, I. and Tyrstrup, M. (2010). 'Well Then—What Now? An Everyday Approach to Managerial Leadership'. *Leadership* 6: 353–72.

Holt, D. (2002). 'Why Do Brands Cause Trouble? A Dialectical Theory of Consumer Culture and Branding'. *Journal of Consumer Culture* 29: 70–90.

Horkheimer, M., and Adorno, T. (1947/1979). *The Dialectics of Enlightenment*. London: Verso.

Hotson, H. (2011). 'Don't Look to the Ivy League'. *London Review of Books* 33(10): 30–2.

Houghton, J., Neck, C., and Manz, C. (2003). 'Self-leadership and Superleadership', in C. Pearce and J. Conger (eds), *Shared Leadership*. Thousand Oaks, CA: Sage.

Huey, J. (1994). 'The New Post-heroic Leadership'. *Fortune* 21: 24–8.

Humphries, M. and Brown, A. (2002). 'Narratives of Organizational Identity and Identification: A Case Study of Hegemony and Resistance'. *Organization Studies* 23(3): 421–47.

Jackall, R. (1988). *Moral Mazes*. New York: Oxford University Press.

Jespersen, J. (1998). 'Hvornår er nok—nok?' *Djøfbladet* 16 (August).

Johansson, A. (1997). *Att förstå rådgivning till småföretagare*. Bjärred: Academia Adacta.

Kairos Futures/Chef (2006). 'Bäst på allt och aldrig nöjd'. Stockholm: Tidningen Chef.

Kärreman, D. and Alvesson, M. (2009). 'Resisting Resistance: On Counter-resistance, Control and Compliance in a Consultancy Firm'. *Human Relations* 62: 1115–44.

——, Sveningsson, S., and Alvesson, M. (2002). 'The Return of the Machine Bureaucracy?' *International Studies of Management and Organization* 32(2): 70–92.

Kasser, T. (2002). *The High Price of Materialism*. Cambridge, MA: MIT Press.

Kincheloe, J. and McLaren, P. (2000). 'Rethinking Critical Theory and Qualitative Research', in N. Denzin and Y. Lincoln (eds), *Handbook of Qualitative Research*. Thousand Oaks, CA: Sage.

Klein, N. (2000). *No Logo*. London: Flamingo.

Kleppestø, S. (1993). *Kultur och identitet*. Stockholm: Nerenius and Santérus.

Knights, D. and Morgan, G. (1991). 'Corporate Strategy, Organisations and Subjectivity: A Critique and Illustration from the Financial Service Industries'. *Organization Studies* 12: 251–73.

—— and Willmott, H. (1989). 'Power and Subjectivity at Work'. *Sociology* 23: 535–58.

Kohut, H. (1971). *The Analysis of the Self*. New York: International University Press.

—— (1977). *The Restoration of the Self*. New York: International University Press.

Korczynski, M. (2005). 'The Point of Selling: Capitalism, Consumption and Contradictions'. *Organization* 12(1): 69–88.

Kovel, J. (1981). *The Age of Desire*. New York: Pantheon.

Kundera, M. (1992). *Immortality*. New York: Grove.

Lair, D., Sullivan, K., and Cheney, G. (2005). 'Marketization and the Recasting of the Professional Self: The Rhetoric and Ethics of Personal Branding'. *Management Communication Quarterly* 18: 307–43.

Lane, R. E. (1978). 'Markets and the Satisfaction of Human Wants'. *Journal of Economic Issues* 12(4): 799–827.

—— (1991). 'Buying Happiness', in *The Market Experience*. Cambridge: Cambridge University Press.

Lasch, C. (1978). *The Culture of Narcissism*. New York: Norton.

—— (1984). *The Mininal Self*. New York: Norton.

Leiss, W. (1978). *The Limits of Satisfaction*. London: Marion Boyers.

—— (1983). 'The Icons of the Marketplace'. *Theory, Culture and Society* 1(3): 10–21.

Lincoln, J. and Kalleberg, A. (1985). 'Work Organization and Workforce Commitment: A Study of Plants and Employees in the US and Japan'. *American Sociological Review* 50: 738–60.

Lukes, S. (1978). 'Authority and Power', in T. Bottomore and R. Nisbet (eds), *A History of Sociological Analysis*. London: Heinemann.

Lundholm, S. (2011). 'An Act of Balance—Hierarchy in Contemporary Work', PhD thesis. Lund: Lund Business Press.

Lyotard, J.-F. (1984). *The Postmodern Condition*. Minneapolis: University of Minnesota Press.

McCloskey, D. and Klamer, A. (1995). 'One Quarter of GDP Is Persuasion'. *American Economic Review* 85(2): 191–5.

McKenna, R. (1991). 'Marketing is Everything.' *Harvard Business Review* (January–February): 65–79.

McMurray, R. (2011). 'The Struggle to Professionalize: An Ethnographic Account of the Occupational Position of Advanced Nurse Practitioners'. *Human Relations* 64(6): 801–22.

McSweeny, B. (2006). 'Do We Live in a Post-Bureaucratic Époque?' *Journal of Organizational Change Management* 19(1): 22–37.

Marcuse, H. (1964). *One-Dimensional Man*. Boston: Beacon Press.

Marginson, S. (2006). 'Dynamics of National and Global Competition in Higher Education'. *Higher Education* 52: 1–39.

Martin, J., Sitkin, S., and Boehm, M. (1985). 'Founders and the Elusiveness of a Cultural Legacy', in P. J. Frost et al. (eds), *Organizational Culture*. Thousand Oaks, CA: Sage.

Meindl, J. (1995). 'The Romance of Leadership as a Follower-Centric Theory: A Social Constructionist Approach'. *Leadership Quarterly* 6: 329–41.

Menand, L. (2011). 'Live and Learn: Why We Have College'. *The New Yorker* (June 6).

Meyer, J. W. and Rowan, B. (1977). 'Institutionalized Organizations: Formal Structure as Myth and Ceremony', in M. Zey-Ferrel and M. Aiken (eds), *Complex Organizations: Critical Perspectives*. Glenview: Scott, Foresman.

Miles, R. et al. (1997). 'Organizing in the Knowledge Age: Anticipating the Cellular Form'. *Academy of Management Executive* 11(4): 7–19.

Miller, D. (2001). 'The Poverty of Morality'. *Journal of Consumer Culture* 1(2): 225–43.

Mintzberg, H. (1983). *Structure in Fives: Designing Effective Organizations*. Englewood Cliffs, NJ: Prentice-Hall.

—— (1990). 'The Design School: Reconsidering the Basic Premises of Strategic Management'. *Strategic Management Journal* 11: 171–95.

Morgan, G. (1992). 'Marketing Discourse and Practice: Towards a Critical Analysis', in M. Alvesson and H. Willmott (eds), *Critical Management Studies*. London: Sage.

Müllern, T. and Stein, J. (2000) *Ledarskap i den nya ekonomin*. Malmö: Liber.

Nicolai, A. T., Schulz, A.-C., and Thomas, T. W. (2010). 'What Wall Street Wants—Exploring the Role of Security Analysts in the Evolution and Spread of Management Concepts'. *Journal of Management Studies* 47: 162–89.

Normann, R. (1977). *Management for Growth*. Chichester: Wiley.

Olins, W. (2000). 'How Brands Are Taken over the Corporation', in M. Schultz et al. (eds), *The Expressive Organization*. Oxford: Oxford University Press.

Oscarsson, E. and Grannas, D. (2002). 'Under- och överutbildning på 2000-talets arbetsmarknad', in K. Abrahamsson et al. (eds), *Utbildning, kompetens och arbete*. Lund: Studentlitteratur.

Östberg, J. and Kaijser, L. (2010). *Konsumtion*. Malmö: Liber.

Packard, V. (1981). *The Hidden Persuaders*. Harmondsworth: Penguin.

Palmer, I. and Hardy, C. (2000). *Thinking about Management*. London: Sage.

Perrow, C. (1978). 'Demystifying Organizations'., in R. Sarri and Y. Heskenfeld (eds), *The Management of Human Services*. New York: Columbia University Press.

Piereson, J. (2011). 'What Is Wrong with Our Universities?' *The New Criterion* 30 (September): 17.

Power, M. (2003). 'Auditing and the Production of Legitimacy'. *Accounting, Organization and Society* 28: 379–94.

Prasad, A., Prasad, P., and Mir, R. (2011). ' "One Mirror in Another": Managing Diversity and the Discourse of Fashion'. *Human Relations* 64(5): 703–24.

Pugno, M. (2009). 'The Easterlin Paradox and the Decline of Social Capital: An Integrated Explanation'. *Journal of Socio-Economics* 38: 590–600.

Ragneklint, R. (2009). *Rationalitet ifrågasatt*. Lövestad: Bokförlaget Akademi och Samhälle.

Reed, M. (2011). 'The Post-bureaucratic Organization and the Control Revolution', in S. Clegg et al. (eds), *Managing Modernity*. Oxford: Oxford University Press.

Reskin, B. and Padavic, I. (1994). *Women and Men at Work*. Thousand Oaks, CA: Pine Forge Press.

Riesman, D. (1950). *The Lonely Crowd*. New Haven, CT: Yale University Press.

Ritzer, G. (2004). *The McDonaldization Thesis*. Thousand Oaks, CA: Sage.

—— (2007). *The Globalization of Nothing*. Thousand Oaks, CA: Pine Forge Press.

Rövik, K. A. (2011). 'From Fashion to Virus: An Alternative Theory of Organizations' Handling of Management Ideas'. *Organization Studies* 32(5): 631–53.

Ruigrok, W., Peck, S., Pettigrew, A. M., and Whittington, R. (1999). 'Corporate Restructuring and New Forms of Organizing Evidence from Europe'. *Management International Review* 39(2): 41–64.

Sahlins, M. (1976). *Culture and Practical Reason*. Chicago: University of Chicago Press.

Salomonsson, K. (2005). 'Kompetensindustrin', in M. Idvall and F. Schoug (eds), *Kunskapssamhällets marknad*. Lund: Studentlitteratur.

Sashkin, M. (2004). 'Transformational Leadership Approaches: A Review and Synthesis', in J. Antonakis et al. (eds), *The Nature of Leadership*. Thousand Oaks, CA: Sage.

Sauder, M. and Espeland, W. E. (2009). 'The Discipline of Rankings: Tight Coupling and Organizational Change'. *American Sociological Review* 74: 63–82.

Schor, J. (2004). *Burn to Buy*. New York: Scribner.

Scitovsky, T. (1976). *The Joyless Economy*. Oxford: Oxford University Press.

Sebrant, U. (2000). *Organiserande och identitet*. Pedagogiska instituionen, Stockholms universitet.

Sennett, R. (1977). *The Fall of Public Man*. New York: Vintage.

—— (1998). *The Corrosion of Character*. New York: Norton.

—— (2006). *The Culture of the New Capitalism*. New Haven, CT: Yale University Press.

Sidhu, R. (2006). *Universities and Globalization*. Mahwah, NJ: Lawrence Erlbaum.

Simmel, G. (1904). 'Fashion', in *Georg Simmel: On Individuality and Social Form*, ed. D. Levine. Chicago: University of Chicago Press, 1971.

Söderberg, J. (2002). 'Att studera konsumtionen. Långa linjer i tänkandet', in G. Ahrne and R. Swedberg (eds), *Ekonomin i samhället*. Lund: Studentlitteratur.

Sohlman, Å. (1996). *Framtidens utbildning—Sverige i internationell konkurrens*. Stockholm: SNS.

SOU (1996). *Livslångt lärande i arbetslivet*. Stockholm: Fritzes.

Spoelstra, S. and ten Bos, R. (2011). 'Leadership', in *Business Ethics and Contemporay Philosophy*. Cambridge: Cambridge University Press.

Stevens, M., Armstrong, E., and Arums, R. (2008). 'Sieve, Incubator, Temple, Hub: Empirical and Theoretical Advances in the Sociology of Higher Education'. *Annual Review of Sociology* 34: 127–51.

Sturdy, A. J., Brocklehurst, M., Winstanley, D., and Littlejohns, M. (2006). 'Management as a (Self) Confidence Trick'. *Organization* 13(6): 841–60.

Suddaby, R. and Greenwood, R. (2001). 'Colonizing Knowledge: Commodification as a Dynamic of Jurisdictional Expansion in Professional Service Firms'. *Human Relations* 54(7): 933–53.

Sveningsson, S. (1999). *Strategisk förändring, makt och kunskap*. Lund: Lund University Press.

—— and Larsson, M. (2006). 'Fantasies of Leadership: Identity Work'. *Leadership* 2(2): 203–24.

Svensson, L. (1990). 'Teori och praktik i professionellas vardagsarbete', in S. Selander (ed.), *Kampen om yrkesutövning, status och kunskap*. Lund: Studentlitteratur.

Sweet, S. and Meiksins, P. (2008). *Changing Contours of Work: Jobs and Opportunities in the New Economy*. Los Angeles: Pine Forge Press.

Tengblad, S (2003). *Den Myndige Medarbetaren*. Malmö: Liber.

Thompson, P. et al. (2000). 'Human Capital or Capitalizing on Humanity? Knowledge, Skills and Competences in Interactive Service Work', in C. Prichard et al. (eds), *Managing Knowledge*. Basingstoke: MacMillan.

—— et al. (2001). 'Ignorant Theory and Knowledgeable Workers: Interrogating the Connections between Knowledge, Skills and Services'. *Journal of Management Studies* 38(7): 923–42.

Twenge, J. and Foster, J. (2010). 'Birth Cohort Increases in Narcissistic Personality Traits among American College Students, 1982–2009'. *Social Psychological and Personality Science* 1(1): 99–106.

——, Konrath, S., Foster, J., Campbell, K., and Bushman, B. (2008). 'Ego Inflating over Time: A Cross-temporal Meta-analysis of the Narcissistic Personality Inventory'. *Journal of Personality* 76(4): 875–97.

Uggla, H. (2001). *Organisation av varumärken*. Malmö: Liber.

Ulver-Sneistrup, S. (2008). *Status Spotting: A Consumer Cultural Exploration into Ordinary Status Consumption of 'Home' and Home Aesthetics*. Lund Studies in Economics and Management 102. Lund: Lund Business Press.

van Reis, M. (1988). 'Begärets strategier: några nedslag i René Girards tänkande'. *Res Publica* 10: 62–72.

Wachtel, P. (1983). *The Poverty of Affluence: A Psychological Portrait of the American Way of Life*. New York: Free Press.

Wallander, J. (2003). *Decentralisation—Why and How to Make It Work the Handelsbanken Case*. Stockholm: SNS.

Watson, T. (1994). *In Search of Management*. London: Routledge.

Wenglén, R. (2005). 'Från dum till klok?', PhD dissertation. Företagsekonomiska institution, Lunds Universitet.

Western, S. (2008). *Leadership: A Critical Text*. London: Sage.

Weymans, W. (2010). 'Democracy, Knowledge and Critique: Rethinking European Universities beyond Tradition and the Market'. *London Review of Education* 8(2): 117–26.

Wilk, R. (2001). 'Consuming morality'. *Journal of Consumer Culture* 1(2): 245–60.

Willmott, H. (2011). 'Back to the Future: What Does Studying Bureaucracy Tells Us?', in S. Clegg et al. (eds), *Managing Modernity*. Oxford: Oxford University Press.

Wolf, A. (2004). 'Education and Economic Performance: Simplistic Theories and Their Policy Consequences'. *Oxford Review of Economic Policy* 20(2): 315–34.

Ydén, K. (2008). *Kriget och karriärsystemet*. Göteborg: BAS.

Zaleznik, A. (1977). 'Managers and Leaders: Are They Different?' *Harvard Business Review* (May–June): 67–8.

Ziehe, T. and Stubenrauch, H. (1982). *Ny ungdom og osaedvanlige laeroprocesser*. Köpenhamn: Politisk Revy.

Zwick, D. and Cayla, J. (2010). 'Inside Marketing: Practices, Ideologies, Devices', in D. Zwick and J. Cayla (eds), *Inside Marketing*. Oxford: Oxford University Press.

Index

Figures are listed as **f**.

Index